MAKING A BETTER WORLD *with the* BAHÁ'Í FAITH

QUOTATIONS

A selection of passages from the Bahá'í holy writings and other materials

Compiled by Nathan Thomas

Copyright © 2013 by Greysands Media, LLC

Cover design by Andrew Johnson

All rights reserved. This book or any portion thereof may not be reproduced or used in any manner whatsoever without the express written permission of the publisher.

First Printing, 2013
ISBN 978-1-939174-05-5

Greysands Media, LLC
www.greysandsmedia.com

THE WHYUNITE? SERIES BOOKS AND VIDEOS

MANY PATHS TO THE BAHÁ'Í FAITH
How people from different faith experiences discover fulfillment in the Bahá'í Faith

QUOTATIONS FOR MANY PATHS TO THE BAHÁ'Í FAITH
Selected passages from the Bahá'í holy writings and other materials

FIRESIDE TALK FOR MANY PATHS TO THE BAHÁ'Í FAITH
A video presentation about the Bahá'í Faith by the author, Nathan Thomas

MANIFEST YOUR POTENTIAL IN THE BAHÁ'Í FAITH
How the beliefs, practices, and vision of the Bahá'í Faith can change your life

QUOTATIONS FOR MANIFESTING YOUR POTENTIAL IN THE BAHÁ'Í FAITH
Selected passages from the Bahá'í holy writings and other materials

FIRESIDE TALK FOR MANIFESTING YOUR POTENTIAL IN THE BAHÁ'Í FAITH
A video presentation about the Bahá'í Faith by the author, Nathan Thomas

MAKING A BETTER WORLD WITH THE BAHÁ'Í FAITH
How Bahá'ís are transforming our world into a more unified, prosperous, and spiritual home for all mankind

QUOTATIONS FOR MAKING A BETTER WORLD WITH THE BAHÁ'Í FAITH
Selected passages from the Bahá'í holy writings and other materials

FIRESIDE TALK FOR MAKING A BETTER WORLD WITH THE BAHÁ'Í FAITH
A video presentation about the Bahá'í Faith by the author, Nathan Thomas

PATHS TO THE BAHÁ'Í FAITH
A nine-part collection of video interviews of Bahá'ís from a variety of backgrounds

Learn more at http://www.whyunite.com

TABLE OF CONTENTS

The WhyUnite? Series Books and Videos.................... iii
Table of Contents v
Preface to the WhyUnite? Series vii

Introduction to Quotations for Making a Better World
with the Bahá'í Faith... 1
   Chapter 1: Welcome to Making a Better World...................... 7
   Chapter 2: What is the Bahá'í Faith? 19

Part I: Aspiring to Universal Goals 29
   Chatper 3: Working Together Toward True Unity 31
   Chapter 4: Creating a Culture of Global Awareness 43
   Chapter 5: Striving for World Peace............................... 53
   Chapter 6: Working for Universal Education 67
   Chapter 7: Promoting the Equality of Men and Women 81
   Chapter 8: Eliminating Prejudice from Our Hearts 97
   Chapter 9: Aligning the World's Faiths............................113
   Chapter 10: Cherishing Our Environment........................... 12
   Chapter 11: Powering the Spiritual Economy....................... 139

Part II: Organizing for Sustainable Change 155
   Chapter 12: Cultivating Effective Communities.................... 157
   Chapter 13: Encouraging Consultative Leadership.................. 171
   Chapter 14: Serving our Spiritual Assemblies..................... 185
   Chapter 15: Cherishing the Universal House of Justice 203
   Chapter 16: Learning through Collective Discovery 221
   Chapter 17: Healing Our World by Healing Our Families............ 239
   Chapter 18: Purifying Our Lives through the Bahá'í Fund 251

Chapter 19: Empowering Youth to Renew Our Communities 267
Chapter 20: Ensuring Unity of Our Community
within the Covenant..281
Chapter 21: Exploring the World in Service to Humanity 295

Part III: Channeling Spiritual Forces.......................307
    Chapter 22: Sharing a Spirit of Faith 309
    Chapter 23: Inspiring an Uplifting Spirit of Morality in Society 325
    Chapter 24: Infusing a Spirit of Service into all Mankind............. 341
    Chapter 25: Cultivating a Spirit of Trust 349

Conclusion 361
    Chapter 26: Deciding How You Will Make a Difference 363

Appendix: Sources and Bibliography 373

PREFACE TO THE WHYUNITE? SERIES

A NEW WORLD RELIGION DEDICATED TO TRANSFORMING HUMANITY

The Bahá'í Faith is a world religion that brings teachings designed to help all of mankind while renewing the spiritual capacities of the human race. Founded by Bahá'u'lláh (meaning "the Glory of God" in Arabic) in the mid-nineteenth century, the goal of the Bahá'í Faith is to bring out the best in humanity. As Bahá'u'lláh wrote, through the teachings of this worldwide faith "every man will advance and develop until he attaineth the station at which he can manifest all the potential forces with which his inmost true self hath been endowed." (*Gleanings from the Writings of Bahá'u'lláh,* no. 27.5).

With practical teachings, a diverse global community, acceptance for of all the world's religions, and a message specifically designed to solve humanity's most pressing needs, the Bahá'í Faith brings a contemporary approach to religion that is unique among all the world's faiths. Bahá'u'lláh writes, "My object is none other than the betterment of the world and the tranquility of its peoples." (*Gleanings from the Writings of Bahá'u'lláh,* no. 131.2).

Today millions of people from every background have found this Faith through the individual investigation of truth. For them, it offers a compelling and fulfilling foundation for their spiritual experience. As 'Abdu'l-Bahá, the son and successor of Bahá'u'lláh said, "Man must walk in many paths and be subjected to various processes in his evolution upward." (*Promulgation of Universal Peace,* p. 295). Throughout all these paths we take in our lives, every person must judge for him or herself what is good and true for their own spiritual journey. For many, that process leads to the Bahá'í Faith.

AN INVITATION TO LEARN MORE WITH THE WHYUNITE? SERIES

The WhyUnite? Series is an individual initiative begun to produce compelling, unique, and practical content about the Bahá'í Faith. Our goal is to develop materials that educate, empower, and inspire people to follow their own path to the truth, to manifest their own potential as spiritual beings, and to make this world a better place in the process. To that end, we are dedicated to the continuous development of books, compilations, videos, and more to help people discover the spiritual richness, endless diversity, and wondrous wisdom offered to humanity through the Bahá'í Faith. Learn more about our work and get involved at www.whyunite.com.

INTRODUCTION TO QUOTATIONS FOR MAKING A BETTER WORLD WITH THE BAHÁ'Í FAITH

2 ❷ Making a Better World with the Bahá'í Faith: QUOTATIONS

Introduction to Quotations for Making a Better World with the Bahá'í Faith

This book is designed to be a companion to the book *Making a Better World with the Bahá'í Faith,* which explores the journey that Bahá'ís are on to help improve the human condition. The Bahá'í Faith offers the world a solution that is comprehensive in its breadth, practical in its approach, and transformative in its potential to change the way we think about who we are, why we exist, and where we are going as one human family. This book addresses many of the social, material, and spiritual problems of our time that the Bahá'í Faith endeavors to solve.

It covers:
- How Bahá'ís promote world peace and global justice at a grassroots level.
- How Bahá'ís work to emancipate women and ensure the equality of all people worldwide.
- How Bahá'ís strive to alleviate economic injustice with a spiritual approach.
- The path to reducing religious intolerance and fanaticism.
- The ways in which Bahá'ís encourage collective learning, discovery and rational thought.
- How the Bahá'ís are building a new global system of organization from the ground up.
- How Bahá'ís work to unleash the capacity of the world in a responsible and ethical manner.
- The ways in which Bahá'ís inspire individuals, families, and youth to realize an enduring purpose for their lives.
- How Bahá'ís support people of all faiths, backgrounds, and causes towards achieving success.

ABOUT THE QUOTATIONS IN THIS BOOK

This book is intended to offer more direct insight into what the Bahá'í Faith directly says on the subjects covered in its companion book, *Making a Better World with the Bahá'í Faith.* It includes many quotations from a wide variety of sources. Many of these sources are authentic documents written by the Founder of the Bahá'í Faith Himself, Bahá'u'lláh, which were often sealed with His personal seal. To that end, any quotations in this book attributed to Bahá'u'lláh are from approved translations of His works. It might be noted that Bahá'ís believe that Bahá'u'lláh revealed the Word of God for this age. Therefore His works are very important to the Bahá'í community. Any reader of His words, though, will soon notice that He revealed His works in many styles. At some times He revealed them as a "lawgiver," at other times He revealed them as a "mystic" or spiritual guide, and at other times as a counselor to His followers. He even revealed works in the voice of God Himself. The reality is, for many people, reading the words of Bahá'u'lláh can take some getting used to. But once people get used to the different tone and language of the Holy Writings, many spend their entire lives exploring the endless meanings and implications of the words revealed by the Founder of this faith.

In addition this book includes many quotations from Bahá'u'lláh's son and successor, 'Abdu'l-Bahá. While 'Abdu'l-Bahá did write many books and letters that can be considered authentic, he also gave many talks throughout his long career as a Central Figure of this Faith. The reader should realize, therefore, that many of the quotations that were gathered from such lectures and forums were written down by observers. Thus some of these passages are not considered authoritative, but can be used for personal edification and spiritual discovery. To that end, the reader should recognize that some of the materials from such works should be balanced with everything else in the Bahá'í Writings that is considered authoritative.

After the Writings of Bahá'u'lláh and 'Abdu'l-Bahá, this book also includes quotations from the grandson of 'Abdu'l-Bahá, the appointed Guardian of the Bahá'í Faith, Shoghi Effendi. These writings include materials, letters, and books that the Guardian wrote to the Bahá'í world, and to individual believers. Sometimes he wrote these letters himself, in other cases they were recorded by his secretaries. The Guardian's writings are considered an authoritative source for guidance and interpretation of the Word of God. And while this material is considered a critical source for understanding the teachings, concepts, and ideas of the Bahá'í Faith, they must also be approached with care when taken from letters to individuals. That is, in some cases direction may have been given to one person that would not necessarily fit the whole of humanity. Therefore, again, Bahá'ís are encouraged to weigh and judge for themselves in these matters with respect to all the other authoritative content we have available to us.

In addition, this book includes writings of the Universal House of Justice, the authoritative word of the supreme governing body of the worldwide Bahá'í community. It also includes works from other sources such as the Bahá'í International Community, which is an agency of the Universal House of Justice that works with non-governmental organizations around the world. These works, while not authoritative, shed insight into the inner workings of the Faith and offer a global perspective on how things should be carried out in the Bahá'í world and beyond.

SUGGESTIONS FOR READING THE QUOTATIONS

It is strongly suggested that the reader explore the book that inspired this collection of quotations, *Making a Better World with the Bahá'í Faith,* before diving fully into the quotes in this book. The fact is, the Bahá'í Faith is rich and nuanced. Many of these quotations are better understood when their context and perspective is considered. In addition, it can also be helpful to read and study these books in book clubs or study classes with other people, including and especially other Bahá'ís. It can be very useful to explore spiritual topics with others, to hear their ideas, their interpretations, and their questions and concerns when one is making his or her own decisions in spiritual development.

Lastly, it is encouraged that new believers take their time when it comes to studying the Bahá'í Writings. This is because it takes patience for many to learn the language of these works, to gain confidence with the terms, to acquire a taste for the grammatical and stylistic approaches, and to build up a solid foundation of understanding that can then be used as a lens to discover, interpret, and cultivate spiritual truths in our lives.

Making a Better World with the Bahá'í Faith: QUOTATIONS

CHAPTER 1:

WELCOME TO MAKING A BETTER WORLD

8 ❓ Making a Better World with the Bahá'í Faith: QUOTATIONS

FROM THE WRITINGS OF BAHÁ'U'LLÁH

1.1 All men have been created to carry forward an ever-advancing civilization.

1.2 All glory be to this Day, the Day in which the fragrances of mercy have been wafted over all created things, a Day so blest that past ages and centuries can never hope to rival it, a Day in which the countenance of the Ancient of Days hath turned towards His holy seat.

1.3 This is the Day whereon the Ocean of God's mercy hath been manifested unto men, the Day in which the Day Star of His loving-kindness hath shed its radiance upon them, the Day in which the clouds of His bountiful favor have overshadowed the whole of mankind. Now is the time to cheer and refresh the down-cast through the invigorating breeze of love and fellowship, and the living waters of friendliness and charity.

1.4 We have, under all circumstances, enjoined on men what is right, and forbidden what is wrong. He Who is the Lord of Being is witness that this Wronged One hath besought from God for His creatures whatever is conducive to unity and harmony, fellowship and concord. By the righteousness of God! This Wronged One is not capable of dissimulation.

1.5 My object is none other than the betterment of the world and the tranquillity of its peoples. The well-being of mankind, its peace and security, are unattainable unless and until its unity is firmly established. This unity can never be achieved so long as the counsels which the Pen of the Most High hath revealed are suffered to pass unheeded.

FROM THE WRITINGS AND UTTERANCES OF 'ABDU'L-BAHÁ

1.6 Then wilt thou see that today these heavenly Teachings are the remedy for a sick and suffering world, and a healing balm for the sores on the body of mankind. They are the spirit of life, the ark of salvation, the magnet to draw down eternal glory, the dynamic power to motivate the inner self of man.

1.7 Wherefore, O loved ones of God! Make ye a mighty effort till you yourselves betoken this advancement and all these confirmations, and become focal centres of God's blessings, daysprings of the light of His unity, promoters of the gifts and graces of civilized life. Be ye in that land vanguards of the perfections of humankind; carry forward the various branches of knowledge, be active and progressive in the field of inventions and the arts. Endeavour to rectify the conduct of men, and seek to excel the whole world in moral character.

1.8 ...Be thou severed from this world, and reborn through the sweet scents of holiness that blow from the realm of the All-Highest. Be thou a summoner to love, and be thou kind to all the human race. Love thou the children of men and share in their sorrows. Be thou of those who foster peace. Offer thy friendship, be worthy of trust. Be thou a balm to every sore, be thou a medicine for every ill. Bind thou the souls together. Recite thou the verses of guidance. Be engaged in the worship of thy Lord, and rise up to lead the people aright. Loose thy tongue and teach, and let thy face be bright with the fire of God's love. Rest thou not for a moment, seek thou to draw no easeful breath. Thus mayest thou become a sign and symbol of God's love, and a banner of His grace.

1.9 Two calls to success and prosperity are being raised from the heights of the happiness of mankind, awakening the slumbering, granting sight to the blind, causing the heedless to become mindful, bestowing hearing upon the deaf, unloosing the tongue of the mute and resuscitating the dead.

The one is the call of civilization, of the progress of the material world. This pertaineth to the world of phenomena, promoteth the principles of material achievement, and is the trainer for the physical accomplishments of mankind. It compriseth the laws, regulations, arts and sciences through which the world of humanity hath developed; laws and regulations which are the outcome of lofty ideals and the result of sound minds, and which have stepped forth into the arena of existence through the efforts of the wise and cultured in past and subsequent ages. The propagator and executive power of this call is just government.

The other is the soul-stirring call of God, Whose spiritual teachings are safeguards of the everlasting glory, the eternal happiness and illumination of the world of humanity, and cause attributes of mercy to be revealed in the human world and the life beyond.

This second call is founded upon the instructions and exhortations of the Lord and the admonitions and altruistic emotions belonging to the realm of morality which, like unto a brilliant light, brighten and illumine the lamp of the realities of mankind. Its penetrative power is the Word of God.

However, until material achievements, physical accomplishments and human virtues are reinforced by spiritual perfections, luminous qualities and characteristics of mercy, no fruit or result shall issue therefrom, nor will the happiness of the world of humanity, which is the ultimate aim, be attained. For although, on the one hand, material achievements and the development of the physical world produce prosperity, which exquisitely manifests its intended aims, on the other hand dangers, severe calamities and violent afflictions are imminent.

Consequently, when thou lookest at the orderly pattern of kingdoms, cities and villages, with the attractiveness of their adornments, the freshness of their natural resources, the refinement of their appliances, the ease of their means of travel, the extent of knowledge available about the world of nature, the great inventions, the colossal enterprises, the noble discoveries and scientific researches, thou wouldst conclude that civilization conducteth to the happiness and the progress of the human world. Yet shouldst thou turn thine eye to the discovery of destructive and infernal machines, to the development of forces of demolition and the invention of fiery implements, which uproot the tree of life, it would become evident and manifest unto thee that civilization is conjoined with barbarism. Progress and barbarism go hand in hand, unless material civilization be confirmed by Divine Guidance, by the revelations of the All-Merciful and by godly virtues, and be reinforced by spiritual conduct, by the ideals of the Kingdom and by the outpourings of the Realm of Might.

1.10 We must use our utmost endeavors in order that the Holy Spirit may influence minds and hearts toward peace, the bounties of God surround, the divine effulgences become successive, human souls advance, minds expand in wider vision, souls become more holy and the world of humanity be rid of its great menace. For the betterment of the world Bahá'u'lláh endured all the hardships, ordeals and vicissitudes of life, sacrificing His very being and comfort, forfeiting His estates, possessions and honor—all that pertains to human existence—not for one year, nay, rather, for nearly fifty years. During this long period He was subjected to persecution and abuse, was cast into prison, was banished from His native land, underwent severities and humiliation and was exiled four times. He was first exiled from Persia to Baghdad, thence to Constantinople, thence to Rumelia and finally to the great prison-fortress of 'Akká in Syria, where He passed the remainder of His life. Every day a new oppression and abuse was heaped upon Him until He winged His flight from the dungeon to the supreme world and returned to His Lord. He endured these ordeals and difficulties in order that this earthly human world might become heavenly, that the illumination of the divine Kingdom should become a reality in human hearts, that the individual members of mankind might progress, the power of the Holy Spirit increase its efficacy and penetration and the happiness of the world of humanity be assured. He desired for all tranquillity and composure and exercised loving-kindness toward the nations regardless of conditions and differences. He addressed humanity, saying, "O humankind! Verily, ye are all the leaves and fruits of one tree; ye are all one. Therefore, associate in friendship; love one another; abandon prejudices of race; dispel forever this gloomy darkness of human ignorance, for the century of light, the Sun of Reality hath appeared. Now is the time for affiliation, and now is the period of unity and concord. For thousands of years ye have been contending in warfare and strife. It is enough. Now is the time for unity. Lay aside all self-purposes, and know for a certainty that all men are the servants of one God Who will bind them together in love and agreement."

1.11 How many blessed souls have longed for this radiant century, their utmost hopes and desires centered upon the happiness and joy of one such day as this. Many the nights they passed sleepless and lamenting until the very morn in longing anticipation of this age, yearning to realize even an hour of this time. God has favored you in this century and has specialized you for the realization of its blessings. Therefore, you must praise and thank God with heart and soul in appreciation of this great opportunity and the attainment of this infinite bestowal—that such doors have been opened before your faces, that such abundance is pouring down from the cloud of mercy and that these refreshing breezes from the paradise of Abha are resuscitating you. You must become of one heart, one spirit and one susceptibility. May you become as the waves of one sea, stars of the same heaven, fruits adorning the same tree, roses of one garden in order that through you the oneness of humanity may establish its temple in the world of mankind, for you are the ones who are called to uplift the cause of unity among the nations of the earth.

1.12 You must thank God that your efforts are high and noble, that your endeavors are worthy, that your intentions are centered upon the Kingdom of God and that your supreme desire is the acquisition of eternal virtues. You must act in accordance with these requirements. A man may be a Bahá'í in name only. If he is a Bahá'í in reality, his deeds and actions will be decisive proofs of it. What are the requirements? Love for mankind, sincerity toward all, reflecting the oneness of the world of humanity, philanthropy, becoming enkindled with the fire of the love of God, attainment to the knowledge of God and that which is conducive to human welfare.

1.13 Praise be to God! The springtime of God is at hand. This century is, verily, the spring season. The world of mind and kingdom of soul have become fresh and verdant by its bestowals. It has resuscitated the whole realm of existence. On one hand, the lights of reality are shining; on the other, the clouds of divine mercy are pouring down the fullness of heavenly bounty. Wonderful material progress is evident, and great spiritual discoveries are being made. Truly, this can be called the miracle of centuries, for it is replete with manifestations of the miraculous. The time has come when all mankind shall be united, when all races shall be loyal to one fatherland, all religions become one religion, and racial and religious bias pass away. It is a day in which the oneness of humankind shall uplift its standard and international peace, like the true morning, flood the world with its light. Therefore, we offer supplications to God, asking Him to dispel these gloomy clouds and uproot these imitations in order that the East and West may become radiant with love and unity, that the nations of the world shall embrace each other and the ideal spiritual brotherhood illumine the world like the glorious sun of the high heavens. This is our hope, our wish and desire. We pray that through the bounty and grace of God we may attain thereto. I am very happy to be present at this meeting which has innate radiance, intelligence, perception and longing to investigate reality. Such meetings are the glory of the world of mankind. I ask the blessing of God in your behalf

1.14 When we observe the world of created phenomena we discover that each atom of the atoms of substance is moving through the various degrees and kingdoms of organic life. For instance, consider the ethereal element which is penetrating and traveling through all the contingent realities. When there is vibration or movement in the ethereal element, the eye is affected by that vibration and beholds what is known as light.

In the same manner the bestowals of God are moving and circulating throughout all created things. This illimitable divine bounty has no beginning and will have no ending. It is moving, circulating and becomes effective wherever capacity is developed to receive it. In every station there is a specialized capacity. Therefore we must be hopeful that through the bounty and favor of God, this spirit of life infusing all created things shall quicken humanity and from its bestowals the human world become a divine world, this earthly kingdom the mirror of the realm of divinity, the virtues and perfections of the world of humanity become unveiled and the image and likeness of God be reflected from this temple.

FROM THE WRITINGS AND LETTERS WRITTEN BY, OR ON BEHALF OF, SHOGHI EFFENDI

1.15 If long-cherished ideals and time-honored institutions, if certain social assumptions and religious formulae have ceased to promote the welfare of the generality of mankind, if they no longer minister to the needs of a continually evolving humanity, let them be swept away and relegated to the limbo of obsolescent and forgotten doctrines. Why should these, in a world subject to the immutable law of change and decay, be exempt from the deterioration that must needs overtake every human institution? For legal standards, political and economic theories are solely designed to safeguard the interests of humanity as a whole, and not humanity to be crucified for the preservation of the integrity of any particular law or doctrine.

FROM THE WRITINGS AND LETTERS WRITTEN BY, OR ON BEHALF OF, THE UNIVERSAL HOUSE OF JUSTICE

1.16 A wider horizon is opening before us, illumined by a growing and universal manifestation of the inherent potentialities of the Cause for ordering human affairs.

1.17 There are spiritual principles, or what some call human values, by which solutions can be found for every social problem. Any well-intentioned group can in a general sense devise practical solutions to its problems, but good intentions and practical knowledge are usually not enough. The essential merit of spiritual principle is that it not only presents a perspective which harmonizes with that which is immanent in human nature, it also induces an attitude, a dynamic, a will, an aspiration, which facilitate the discovery and implementation of practical measures. Leaders of governments and all in authority would be well served in their efforts to solve problems if they would first seek to identify the principles involved and then be guided by them.

1.18 It is understandable that Bahá'ís who witness the miserable conditions under which so many human beings have to live, or who hear of a sudden disaster that has struck a certain area of the world, are moved to do something practical to ameliorate those conditions and to help their suffering fellow-mortals.

There are many ways in which help can be rendered. Every Bahá'í has the duty to acquire a trade or profession through which he will earn that wherewith he can support himself and his family; in the choice of such work he can seek those activities which are of benefit to his fellow-men and not merely those which promote his personal interests, still less those whose effects are actually harmful.

There are also the situations in which an individual Bahá'í or a Spiritual Assembly is confronted with an urgent need which neither justice nor compassion could allow to go unheeded and unhelped. How many are the stories told of 'Abdu'l-Bahá in such situations, when He would even take off a garment He was wearing and give it to a shivering man in rags.

But in our concern for such immediate obvious calls upon our succour we must not allow ourselves to forget the continuing, appalling burden of suffering under which millions of human beings are always groaning—a burden which they have bourne for century upon century and which it is the Mission of Bahá'u'lláh to lift at last. the principal cause of this suffering, which one can witness wherever one turns, is the corruption of human morals and the prevalence of prejudice, suspicion, hatred, untrustworthiness, selfishness and tyranny among men. It is not merely material well-being that people need. What they desperately need is to know how to live their lives—they need to know who they are', to what purpose they exist, and how they should act towards one another; and, once they know the answers to these questions they need to be helped to gradually apply these answers to every-day behavior. It is to the solution of this basic problem of mankind that the greater part of all our energy and resources should be directed...

1.19 Central to Bahá'u'lláh's mission, therefore, has been the creation of a global community that would reflect the oneness of humankind. The ultimate testimony that the Bahá'í community can summon in vindication of His mission is the example of unity that His teachings have produced. As it enters the twenty-first century, the Bahá'í Cause is a phenomenon unlike anything else the world has seen. After decades of effort, in which surges of growth alternated with long stretches of consolidation, often shadowed by setbacks, the Bahá'í community comprises several million people representative of virtually every ethnic, cultural, social and religious background on earth, administering their collective affairs without the intervention of a clergy, through democratically elected institutions. The many thousands of localities in which it has put down its roots are to be found in every country, territory and significant island group, from the Arctic to Tierra del Fuego, from Africa to the Pacific. The assertion that this community may today already constitute the most diverse and geographically widespread of any similarly organized body of people on the planet is unlikely to be challenged by one familiar with the evidence.

18 ❷ Making a Better World with the Bahá'í Faith: QUOTATIONS

CHAPTER 2:

WHAT IS THE BAHÁ'Í FAITH?

FROM THE WRITINGS OF BAHÁ'U'LLÁH

2.1 Great indeed is this Day! The allusions made to it in all the sacred Scriptures as the Day of God attest its greatness. The soul of every Prophet of God, of every Divine Messenger, hath thirsted for this wondrous Day. All the diverse kindreds of the earth have, likewise, yearned to attain it. No sooner, however, had the Day Star of His Revelation manifested itself in the heaven of God's Will, than all, except those whom the Almighty was pleased to guide, were found dumbfounded and heedless.

2.2 We desire but the good of the world and the happiness of the nations; yet they deem Us a stirrer up of strife and sedition worthy of bondage and banishment.... That all nations should become one in faith and all men as brothers; that the bonds of affection and unity between the sons of men should be strengthened; that diversity of religion should cease, and differences of race be annulled—what harm is there in this?... Yet so it shall be; these fruitless strifes, these ruinous wars shall pass away, and the 'Most Great Peace' shall come.... Yet do We see your kings and rulers lavishing their treasures more freely on means for the destruction of the human race than on that which would conduce to the happiness of mankind.... These strifes and this bloodshed and discord must cease, and all men be as one kindred and one family.... Let not a man glory in this, that he loves his country; let him rather glory in this, that he loves his kind...

2.3 We, verily, have come to unite and weld together all that dwell on earth.

2.4 Give ear unto the verses of God which He Who is the sacred Lote-Tree reciteth unto you. They are assuredly the infallible balance, established by God, the Lord of this world and the next. Through them the soul of man is caused to wing its flight towards the Dayspring of Revelation, and the heart of every true believer is suffused with light. Such are the laws which God hath enjoined upon you, such His commandments prescribed unto you in His Holy Tablet; obey them with joy and gladness, for this is best for you, did ye but know.

2.5 I was but a man like others, asleep upon My couch, when lo, the breezes of the All-Glorious were wafted over Me, and taught Me the knowledge of all that hath been. This thing is not from Me, but from One Who is Almighty and All-Knowing. And He bade Me lift up My voice between earth and heaven, and for this there befell Me what hath caused the tears of every man of understanding to flow. The learning current amongst men I studied not; their schools I entered not. Ask of the city wherein I dwelt, that thou mayest be well assured that I am not of them who speak falsely. This is but a leaf which the winds of the will of thy Lord, the Almighty, the All-Praised, have stirred. Can it be still when the tempestuous winds are blowing? Nay, by Him Who is the Lord of all Names and Attributes! They move it as they list. The evanescent is as nothing before Him Who is the Ever-Abiding. His all-compelling summons hath reached Me, and caused Me to speak His praise amidst all people. I was indeed as one dead when His behest was uttered. The hand of the will of thy Lord, the Compassionate, the Merciful, transformed Me.

2.6 While engulfed in tribulations I heard a most wondrous, a most sweet voice, calling above My head. Turning My face, I beheld a Maiden—the embodiment of the remembrance of the name of My Lord—suspended in the air before Me. So rejoiced was she in her very soul that her countenance shone with the ornament of the good pleasure of God, and her cheeks glowed with the brightness of the All-Merciful. Betwixt earth and heaven she was raising a call which captivated the hearts and minds of men. She was imparting to both My inward and outer being tidings which rejoiced My soul, and the souls of God's honoured servants.

Pointing with her finger unto My head, she addressed all who are in heaven and all who are on earth, saying: By God! This is the Best-Beloved of the worlds, and yet ye comprehend not. This is the Beauty of God amongst you, and the power of His sovereignty within you, could ye but understand. This is the Mystery of God and His Treasure, the Cause of God and His glory unto all who are in the kingdoms of Revelation and of creation, if ye be of them that perceive. This is He Whose Presence is the ardent desire of the denizens of the Realm of eternity, and of them that dwell within the Tabernacle of glory, and yet from His Beauty do ye turn aside.

FROM THE WRITINGS AND UTTERANCES OF 'ABDU'L-BAHÁ

2.7 When delivering the glad tidings, speak out and say: the Promised One of all the world's peoples hath now been made manifest. For each and every people, and every religion, await a Promised One, and Bahá'u'lláh is that One Who is awaited by all; and therefore the Cause of Bahá'u'lláh will bring about the oneness of mankind, and the tabernacle of unity will be upraised on the heights of the world, and the banners of the universality of all humankind will be unfurled on the peaks of the earth. When thou dost loose thy tongue to deliver this great good news, this will become the means of teaching the people.

2.8 Unless these Teachings are effectively spread among the people, until the old ways, the old concepts, are gone and forgotten, this world of being will find no peace, nor will it reflect the perfections of the Heavenly Kingdom. Strive ye with all your hearts to make the heedless conscious, to waken those who sleep, to bring knowledge to the ignorant, to make the blind to see, the deaf to hear, and restore the dead to life.

2.9 Throughout the world generally war and dissension prevailed. At this time Bahá'u'lláh appeared in Persia and began devoting Himself to the uplift and education of the people. He united divergent sects and creeds, removed religious, racial, patriotic and political prejudices and established a strong bond of unity and reconciliation among varying degrees and classes of mankind. The enmity then existing among the people was so bitter and intense that even ordinary association was out of the question. They would not meet and consult with each other at all. Through the power of the teachings of Bahá'u'lláh the most wonderful results were witnessed. He removed the prejudices and hatred from human hearts and wrought such transformation in their attitudes toward each other that today in Persia there is perfect accord among hitherto bigoted religionists, varying sects and divergent classes. This was not an easy accomplishment, for Bahá'u'lláh underwent severe trials, great difficulties and violent persecution. He was imprisoned, tortures were inflicted upon Him, and finally He was banished from His native land. He bore every ordeal and infliction cheerfully. In His successive exiles from country to country up to the time of His ascension from this world, He was enabled to promulgate His teachings, even from prison. Wherever His oppressors sent Him, He hoisted the standard of the oneness of the world of humanity and promulgated the principles of the unity of mankind. Some of these principles are as follows. First, it is incumbent upon all mankind to investigate truth. If such investigation be made, all should agree and be united, for truth or reality is not multiple; it is not divisible. The different religions have one truth underlying them; therefore, their reality is one.

2.10 From time immemorial the divine teachings have been successively revealed, and the bounties of the Holy Spirit have ever been emanating. All the teachings are one reality, for reality is single and does not admit multiplicity. Therefore, the divine Prophets are one, inasmuch as They reveal the one reality, the Word of God. Abraham announced teachings founded upon reality, Moses proclaimed reality, Christ established reality and Bahá'u'lláh was the Messenger and Herald of reality. But humanity, having forsaken the one essential and fundamental reality which underlies the religion of God, and holding blindly to imitations of ancestral forms and interpretations of belief, is separated and divided in the strife, contention and bigotry of various sects and religious factions. If all should be true to the original reality of the Prophet and His teaching, the peoples and nations of the world would become unified, and these differences which cause separation would be lost sight of. To accomplish this great and needful unity in reality, Bahá'u'lláh appeared in the Orient and renewed the foundations of the divine teachings. His revelation of the Word embodies completely the teachings of all the Prophets, expressed in principles and precepts applicable to the needs and conditions of the modern world, amplified and adapted to present-day questions and critical human problems. That is to say, the words of Bahá'u'lláh are the essences of the words of the Prophets of the past. They are the very spirit of the age and the cause of the unity and illumination of the East and the

West. The followers of His teachings are in conformity with the precepts and commands of all the former heavenly Messengers. Differences and dissensions, which destroy the foundations of the world of humanity and are contrary to the will and good pleasure of God, disappear completely in the light of the revelation of Bahá'u'lláh; difficult problems are solved, unity and love are established. For the good pleasure of God is the effulgence of love and the establishment of unity and fellowship in the human world, whereas discord, contention, warfare and strife are satanic outcomes and contrary to the will of the Merciful. In order that human souls, minds and spirits may attain advancement, tranquillity and vision in broader horizons of unity and knowledge, Bahá'u'lláh proclaimed certain principles or teachings, some of which I will mention.

2.11 Briefly, the Blessed Perfection bore all these ordeals and calamities in order that our hearts might become enkindled and radiant, our spirits be glorified, our faults become virtues, our ignorance be transformed into knowledge; in order that we might attain the real fruits of humanity and acquire heavenly graces; in order that, although pilgrims upon earth, we should travel the road of the heavenly Kingdom, and, although needy and poor, we might receive the treasures of eternal life. For this has He borne these difficulties and sorrows.

FROM THE WRITINGS AND LETTERS WRITTEN BY, OR ON BEHALF OF, SHOGHI EFFENDI

2.12 The Bahá'í Faith upholds the unity of God, recognizes the unity of His Prophets, and inculcates the principle of the oneness and wholeness of the entire human race. it proclaims the necessity and the inevitability of the unification of mankind, asserts that it is gradually approaching, and claims that nothing short of the transmuting spirit of God, working through His chosen Mouthpiece in this day, can ultimately succeed in bringing it about. It, moreover, enjoins upon its followers the primary duty of an unfettered search after truth, condemns all manner of prejudice and superstition, declares the purpose of religion to be the promotion of amity and concord, proclaims its essential harmony with science, and recognizes it as the foremost agency for the pacification and the orderly progress of human society. It unequivocally maintains the principle of equal rights, opportunities and privileges for men and women, insists on compulsory education, eliminates extremes of poverty and wealth, abolishes the institution of priesthood, prohibits slavery, asceticism, mendicancy and monasticism, prescribes monogamy, discourages divorce, emphasizes the necessity of strict obedience to one's government, exalts any work performed in the spirit of service to the level of worship, urges either the creation or selection of an auxiliary international language, and delineates the outlines of those institutions that must establish and perpetuate the general peace of mankind.

2.13 The independent search after truth, unfettered by superstition or tradition; the oneness of the entire human race, the pivotal principle and fundamental doctrine of the Faith; the basic unity of all religions; the condemnation of all forms of prejudice, whether religious, racial, class or national; the harmony which must exist between religion and science; the equality of men and women, the two wings on which the bird of human kind is able to soar; the introduction of compulsory education; the adoption of a universal auxiliary language; the abolition of the extremes of wealth and poverty; the institution of a world tribunal for the adjudication of disputes between nations; the exaltation of work, performed in the spirit of service, to the rank of worship; the glorification of justice as the ruling principle in human society, and of religion as a bulwark for the protection of all peoples and nations; and the establishment of a permanent and universal peace as the supreme goal of all mankind—these stand out as the essential elements of that Divine polity which He proclaimed to leaders of public thought as well as to the masses at large in the course of these missionary journeys.

FROM THE WRITINGS AND LETTERS WRITTEN BY, OR ON BEHALF OF, THE UNIVERSAL HOUSE OF JUSTICE

2.14 The Bahá'í Faith regards the current world confusion and calamitous condition in human affairs as a natural phase in an organic process leading ultimately and irresistibly to the unification of the human race in a single social order whose boundaries are those of the planet. The human race, as a distinct, organic unit, has passed through evolutionary stages analogous to the stages of infancy and childhood in the lives of its individual members, and is now in the culminating period of its turbulent adolescence approaching its long-awaited coming of age.

2.15 ...Whatever suffering and turmoil the years immediately ahead may hold, however dark the immediate circumstances, the Bahá'í community believes that humanity can confront this supreme trial with confidence in its ultimate outcome. Far from signalizing the end of civilization, the convulsive changes towards which humanity is being ever more rapidly impelled will serve to release the "potentialities inherent in the station of man" and reveal "the full measure of his destiny on earth, the innate excellence of his reality".

PART I: ASPIRING TO UNIVERSAL GOALS

30 ❓ Making a Better World with the Bahá'í Faith: QUOTATIONS

CHATPER 3:

WORKING TOGETHER TOWARD TRUE UNITY

FROM THE WRITINGS OF BAHÁ'U'LLÁH

3.1   O Thou Who art the Lord of Lords! I testify that Thou art the Lord of all creation, and the Educator of all beings, visible and invisible. I bear witness that Thy power hath encompassed the entire universe, and that the hosts of the earth can never dismay Thee, nor can the dominion of all peoples and nations deter Thee from executing Thy purpose. I confess that Thou hast no desire except the regeneration of the whole world, and the establishment of the unity of its peoples, and the salvation of all them that dwell therein.

3.2   It is binding and incumbent upon the peoples of the world, one and all, to extend aid unto this momentous Cause which is come from the heaven of the Will of the ever-abiding God, that perchance the fire of animosity which blazeth in the hearts of some of the peoples of the earth may, through the living waters of divine wisdom and by virtue of heavenly counsels and exhortations, be quenched, and the light of unity and concord may shine forth and shed its radiance upon the world.

3.3   O SON OF MAN! My eternity is My creation, I have created it for thee. Make it the garment of thy temple. My unity is My handiwork; I have wrought it for thee; clothe thyself therewith, that thou mayest be to all eternity the revelation of My everlasting being.

3.4   I bear witness, O my God, that Thou hast created me to know Thee and to worship Thee.

3.5   The Pen of the Most High hath, at all times and under all conditions, remembered, with joy and tenderness, His loved ones, and hath counselled them to follow in His way. Well is it with him whom the changes and chances of this world have failed to deter from recognizing the Day Spring of the Unity of God, who hath quaffed, with unswerving resolve, and in the name of the Self-Subsisting, the sealed wine of His Revelation. Such a man shall be numbered with the inmates of Paradise, in the Book of God, the Lord of all worlds.

FROM THE WRITINGS AND UTTERANCES OF 'ABDU'L-BAHÁ

3.6   For a single purpose were the Prophets, each and all, sent down to earth; for this was Christ made manifest, for this did Bahá'u'lláh raise up the call of the Lord: that the world of man should become the world of God, this nether realm the Kingdom, this darkness light, this satanic wickedness all the virtues of heaven—and unity, fellowship and love be won for the whole human race, that the organic unity should reappear and the bases of discord be destroyed and life everlasting and grace everlasting become the harvest of mankind.

3.7   ...In cycles gone by, though harmony was established, yet, owing to the absence of means, the unity of all mankind could not have been achieved. Continents remained widely divided, nay even among the peoples of one and the same continent association and interchange of thought were wellnigh impossible. Consequently intercourse, understanding and unity amongst all the peoples and kindreds of the earth were unattainable. In this day, however, means of communication have multiplied, and the five continents of the earth have virtually merged into one. And for everyone it is now easy to travel to any land, to associate and exchange views with its peoples, and to become familiar, through publications, with the conditions, the religious beliefs and the thoughts of all men. In like manner all the members of the human family, whether peoples or governments, cities or villages, have become increasingly interdependent. For none is self-sufficiency any longer possible, inasmuch as political ties unite all peoples and nations, and the bonds of trade and industry, of agriculture and education, are being strengthened every day. Hence the unity of all mankind can in this day be achieved. Verily this is none other but one of the wonders of this wondrous age, this glorious century. Of this past ages have been deprived, for this century—the century of light—hath been endowed with unique and unprecedented glory, power and illumination. Hence the miraculous unfolding of a fresh marvel every day. Eventually it will be seen how bright its candles will burn in the assemblage of man.

Behold how its light is now dawning upon the world's darkened horizon. The first candle is unity in the political realm, the early glimmerings of which can now be discerned. The second candle is unity of thought in world undertakings, the consummation of which will erelong be witnessed. The third candle is unity in freedom which will surely come to pass. The fourth candle is unity in religion which is the corner-stone of the foundation itself, and which, by the power of God, will be revealed in all its splendour. The fifth candle is the unity of nations—a unity which in this century will be securely established, causing all the peoples of the world to regard themselves as citizens of one common fatherland. The sixth candle is unity of races, making of all that dwell on earth peoples and kindreds of one race. The seventh candle is unity of language, i.e., the choice of a universal tongue in which all peoples will be instructed and converse. Each and every one of these will inevitably come to pass, inasmuch as the power of the Kingdom of God will aid and assist in their realization.

3.8 O ye lovers of this wronged one! Cleanse ye your eyes, so that ye behold no man as different from yourselves. See ye no strangers; rather see all men as friends, for love and unity come hard when ye fix your gaze on otherness. And in this new and wondrous age, the Holy Writings say that we must be at one with every people; that we must see neither harshness nor injustice, neither malevolence, nor hostility, nor hate, but rather turn our eyes toward the heaven of ancient glory. For each of the creatures is a sign of God, and it was by the grace of the Lord and His power that each did step into the world; therefore they are not strangers, but in the family; not aliens, but friends, and to be treated as such.

Wherefore must the loved ones of God associate in affectionate fellowship with stranger and friend alike, showing forth to all the utmost loving-kindness, disregarding the degree of their capacity, never asking whether they deserve to be loved. In every instance let the friends be considerate and infinitely kind. Let them never be defeated by the malice of the people, by their aggression and their hate, no matter how intense. If others hurl their darts against you, offer them milk and honey in return; if they poison your lives, sweeten their souls; if they injure you, teach them how to be comforted; if they inflict a wound upon you, be a balm to their sores; if they sting you, hold to their lips a refreshing cup.

3.9 Today the world of humanity is in need of international unity and conciliation. To establish these great fundamental principles a propelling power is needed. It is self-evident that the unity of the human world and the Most Great Peace cannot be accomplished through material means. They cannot be established through political power, for the political interests of nations are various and the policies of peoples are divergent and conflicting. They cannot be founded through racial or patriotic power, for these are human powers, selfish and weak. The very nature of racial differences and patriotic prejudices prevents the realization of this unity and agreement. Therefore, it is evidenced that the promotion of the oneness of the kingdom of humanity, which is the essence of the teachings of all the Manifestations of God, is impossible except through the divine power and breaths of the Holy Spirit. Other powers are too weak and are incapable of accomplishing this.

3.10 The first teaching of Bahá'u'lláh is the investigation of reality. Man must seek reality himself, forsaking imitations and adherence to mere hereditary forms. As the nations of the world are following imitations in lieu of truth and as imitations are many and various, differences of belief have been productive of strife and warfare. So long as these imitations remain, the oneness of the world of humanity is impossible. Therefore, we must investigate reality in order that by its light the clouds and darkness may be dispelled. Reality is one reality; it does not admit multiplicity or division.

3.11 The body politic today is greatly in need of a physician. It is similar to a human body afflicted with severe ailments. A doctor diagnoses the case and prescribes treatment. He does not prescribe, however, until he has made the diagnosis. The disease which afflicts the body politic is lack of love and absence of altruism. In the hearts of men no real love is found, and the condition is such that, unless their susceptibilities are quickened by some power so that unity, love and accord may develop within them, there can be no healing, no agreement among mankind. Love and unity are the needs of the body politic today. Without these there can be no progress or prosperity attained. Therefore, the friends of God must adhere to the power which will create this love and unity in the hearts of the sons of men. Science cannot cure the illness of the body politic. Science cannot create amity and fellowship in human hearts. Neither can patriotism nor racial allegiance effect a remedy. It must be accomplished solely through the divine bounties and spiritual bestowals which have descended from God in this day for that purpose. This is an exigency of the times, and the divine remedy has been provided. The spiritual teachings of the religion of God can alone create this love, unity and accord in human hearts.

3.12 Likewise, in the world of minds and souls, fellowship, which is an expression of composition, is conducive to life, whereas discord, which is an expression of decomposition, is the equivalent of death. Without cohesion among the individual elements which compose the body politic, disintegration and decay must inevitably follow and life be extinguished. Ferocious animals have no fellowship. The vultures and tigers are solitary, whereas domestic animals live together in complete harmony. The sheep, black and white, associate without discord. Birds of various species and colors wing their flight and feed together without a trace of enmity or disagreement. Therefore, in the world of humanity it is wise and seemly that all the individual members should manifest unity and affinity. In the clustered jewels of the races may the blacks be as sapphires and rubies and the whites as diamonds and pearls. The composite beauty of humanity will be witnessed in their unity and blending. How glorious the spectacle of real unity among mankind! How conducive to peace, confidence and happiness if races and nations were united in fellowship and accord! The Prophets of God were sent into the world upon this mission of unity and agreement: that these long-separated sheep might flock together. When the sheep separate, they are exposed to danger, but in a flock and under protection of the shepherd they are safe from the attack of all ferocious enemies.

3.13 The unity which is productive of unlimited results is first a unity of mankind which recognizes that all are sheltered beneath the overshadowing glory of the All-Glorious, that all are servants of one God; for all breathe the same atmosphere, live upon the same earth, move beneath the same heavens, receive effulgence from the same sun and are under the protection of one God. This is the most great unity, and its results are lasting if humanity adheres to it; but mankind has hitherto violated it, adhering to sectarian or other limited unities such as racial, patriotic or unity of self-interests; therefore, no great results have been forthcoming. Nevertheless, it is certain that the radiance and favors of God are encompassing, minds have developed, perceptions have become acute, sciences and arts are widespread, and capacity exists for the proclamation and promulgation of the real and ultimate unity of mankind, which will bring forth marvelous results. It will reconcile all religions, make warring nations loving, cause hostile kings to become friendly and bring peace and happiness to the human world. It will cement together the Orient and Occident, remove forever the foundations of war and upraise the ensign of the Most Great Peace. These limited unities are, therefore, signs of that great unity which will make all the human family one by being productive of the attractions of conscience in mankind.

3.14 In the world of existence there are various bonds which unite human hearts, but not one of these bonds is completely effective. The first and foremost is the bond of family relationship, which is not an efficient unity, for how often it happens that disagreement and divergence rend asunder this close tie of association. The bond of patriotism may be a means of fellowship and agreement, but oneness of native land will not completely cement human hearts; for if we review history, we shall find that people of the same race and native land have frequently waged war against each other. Often in civil strife they have shed the same racial blood and destroyed the possessions of their own native kind. Therefore, this bond is not sufficient. Another means of seeming unity is the bond of political association, where governments and rulers have been allied for reasons of intercourse and mutual protection, but which agreement and union afterward became subject to change and violent hatred even to the extreme of war and bloodshed. It is evident that political oneness is not permanently effective.

The source of perfect unity and love in the world of existence is the bond and oneness of reality. When the divine and fundamental reality enters human hearts and lives, it conserves and protects all states and conditions of mankind, establishing that intrinsic oneness of the world of humanity which can only come into being through the efficacy of the Holy Spirit. For the Holy Spirit is like unto the life in the human body, which blends all differences of parts and members in unity and agreement. Consider how numerous are these parts and members, but the oneness of the animating spirit of life unites them all in perfect combination. It establishes such a unity in the bodily organism that if any part is subjected to injury or becomes diseased, all the other parts and functions sympathetically respond and suffer, owing to the perfect oneness existing. Just as the human spirit of life is the cause of coordination among the various parts of the human organism, the Holy Spirit is the controlling cause of the unity and coordination of mankind. That is to say, the bond or oneness of humanity cannot be effectively established save through the power of the Holy Spirit, for the world of humanity is a composite body, and the Holy Spirit is the animating principle of its life.

3.15 This is the day when pure hearts have a portion of the everlasting bounties and sanctified souls are being illumined by the eternal manifestations. Praise be to God! You are believers in God, assured by the words of God and turning to the Kingdom of God. You have heard the divine call. Your hearts are moved by the breezes of the paradise of Abha. You have good intentions; your purpose is the good pleasure of God; you desire to serve in the Kingdom of the Merciful One. Therefore, arise in the utmost power. Be in perfect unity. Never become angry with one another. Let your eyes be directed toward the kingdom of truth and not toward the world of creation. Love the creatures for the sake of God and not for themselves. You will never become angry or impatient if you love them for the sake of God. Humanity is not perfect. There are imperfections in every human being, and you will always become unhappy if you look toward the people themselves. But if you look toward God, you will love them and be kind to them, for the world of God is the world of perfection and complete mercy. Therefore, do not look at the shortcomings of anybody; see with the sight of forgiveness. The imperfect eye beholds imperfections. The eye that covers faults looks toward the Creator of souls. He created them, trains and provides for them, endows them with capacity and life, sight and hearing; therefore, they are the signs of His grandeur. You must love and be kind to everybody, care for the poor, protect the weak, heal the sick, teach and educate the ignorant.

FROM THE WRITINGS AND LETTERS WRITTEN BY, OR ON BEHALF OF, SHOGHI EFFENDI

3.16   ... the condition that the world is in is bringing many issues to a head. It would be perhaps impossible to find a nation or people not in a state of crisis today. The materialism, the lack of true religion and the consequent baser forces in human nature which are being released, have brought the whole world to the brink of probably the greatest crisis it has ever faced or will have to face. The Bahá'ís are a part of the world. They too feel the great pressures which are brought to bear upon all people today, whoever and wherever they may be. On the other hand, the Divine Plan, which is the direct method of working towards the establishment of peace and World Order, has perforce reached an important and challenging point in its unfoldment; because of the desperate needs of the world, the Bahá'ís find themselves, even though so limited in numbers, in financial strength and in prestige, called upon to fulfill a great responsibility.

FROM THE WRITINGS AND LETTERS WRITTEN BY, OR ON BEHALF OF, THE UNIVERSAL HOUSE OF JUSTICE

3.17 In the midst of a civilization torn by strifes and enfeebled by materialism, the people of Baha are building a new world. We face at this time opportunities and responsibilities of vast magnitude and great urgency. Let each believer in his inmost heart resolve not to be seduced by the ephemeral allurements of the society around him nor to be drawn into its feuds and short-lived enthusiasms, but instead to transfer all he can from the old world to that new one which is the vision of his longing and will be the fruit of his labours.

3.18 At the very core of the aims of the Faith are the establishment of justice and unity in the world, the removal of prejudice and enmity from among all people, the awakening of compassion and understanding in the hearts of all men and women, and the raising of all souls to a new level of spirituality and behavior through the vitalizing influence of divine Revelation. The course set forth by Bahá'u'lláh for the attainment of these aims is the double task of simultaneously building an ideal society and perfecting the behavior of individuals. For this dual and reciprocal transformation He has not only revealed laws, principles and truths attuned to the needs of this age, but has established the very nucleus and patter of those institutions which are to evolve into the structure of the divinely purposed world society.

OTHER SOURCES

3.19 Within the context of the history of civilization, the objective of the succession of divine Manifestations has been to prepare human consciousness for the race's unification as a single species, indeed as a single organism capable of taking up the responsibility for its collective future: "He Who is your Lord, the All-Merciful," Bahá'u'lláh says, "cherisheth in His heart the desire of beholding the entire human race as one soul and one body." Not until humanity has accepted its organic oneness can it meet even its immediate challenges, let alone those that lie ahead: "The well-being of mankind," Bahá'u'lláh insists, "its peace and security, are unattainable unless and until its unity is firmly established." Only a unified global society can provide its children with the sense of inner assurance implied in one of Bahá'u'lláh's prayers to God: "Whatever duty Thou hast prescribed unto Thy servants of extolling to the utmost Thy majesty and glory is but a token of Thy grace unto them, that they may be enabled to ascend unto the station conferred upon their own inmost being, the station of the knowledge of their own selves." Paradoxically, it is only by achieving true unity that humanity can fully cultivate its diversity and individuality. This is the goal which the missions of all of the Manifestations of God known to history have served, the Day of "one fold and one shepherd." Its attainment, Bahá'u'lláh says, is the stage of civilization upon which the human race is now entering. (Baha'i International Community, 1992 May 29, *Statement on Baha'u'llah*, p. 15)

CHAPTER 4:

CREATING A CULTURE OF GLOBAL AWARENESS

44 ❓ Making a Better World with the Bahá'í Faith: QUOTATIONS

FROM THE WRITINGS OF BAHÁ'U'LLÁH

4.1 Likewise He saith: Among the things which are conducive to unity and concord and will cause the whole earth to be regarded as one country is that the divers languages be reduced to one language and in like manner the scripts used in the world be confined to a single script. It is incumbent upon all nations to appoint some men of understanding and erudition to convene a gathering and through joint consultation choose one language from among the varied existing languages, or create a new one, to be taught to the children in all the schools of the world.

The day is approaching when all the peoples of the world will have adopted one universal language and one common script. When this is achieved, to whatsoever city a man may journey, it shall be as if he were entering his own home. These things are obligatory and absolutely essential. It is incumbent upon every man of insight and understanding to strive to translate that which hath been written into reality and action.

4.2 From the beginning of time the light of unity hath shed its divine radiance upon the world, and the greatest means for the promotion of that unity is for the peoples of the world to understand one another's writing and speech. In former Epistles We have enjoined upon the Trustees of the House of Justice either to choose one language from among those now existing or to adopt a new one, and in like manner to select a common script, both of which should be taught in all the schools of the world. Thus will the earth be regarded as one country and one home. The most glorious fruit of the tree of knowledge is this exalted word: Of one tree are all ye the fruit, and of one bough the leaves. Let not man glory in this that he loveth his country, let him rather glory in this that he loveth his kind. Concerning this We have previously revealed that which is the means of the reconstruction of the world and the unity of nations. Blessed are they that attain thereunto. Blessed are they that act accordingly

4.3 This decree hath formerly streamed forth from the Pen of the Most High: It behoveth the sovereigns of the world—may God assist them—or the ministers of the earth to take counsel together and to adopt one of the existing languages or a new one to be taught to children in schools throughout the world, and likewise one script. Thus the whole earth will come to be regarded as one country. Well is it with him who hearkeneth unto His Call and observeth that whereunto he is bidden by God, the Lord of the Mighty Throne.

4.4 O members of parliaments throughout the world! Select ye a single language for the use of all on earth, and adopt ye likewise a common script. God, verily, maketh plain for you that which shall profit you and enable you to be independent of others. He, of a truth, is the Most Bountiful, the All-Knowing, the All-Informed. This will be the cause of unity, could ye but comprehend it, and the greatest instrument for promoting harmony and civilization, would that ye might understand!

4.5 Languages must be reduced to one common language to be taught in all the schools of the world.

4.6 Take pride not in love for yourselves but in love for your fellow-creatures. Glory not in love for your country, but in love for all mankind.

4.7 This is the Day whereon the Ocean of God's mercy hath been manifested unto men, the Day in which the Day Star of His loving-kindness hath shed its radiance upon them, the Day in which the clouds of His bountiful favor have overshadowed the whole of mankind.

FROM THE WRITINGS AND UTTERANCES OF 'ABDU'L-BAHÁ

4.8 Wherefore, O ye beloved of the Lord, bestir yourselves, do all in your power to be as one, to live in peace, each with the others: for ye are all the drops from but one ocean, the foliage of one tree, the pearls from a single shell, the flowers and sweet herbs from the same one garden. And achieving that, strive ye to unite the hearts of those who follow other faiths.

For one another must ye give up even life itself. To every human being must ye be infinitely kind. Call none a stranger; think none to be your foe. Be ye as if all men were your close kin and honoured friends. Walk ye in such wise that this fleeting world will change into a splendour and this dismal heap of dust become a palace of delights. Such is the counsel of 'Abdu'l-Bahá, this hapless servant.

4.9 Care for the stranger as for one of your own; show to alien souls the same loving kindness ye bestow upon your faithful friends.

4.10 And among the teachings of Bahá'u'lláh is the origination of one language that may be spread universally among the people. This teaching was revealed from the pen of Bahá'u'lláh in order that this universal language may eliminate misunderstandings from among mankind.

4.11 We must now highly resolve to arise and lay hold of all those instrumentalities that promote the peace and well-being and happiness, the knowledge, culture and industry, the dignity, value and station, of the entire human race. Thus, through the restoring waters of pure intention and unselfish effort, the earth of human potentialities will blossom with its own latent excellence and flower into praiseworthy qualities, and bear and flourish until it comes to rival that rosegarden of knowledge which belonged to our forefathers.

4.12 Bahá'u'lláh has proclaimed the adoption of a universal language. A language shall be agreed upon by which unity will be established in the world. Each person will require training in two languages: his native tongue and the universal auxiliary form of speech. This will facilitate intercommunication and dispel the misunderstandings which the barriers of language have occasioned in the world. All people worship the same God and are alike His servants. When they are able to communicate freely, they will associate in friendship and concord, entertain the greatest love and fellowship for each other, and in reality the Orient and Occident will embrace in unity and agreement

4.13   ... a universal language shall be adopted and be taught by all the schools and institutions of the world. A committee appointed by national bodies of learning shall select a suitable language to be used as a medium of international communication. All must acquire it. This is one of the great factors in the unification of man.

4.14   All mankind must attain to spiritual fraternity—that is to say, fraternity in the Holy Spirit—for patriotic, racial and political fraternity are of no avail. Their results are meager; but divine fraternity, spiritual fraternity, is the cause of unity and amity among mankind. As heretofore material civilization has been extended, the divine civilization must now be promulgated. Until the two agree, real happiness among mankind will be unknown. By mere intellectual development and power of reason, man cannot attain to his fullest degree—that is to say, by means of intellect alone he cannot accomplish the progress effected by religion. For the philosophers of the past strove in vain to revivify the world of mankind through the intellectual faculty. The most of which they were capable was educating themselves and a limited number of disciples; they themselves have confessed failure. Therefore, the world of humanity must be confirmed by the breath of the Holy Spirit in order to receive universal education. Through the infusion of divine power all nations and peoples become quickened, and universal happiness is possible.

4.15   Let not conventionality cause you to seem cold and unsympathetic when you meet strange people from other countries. Do not look at them as though you suspected them of being evil-doers, thieves and boors. You think it necessary to be very careful, not to expose yourselves to the risk of making acquaintance with such, possibly, undesirable people.

   I ask you not to think only of yourselves. Be kind to the strangers, whether come they from Turkey, Japan, Persia, Russia, China or any other country in the world.

> Help to make them feel at home; find out where they are staying, ask if you may render them any service; try to make their lives a little happier.
>
> In this way, even if, sometimes, what you at first suspected should be true, still go out of your way to be kind to them—this kindness will help them to become better.
>
> After all, why should any foreign people be treated as strangers?
>
> Let those who meet you know, without your proclaiming the fact, that you are indeed a Bahá'í.

FROM THE WRITINGS AND LETTERS WRITTEN BY, OR ON BEHALF OF, SHOGHI EFFENDI

4.16 Let there be no misgivings as to the animating purpose of the world-wide Law of Bahá'u'lláh. Far from aiming at the subversion of the existing foundations of society, it seeks to broaden its basis, to remold its institutions in a manner consonant with the needs of an ever-changing world. It can conflict with no legitimate allegiances, nor can it undermine essential loyalties. Its purpose is neither to stifle the flame of a sane and intelligent patriotism in men's hearts, nor to abolish the system of national autonomy so essential if the evils of excessive centralization are to be avoided. It does not ignore, nor does it attempt to suppress, the diversity of ethnical origins, of climate, of history, of language and tradition, of thought and habit, that differentiate the peoples and nations of the world. It calls for a wider loyalty, for a larger aspiration than any that has animated the human race. It insists upon the subordination of national impulses and interests to the imperative claims of a unified world. It repudiates excessive centralization on one hand, and disclaims all attempts at uniformity on the other. Its watchword is unity in diversity such as 'Abdu'l-Bahá Himself has explained...

4.17 The Revelation of Bahá'u'lláh, whose supreme mission is none other but the achievement of this organic and spiritual unity of the whole body of nations, should, if we be faithful to its implications, be regarded as signalizing through its advent the coming of age of the entire human race. It should be viewed not merely as yet another spiritual revival in the ever-changing fortunes of mankind, not only as a further stage in a chain of progressive Revelations, nor even as the culmination of one of a series of recurrent prophetic cycles, but rather as marking the last and highest stage in the stupendous evolution of man's collective life on this planet. The emergence of a world community, the consciousness of world citizenship, the founding of a world civilization and culture—all of which must synchronize with the initial stages in the unfoldment of the Golden Age of the Bahá'í Era—should, by their very nature, be regarded, as far as this planetary life is concerned, as the furthermost limits in the organization of human society, though man, as an individual, will, nay must indeed as a result of such a consummation, continue indefinitely to progress and develop.

4.18 Also, you raise the question of what will be the source of inspiration to Bahá'í musicians and composers; the music of the past or the Word? We cannot possibly foresee, standing as we do on the threshold of Bahá'í culture, what forms and characteristics the arts of the future, inspired by this Mighty New Revelation, will have. All we can be sure of is that they will be wonderful; as every Faith has given rise to a culture which flowered in different forms, so too our beloved Faith may be expected to do the same thing. It is premature to try and grasp what they will be at present.

4.19 Regarding the whole question of an international language and its relation to the Faith: We, as Bahá'ís, are very anxious to see a universal auxiliary tongue adopted as soon as possible; we are not the protagonists of any one language to fill this post. If the governments of the world agree on an existing language, or a constructed, new tongue, to be used internationally, we would heartily support it because we desire to see this step in the unification of the human race take place as soon as possible.

FROM THE WRITINGS AND LETTERS WRITTEN BY, OR ON BEHALF OF, THE UNIVERSAL HOUSE OF JUSTICE

4.20 A fundamental lack of communication between peoples seriously undermines efforts towards world peace. Adopting an international auxiliary language would go far to resolving this problem and necessitates the most urgent attention.

4.21 In recent years, the House of Justice has taken the opportunity provided by its Ridvan messages to draw the attention of the worldwide Bahá'í community to the profound significance of the events occurring in the wider society as humanity exhibits a growing consciousness of the unity of the nations and peoples of the planet.

4.22 Humanity's crying need will not be met by a struggle among competing ambitions or by protest against one or another of the countless wrongs afflicting a desperate age. It calls, rather, for a fundamental change of consciousness, for a wholehearted embrace of Bahá'u'lláh's teaching that the time has come when each human being on earth must learn to accept responsibility for the welfare of the entire human family. Commitment to this revolutionizing principle will increasingly empower individual believers and Bahá'í institutions alike in awakening others to the Day of God and to the latent spiritual and moral capacities that can change this world into another world. We demonstrate this commitment, Shoghi Effendi tells us, by our rectitude of conduct towards others, by the discipline of our own natures, and by our complete freedom from the prejudices that cripple collective action in the society around us and frustrate positive impulses towards change.

OTHER SOURCES

4.23 The Bahá'í International Community is confident—because of its experience in bringing together in harmony members of nearly every religion and culture on earth—that even deeply rooted religious prejudices melt away in an environment of humility, compassion, and an earnest search for truth. (Bahá'í International Community, 1993 Aug 03, *Ending Religious Intolerance*)

4.24 We foresee that eventually, the world cannot but adopt a single, universally agreed-upon auxiliary language and script to be taught in schools worldwide, as a supplement to the language or languages of each country. The objective would be to facilitate the transition to a global society through better communication among nations, reduction of administrative costs for businesses, governments and others involved in global enterprise, and a general fostering of more cordial relations between all members of the human family. (Baha'i International Community, 1995 Oct, *Turning Point For All Nations*)

4.25 Implicit in these paragraphs is a perspective which represents the most challenging feature of Bahá'u'lláh's exposition of the function of the Manifestation of God. Divine Revelation is, He says, the motive power of civilization. When it occurs, its transforming effect on the minds and souls of those who respond to it is replicated in the new society that slowly takes shape around their experience. A new center of loyalty emerges that can win the commitment of peoples from the widest range of cultures; music and the arts seize on symbols that mediate far richer and more mature inspirations; a radical redefinition of concepts of right and wrong makes possible the formulation of new codes of civil law and conduct; new institutions are conceived in order to give expression to impulses of moral responsibility previously ignored or unknown: "He was in the world, and the world was made by him..." As the new culture evolves into a civilization, it assimilates achievements and insights of past eras in a multitude of fresh permutations. Features of past cultures that cannot be incorporated atrophy or are taken up by marginal elements among the population. The Word of God creates new possibilities within both the individual consciousness and human relationships. (Baha'i International Community, 1992 May 29, *Statement on Bahá'u'lláh*, p. 13)

CHAPTER 5:

STRIVING FOR WORLD PEACE

Making a Better World with the Bahá'í Faith: QUOTATIONS

FROM THE WRITINGS OF BAHÁ'U'LLÁH

5.1 Soon will the present-day order be rolled up, and a new one spread out in its stead. Verily, thy Lord speaketh the truth, and is the Knower of things unseen.

5.2 The Great Being, wishing to reveal the prerequisites of the peace and tranquillity of the world and the advancement of its peoples, hath written: The time must come when the imperative necessity for the holding of a vast, an all-embracing assemblage of men will be universally realized. The rulers and kings of the earth must needs attend it, and, participating in its deliberations, must consider such ways and means as will lay the foundations of the world's Great Peace amongst men. Such a peace demandeth that the Great Powers should resolve, for the sake of the tranquility of the peoples of the earth, to be fully reconciled among themselves. Should any king take up arms against another, all should unitedly arise and prevent him. If this be done, the nations of the world will no longer require any armaments, except for the purpose of preserving the security of their realms and of maintaining internal order within their territories. This will ensure the peace and composure of every people, government and nation. We fain would hope that the kings and rulers of the earth, the mirrors of the gracious and almighty name of God, may attain unto this station, and shield mankind from the onslaught of tyranny. …The day is approaching when all the peoples of the world will have adopted one universal language and one common script. When this is achieved, to whatsoever city a man may journey, it shall be as if he were entering his own home. These things are obligatory and absolutely essential. It is incumbent upon every man of insight and understanding to strive to translate that which hath been written into reality and action.... That one indeed is a man who, today, dedicateth himself to the service of the entire human race. The Great Being saith: Blessed and happy is he that ariseth to promote the best interests of the peoples and kindreds of the earth. In another passage He hath proclaimed: It is not for him to pride himself who loveth his own country, but rather for him who loveth the whole world. The earth is but one country, and mankind its citizens.

5.3 THIS is the Day in which God's most excellent favours have been poured out upon men, the Day in which His most mighty grace hath been infused into all created things. It is incumbent upon all the peoples of the world to reconcile their differences, and, with perfect unity and peace, abide beneath the shadow of the Tree of His care and loving-kindness. It behoveth them to cleave to whatsoever will, in this Day, be conducive to the exaltation of their stations, and to the promotion of their best interests. Happy are those whom the all-glorious Pen was moved to remember, and blessed are those men whose names, by virtue of Our inscrutable decree, We have preferred to conceal.

5.4 Let none contend with another, and let no soul slay another; this, verily, is that which was forbidden you in a Book that hath lain concealed within the Tabernacle of glory.

5.5 Know thou that We have annulled the rule of the sword, as an aid to Our Cause, and substituted for it the power born of the utterance of men.

5.6 Say: Sow not, O people, the seeds of dissension amongst men, and contend not with your neighbor. Be patient under all conditions, and place your whole trust and confidence in God. Aid ye your Lord with the sword of wisdom and of utterance. This indeed well becometh the station of man. To depart from it would be unworthy of God, the Sovereign Lord of all, the Glorified.

5.7 Lay not aside the fear of God, O kings of the earth, and beware that ye transgress not the bounds which the Almighty hath fixed. Observe the injunctions laid upon you in His Book, and take good heed not to overstep their limits. Be vigilant, that ye may not do injustice to anyone, be it to the extent of a grain of mustard seed. Tread ye the path of justice, for this, verily, is the straight path.

Compose your differences, and reduce your armaments, that the burden of your expenditures may be lightened, and that your minds and hearts may be tranquillized. Heal the dissensions that divide you, and ye will no longer be in need of any armaments except what the protection of your cities and territories demandeth. Fear ye God, and take heed not to outstrip the bounds of moderation, and be numbered among the extravagant.

We have learned that you are increasing your outlay every year, and are laying the burden thereof on your subjects. This, verily, is more than they can bear, and is a grievous injustice. Decide justly between men, and be ye the emblems of justice amongst them. This, if ye judge fairly, is the thing that behoveth you, and beseemeth your station.

Beware not to deal unjustly with any one that appealeth to you, and entereth beneath your shadow. Walk ye in the fear of God, and be ye of them that lead a godly life. Rest not on your power, your armies, and treasures. Put your whole trust and confidence in God, Who hath created you, and seek ye His help in all your affairs. Succor cometh from Him alone. He succoreth whom He will with the hosts of the heavens and of the earth.

5.8 The winds of despair are, alas, blowing from every direction, and the strife that divideth and afflicteth the human race is daily increasing. The signs of impending convulsions and chaos can now be discerned, inasmuch as the prevailing order appeareth to be lamentably defective.

5.9 Now that ye have refused the Most Great Peace, hold ye fast unto this, the Lesser Peace, that haply ye may in some degree better your own condition and that of your dependents.

O rulers of the earth! Be reconciled among yourselves, that ye may need no more armaments save in a measure to safeguard your territories and dominions. Beware lest ye disregard the counsel of the All-Knowing, the Faithful.

Be united, O kings of the earth, for thereby will the tempest of discord be stilled amongst you, and your peoples find rest, if ye be of them that comprehend. Should any one among you take up arms against another, rise ye all against him, for this is naught but manifest justice.

FROM THE WRITINGS AND UTTERANCES OF 'ABDU'L-BAHÁ

5.10 As to the patriotic prejudice, this is also due to absolute ignorance, for the surface of the earth is one native land. Every one can live in any spot on the terrestrial globe. Therefore all the world is man's birthplace. These boundaries and outlets have been devised by man. In the creation, such boundaries and outlets were not assigned. Europe is one continent, Asia is one continent, Africa is one continent, Australia is one continent, but some of the souls, from personal motives and selfish interests, have divided each one of these continents and considered a certain part as their own country. God has set up no frontier between France and Germany; they are continuous. Yea, in the first centuries, selfish souls, for the promotion of their own interests, have assigned boundaries and outlets and have, day by day, attached more importance to these, until this led to intense enmity, bloodshed and rapacity in subsequent centuries. In the same way this will continue indefinitely, and if this conception of patriotism remains limited within a certain circle, it will be the primary cause of the world's destruction. No wise and just person will acknowledge these imaginary distinctions. Every limited area which we call our native country we regard as our motherland, whereas the terrestrial globe is the motherland of all, and not any restricted area. In short, for a few days we live on this earth and eventually we are buried in it, it is our eternal tomb. Is it worth while that we should engage in bloodshed and tear one another to pieces for this eternal tomb? Nay, far from it, neither is God pleased with such conduct nor would any sane man approve of it.

5.11 True civilization will unfurl its banner in the midmost heart of the world whenever a certain number of its distinguished and high-minded sovereigns—the shining exemplars of devotion and determination—shall, for the good and happiness of all mankind, arise, with firm resolve and clear vision, to establish the Cause of Universal Peace. They must make the Cause of Peace the object of general consultation, and seek by every means in their power to establish a Union of the nations of the world. They must conclude a binding treaty and establish a covenant, the provisions of which shall be sound, inviolable and definite. They must proclaim it to all the world and obtain for it the sanction of all the human race. This supreme and noble undertaking—the real source of the peace and well-being of all the world—should be regarded as sacred by all that dwell on earth. All the forces of humanity must be mobilized to ensure the stability and permanence of this Most Great Covenant. In this all-embracing Pact the limits and frontiers of each and every nation should be clearly fixed, the principles underlying the relations of governments towards one another definitely laid down, and all international agreements and obligations ascertained. In like manner, the size of the armaments of every government should be strictly limited, for if the preparations for war and the military forces of any nation should be allowed to increase, they will arouse the suspicion of others. The fundamental principle underlying this solemn Pact should be so fixed that if any government later violate any one of its provisions, all the governments on earth should arise to reduce it to utter submission, nay the human race as a whole should resolve, with every power at its disposal, to destroy that government. Should this greatest of all remedies be applied to the sick body of the world, it will assuredly recover from its ills and will remain eternally safe and secure.

5.12 The apparatus of conflict will, as preparations go on at their present rate, reach the point where war will become something intolerable to mankind.

5.13 ... All are the servants of God and members of one human family. God has created all, and all are His children. He rears, nourishes, provides for and is kind to all. Why should we be unjust and unkind? This is the policy of God, the lights of which have shone throughout the world. His sun bestows its effulgence unsparingly upon all; His clouds send down rain without distinction or favor; His breezes refresh the whole earth. It is evident that humankind without exception is sheltered beneath His mercy and protection. Some are imperfect; they must be perfected. The ignorant must be taught, the sick healed, the sleepers awakened. The child must not be oppressed or censured because it is undeveloped; it must be patiently trained. The sick must not be neglected because they are ailing; nay, rather, we must have compassion upon them and bring them healing. Briefly, the old conditions of animosity, bigotry and hatred between the religious systems must be dispelled and the new conditions of love, agreement and spiritual brotherhood be established among them.

5.14 The world is in greatest need of international peace. Until it is established, mankind will not attain composure and tranquility. It is necessary that the nations and governments organize an international tribunal to which all their disputes and differences shall be referred. The decision of that tribunal shall be final. Individual controversy will be adjudged by a local tribunal. International questions will come before the universal tribunal, and so the cause of warfare will be taken away.

5.15 He promulgated the adoption of the same course of education for man and woman. Daughters and sons must follow the same curriculum of study, thereby promoting unity of the sexes. When all mankind shall receive the same opportunity of education and the equality of men and women be realized, the foundations of war will be utterly destroyed. Without equality this will be impossible because all differences and distinction are conducive to discord and strife. Equality between men and women is conducive to the abolition of warfare for the reason that women will never be willing to sanction it. Mothers will not give their sons as sacrifices upon the battlefield after twenty years of anxiety and loving devotion in rearing them from infancy, no matter what cause they are called upon to defend. There is no doubt that when women obtain equality of rights, war will entirely cease among mankind.

FROM THE WRITINGS AND LETTERS WRITTEN BY, OR ON BEHALF OF, SHOGHI EFFENDI

5.16   It is still his firm conviction that the believers, while expressing their readiness to unreservedly obey any directions that the authorities may issue concerning national service in time of war, should also, and while there is yet no outbreak of hostilities, appeal to the government for exemption from active military service in a combatant capacity, stressing the fact that in doing so they are not prompted by any selfish considerations but by the sole and supreme motive of upholding the Teachings of their Faith, which make it a moral obligation for them to desist from any act that would involve them in direct warfare with their fellow-humans of any other race or nation. The Bahá'í Teachings, indeed, condemn, emphatically and unequivocally, any form of physical violence, and warfare in the battlefield is obviously a form, and perhaps the worst form which such violence can assume.

There are many other avenues through which the believers can assist in times of war by enlisting in services of a non-combatant nature—services that do not involve the direct shedding of blood—such as ambulance work, anti-air raid precaution service, office and administrative works, and it is for such types of national service that they should volunteer.

It is immaterial whether such activities would still expose them to dangers, either at home or in the front, since their desire is not to protect their lives, but to desist from any acts of wilful murder.

The friends should consider it their conscientious duty, as loyal members of the Faith, to apply for such exemption, even though there may be slight prospect of their obtaining the consent and approval of the authorities to their petition. It is most essential that in times of such national excitement and emergency as those through which so many countries in the world are now passing that the believers should not allow themselves to be carried away by the passions agitating the masses, and act in a manner that would make them deviate from the path of wisdom and moderation, and lead them to violate, however reluctantly and indirectly, the spirit as well as the letter of the Teachings.

FROM THE WRITINGS AND LETTERS WRITTEN BY, OR ON BEHALF OF, THE UNIVERSAL HOUSE OF JUSTICE

5.17 The primary question to be resolved is how the present world, with its entrenched pattern of conflict, can change to a world in which harmony and co-operation will prevail.

5.18 Two points bear emphasizing in all these issues. One is that the abolition of war is not simply a matter of signing treaties and protocols; it is a complex task requiring a new level of commitment to resolving issues not customarily associated with the pursuit of peace. Based on political agreements alone, the idea of collective security is a chimera. The other point is that the primary challenge in dealing with issues of peace is to raise the context to the level of principle, as distinct from pure pragmatism. For, in essence, peace stems from an inner state supported by a spiritual or moral attitude, and it is chiefly in evoking this attitude that the possibility of enduring solutions can be found.

5.19 The Great Peace towards which people of goodwill throughout the centuries have inclined their hearts, of which seers and poets for countless generations have expressed their vision, and for which from age to age the sacred scriptures of mankind have constantly held the promise, is now at long last within the reach of the nations. For the first time in history it is possible for everyone to view the entire planet, with all its myriad diversified peoples, in one perspective. World peace is not only possible but inevitable.

5.20 Whether peace is to be reached only after unimaginable horrors precipitated by humanity's stubborn clinging to old patterns of behaviour, or is to be embraced now by an act of consultative will, is the choice before all who inhabit the earth. At this critical juncture when the intractable problems confronting nations have been fused into one common concern for the whole world, failure to stem the tide of conflict and disorder would be unconscionably irresponsible.

5.21 To choose such a course is not to deny humanity's past but to understand it. The Bahá'í Faith regards the current world confusion and calamitous condition in human affairs as a natural phase in an organic process leading ultimately and irresistibly to the unification of the human race in a single social order whose boundaries are those of the planet. The human race, as a distinct, organic unit, has passed through evolutionary stages analogous to the stages of infancy and childhood in the lives of its individual members, and is now in the culminating period of its turbulent adolescence approaching its long-awaited coming of age.

5.22 World order can be founded only on an unshakeable consciousness of the oneness of mankind, a spiritual truth which all the human sciences confirm. Anthropology, physiology, psychology, recognize only one human species, albeit infinitely varied in the secondary aspects of life. Recognition of this truth requires abandonment of prejudice—prejudice of every kind-race, class, colour, creed, nation, sex, degree of material civilization, everything which enables people to consider themselves superior to others.

5.23 The experience of the Bahá'í community may be seen as an example of this enlarging unity. It is a community of some three to four million people drawn from many nations, cultures, classes and creeds, engaged in a wide range of activities serving the spiritual, social and economic needs of the peoples of many lands. It is a single social organism, representative of the diversity of the human family, conducting its affairs through a system of commonly accepted consultative principles, and cherishing equally all the great outpourings of divine guidance in human history. Its existence is yet another convincing proof of the practicality of its Founder's vision of a united world, another evidence that humanity can live as one global society, equal to whatever challenges its coming of age may entail. If the Bahá'í experience can contribute in whatever measure to reinforcing hope in the unity of the human race, we are happy to offer it as a model for study.

5.24 World order can be founded only on an unshakeable consciousness of the oneness of mankind, a spiritual truth which all the human sciences confirm. Anthropology, physiology, psychology, recognize only one human species, albeit infinitely varied in the secondary aspects of life. Recognition of this truth requires abandonment of prejudice—prejudice of every kind—race, class, colour, creed, nation, sex, degree of material civilization, everything which enables people to consider themselves superior to others.

5.25 Acceptance of the oneness of mankind is the first fundamental prerequisite for reorganization and administration of the world as one country, the home of humankind. Universal acceptance of this spiritual principle is essential to any successful attempt to establish world peace. It should therefore be universally proclaimed, taught in schools, and constantly asserted in every nation as preparation for the organic change in the structure of society which it implies.

In the Bahá'í view, recognition of the oneness of mankind "calls for no less than the reconstruction and the demilitarization of the whole civilized world—a world organically unified in all the essential aspects of its life, its political machinery, its spiritual aspiration, its trade and finance, its script and language, and yet infinite in the diversity of the national characteristics of its federated units."

5.26 The holding of this mighty convocation is long overdue.

With all the ardour of our hearts, we appeal to the leaders of all nations to seize this opportune moment and take irreversible steps to convoke this world meeting. All the forces of history impel the human race towards this act which will mark for all time the dawn of its long-awaited maturity.

5.27 Disunity is a danger that the nations and peoples of the earth can no longer endure; the consequences are too terrible to contemplate, too obvious to require any demonstration. "The well-being of mankind," Bahá'u'lláh wrote more than a century ago, "its peace and security, are unattainable unless and until its unity is firmly established." In observing that "mankind is groaning, is dying to be led to unity, and to terminate its age-long martyrdom", Shoghi Effendi further commented that: "Unification of the whole of mankind is the hall-mark of the stage which human society is now approaching. Unity of family, of tribe, of citystate, and nation have been successively attempted and fully established. World unity is the goal towards which a harassed humanity is striving. Nation-building has come to an end. The anarchy inherent in state sovereignty is moving towards a climax. A world, growing to maturity, must abandon this fetish, recognize the oneness and wholeness of human relationships, and establish once for all the machinery that can best incarnate this fundamental principle of its life.

OTHER SOURCES

5.28   World Peace, a hallmark of the emerging global civilization, will be realized as a tangible expression of the principle of the oneness of humankind. This assurance is given in the teachings of Bahá'u'lláh.

Such a peace will result from the culmination of two distinct but simultaneous and mutually reinforcing processes: one leading to the spiritual unity of the human race, referred to as the "Most Great Peace"; the other to the political unity of nations and known as the "Lesser Peace". The former is a distant goal, requiring a monumental change in human conduct that only religious faith can ensure; the other is more immediate and can already be detected on the political horizon. The one is directly related to the efforts of the Bahá'í community in promoting the pivotal principle of their Faith; the other is dependent on the actions of world political leaders and not on any Bahá'í plan or action.

The political unity of nations implies the achievement of a relationship among them that will enable them to resolve questions of international import through consultation rather than war and that will lead to the establishment of a world government. The attainment of peace in the political realm is discernible through the workings of a process that can be seen as having been definitely established in the twentieth century amid the terror and turmoil that have characterized so much of this period. It is noteworthy that the majority of the nations have come into being during this century and that they have opted for peaceful relations with one another by joining in the membership of the United Nations and through participation in regional organizations that facilitate their working together. Moreover, the process of political unification is gaining acceleration through the awakening of a consciousness of peace among the world's peoples that validates the work of the

United Nations, and through advances in science and technology, which have already contracted and transformed the world into a single complex organism.

The horrific experiences of two world wars which gave birth at first to the League of Nations and then to the United Nations; the frequency with which world leaders, particularly in the decade of the nineties, have met and agreed on the resolution of global issues; the call for a global order that issued from the participation of these leaders in the celebration of the fiftieth anniversary of the United Nations; the multiplication of organizations of civil society that focus attention on a variety of international concerns through the operation of an ever-expanding network of activities; the widespread debates on the need for global governance and numerous organized efforts towards world peace; the emergence of international tribunals; the rapid developments in communications technology that have made the planet borderless—these are among the voluminous evidences of a momentum toward peaceful international relations that has clearly become irreversible.

The Bahá'í writings indicate that peace among the nations will be established in the twentieth century; they do say, however, that a universal fermentation and horrendous social upheavals would mark the transition from a warlike world to a peaceful one, but they do not point to the occurrence of any specific cataclysmic event at the end of the century. Inevitably, the movement leading to world unity must encounter opposing tendencies rooted in stubborn habits of chauvinism and partisanship that refuse to yield to the expectations of a new age. The torturous suffering imposed by such conditions as poverty, war, violence, fanaticism, disease, and degradation of the environment, to which masses of people are subjected, is a consequence of this opposition. Hence, before the peace of nations matures into a comprehensive reality, it must pass through difficult stages, not unlike those experienced by individual nations until their internal consolidation was achieved. But that the process toward peace is far advanced can hardly be denied. (Baha'i International Community, 1999 Mar 20, *Peace Among the Nations*)

CHAPTER 6:

WORKING FOR UNIVERSAL EDUCATION

68 ❓ Making a Better World with the Bahá'í Faith: QUOTATIONS

FROM THE WRITINGS OF BAHÁ'U'LLÁH

6.1 Man is the supreme Talisman. Lack of a proper education hath, however, deprived him of that which he doth inherently possess. Through a word proceeding out of the mouth of God he was called into being; by one word more he was guided to recognize the Source of his education; by yet another word his station and destiny were safeguarded. The Great Being saith: Regard man as a mine rich in gems of inestimable value. Education can, alone, cause it to reveal its treasures, and enable mankind to benefit therefrom.

6.2 Be not the cause of grief, much less of discord and strife. The hope is cherished that ye may obtain true education in the shelter of the tree of His tender mercies and act in accordance with that which God desireth.

6.3 Beseech ye the One true God that He may, through the power of the hand of loving-kindness and spiritual education, purge and purify certain souls from the defilement of evil passions and corrupt desires, that they may arise and unloose their tongues for the sake of God, that perchance the evidences of injustice may be blotted out and the splendour of the light of justice may shed its radiance upon the whole world. The people are ignorant, and they stand in need of those who will expound the truth.

6.4 Please God, the peoples of the world may be led, as the result of the high endeavours exerted by their rulers and the wise and learned amongst men, to recognize their best interests.

6.5 To whatever place We may be banished, however great the tribulation We may suffer, they who are the people of God must, with fixed resolve and perfect confidence, keep their eyes directed towards the Day Spring of Glory, and be busied in whatever may be conducive to the betterment of the world and the education of its peoples.

6.6   Address yourselves to the promotion of the well-being and tranquility of the children of men. Bend your minds and wills to the education of the peoples and kindreds of the earth, that haply the dissensions that divide it may, through the power of the Most Great Name, be blotted out from its face, and all mankind become the upholders of one Order, and the inhabitants of one City. Illumine and hallow your hearts; let them not be profaned by the thorns of hate or the thistles of malice. Ye dwell in one world, and have been created through the operation of one Will. Blessed is he who mingleth with all men in a spirit of utmost kindliness and love.

6.7   The purpose underlying Their revelation hath been to educate all men, that they may, at the hour of death, ascend, in the utmost purity and sanctity and with absolute detachment, to the throne of the Most High.

6.8   We have decreed, O people, that the highest and last end of all learning be the recognition of Him Who is the Object of all knowledge…

6.9   Consider, for instance, the revelation of the light of the Name of God, the Educator. Behold, how in all things the evidences of such a revelation are manifest, how the betterment of all beings dependeth upon it. This education is of two kinds. The one is universal. Its influence pervadeth all things and sustaineth them. It is for this reason that God hath assumed the title, "Lord of all worlds." The other is confined to them that have come under the shadow of this Name, and sought the shelter of this most mighty Revelation.

6.10 We prescribe unto all men that which will lead to the exaltation of the Word of God amongst His servants, and likewise, to the advancement of the world of being and the uplift of souls. To this end, the greatest means is education of the child. To this must each and all hold fast. We have verily laid this charge upon you in manifold Tablets as well as in My Most Holy Book. Well is it with him who deferreth thereto. We ask of God that He will assist each and every one to obey this inescapable command that hath appeared and been caused to descend through the Pen of the Ancient of Days.

6.11 Strain every nerve to acquire both inner and outer perfections, for the fruit of the human tree hath ever been and will ever be perfections both within and without. It is not desirable that a man be left without knowledge or skills, for he is then but a barren tree. Then, so much as capacity and capability allow, ye needs must deck the tree of being with fruits such as knowledge, wisdom, spiritual perception and eloquent speech.

6.12 Man is even as steel, the essence of which is hidden: through admonition and explanation, good counsel and education, that essence will be brought to light. If, however, he be allowed to remain in his original condition, the corrosion of lusts and appetites will effectively destroy him.

6.13 There are many things which will, if neglected, be wasted, and come to nothing. How often in this world do we see a child who has lost his parents and who, unless attention be devoted to his education and training, can produce no fruit...

6.14 How resplendent the luminaries of knowledge that shine in an atom, and how vast the oceans of wisdom that surge within a drop! To a supreme degree is this true of man, who, among all created things, hath been invested with the robe of such gifts, and hath been singled out for the glory of such distinction. For in him are potentially revealed all the attributes and names of God to a degree that no other created being hath excelled or surpassed. All these names and attributes are applicable to him. Even as He hath said: 'Man is My mystery, and I am his mystery.'

FROM THE WRITINGS AND UTTERANCES OF 'ABDU'L-BAHÁ

6.15 O handmaids of the Merciful! Render ye thanks unto the Ancient Beauty that ye have been raised up and gathered together in this mightiest of centuries, this most illumined of ages. As befitting thanks for such a bounty, stand ye staunch and strong in the Covenant and, following the precepts of God and the holy Law, suckle your children from their infancy with the milk of a universal education, and rear them so that from their earliest days, within their inmost heart, their very nature, a way of life will be firmly established that will conform to the divine Teachings in all things.

For mothers are the first educators, the first mentors; and truly it is the mothers who determine the happiness, the future greatness, the courteous ways and learning and judgement, the understanding and the faith of their little ones.

6.16 Were there no educator, all souls would remain savage, and were it not for the teacher, the children would be ignorant creatures.

It is for this reason that, in this new cycle, education and training are recorded in the Book of God as obligatory and not voluntary. That is, it is enjoined upon the father and mother, as a duty, to strive with all effort to train the daughter and the son, to nurse them from the breast of knowledge and to rear them in the bosom of sciences and arts. Should they neglect this matter, they shall be held responsible and worthy of reproach in the presence of the stern Lord.

6.17 But the difference of the qualities with regard to culture is very great, for education has great influence. Through education the ignorant become learned; the cowardly become valiant. Through cultivation the crooked branch becomes straight; the acid, bitter fruit of the mountains and woods becomes sweet and delicious; and the five-petaled flower becomes hundred petaled. Through education savage nations become civilized, and even the animals become domesticated. Education must be considered as most important, for as diseases in the world of bodies are extremely contagious, so, in the same way, qualities of spirit and heart are extremely contagious. Education has a universal influence, and the differences caused by it are very great.

6.18 O Company of God! To each created thing, the Ancient Sovereignty hath portioned out its own perfection, its particular virtue and special excellence, so that each in its degree may become a symbol denoting the sublimity of the true Educator of humankind, and that each, even as a crystalline mirror, may tell of the grace and splendour of the Sun of Truth.

And from amongst all creatures He hath singled out man, to grant him His most wondrous gift, and hath made him to attain the bounties of the Company on High. That most precious of gifts is attainment unto His unfailing guidance, that the inner reality of humankind should become as a niche to hold this lamp; and when the scattering splendours of this light do beat against the bright glass of the heart, the heart's purity maketh the beams to blaze out even stronger than before, and to shine in glory on the minds and souls of men.

The attainment of the most great guidance is dependent upon knowledge and wisdom, and on being informed as to the mysteries of the Holy Words. Wherefore must the loved ones of God, be they young or old, be they men or women, each one according to his capabilities, strive to acquire the various branches of knowledge, and to increase his understanding of the mysteries of the Holy Books, and his skill in marshalling the divine proofs and evidences.

The eminent Sadru's-Sudur, who hath verily attained a most exalted station in the Retreats of Bliss, inaugurated the teaching meeting. He was the first blessed soul to lay the foundation of this momentous institution. God be praised, during the course of his life he educated persons who today are strong and eloquent advocates of the Lord God, disciples who are indeed pure and spiritual descendants of him who was so close to the Holy Threshold. After his passing, certain blessed individuals took steps to perpetuate his teaching work, and when He learned of it, this Captive's heart rejoiced.

At this time, likewise, I most urgently request the friends of God to make every effort, as much as lieth within their competence, along these lines. The harder they strive to widen the scope of their knowledge, the better and more gratifying will be the result. Let the loved ones of God, whether young or old, whether male or female, each according to his capabilities, bestir themselves and spare no efforts to acquire the various current branches of knowledge, both spiritual and secular, and of the arts. Whensoever they gather in their meetings let their conversation be confined to learned subjects and to information on the knowledge of the day.

If they do thus, they will flood the world with the Manifest Light, and change this dusty earth into gardens of the Realm of Glory.

6.19 In these days there are new schools of philosophy blindly claiming that the world of nature is perfect. If this is true, why are children trained and educated in schools, and what is the need of extended courses in sciences, arts and letters in colleges and universities? What would be the result if humanity were left in its natural condition without education or training? All scientific discoveries and attainments are the outcomes of knowledge and education. The telegraph, phonograph, telephone were latent and potential in the world of nature but would never have come forth into the realm of visibility unless man through education had penetrated and discovered the laws which control them. All the marvelous developments and miracles of what we call civilization would have remained hidden, unknown and, so to speak, nonexistent, if man had remained in his natural condition, deprived of the bounties, blessings and benefits of education and mental culture. The intrinsic difference between the ignorant man and the astute philosopher is that the former has not been lifted out of his natural condition, while the latter has undergone systematic training and education in schools and colleges until his mind has awakened and unfolded to higher realms of thought and perception; otherwise, both are human and natural.

6.20 Nevertheless, although capacities are not the same, every member of the human race is capable of education.

6.21 ... education is essential, and all standards of training and teaching throughout the world of mankind should be brought into conformity and agreement; a universal curriculum should be established, and the basis of ethics be the same.

6.22 Bahá'u'lláh has announced that inasmuch as ignorance and lack of education are barriers of separation among mankind, all must receive training and instruction. Through this provision the lack of mutual understanding will be remedied and the unity of mankind furthered and advanced. Universal education is a universal law. It is, therefore, incumbent upon every father to teach and instruct his children according to his possibilities. If he is unable to educate them, the body politic, the representative of the people, must provide the means for their education.

6.23 If a child is left in its natural state and deprived of education, there is no doubt that it will grow up in ignorance and illiteracy, its mental faculties dulled and dimmed; in fact it will become like an animal...

FROM THE WRITINGS AND LETTERS WRITTEN BY, OR ON BEHALF OF, SHOGHI EFFENDI

6.24 The Bahá'í Faith ... advocates compulsory education...

6.25 In philanthropic enterprises and acts of charity, in promotion of the general welfare and furtherance of the public good including that of every group without any exceptions whatever, let the beloved of God attract the favourable attention of all, and lead all the rest.

Let them, freely and without charge, open the doors of their schools and their higher institutions for the study of sciences and the liberal arts, to non-Bahá'í children and youth who are poor and in need.

... and next is the propagation of learning and the promulgation of Bahá'í rules of conduct, practices and laws. At this time, when the nation has awakened out of its sleep of negligence, and the Government has begun to consider the promotion and expansion of its educational establishment, let the Bahá'í representatives in that country arise in such a manner that as a result of their high endeavours in every hamlet, village and town, of every province and district, preliminary measures will be taken for the setting up of institutions for the study of sciences, the liberal arts and religion. Let Bahá'í children without any exceptions learn the fundamentals of reading and writing and familiarize themselves with the rules of conduct, the customs, practices and laws as set forth in the Book of God; and let them, in the new branches of knowledge, in the arts and technology of the day, in pure and praiseworthy characteristics—Bahá'í conduct, the Bahá'í way of life—become so distinguished above the rest that all other communities, whether

Islamic, Zoroastrian, Christian, Judaic or materialist, will of their own volition and most gladly enter their children in such advanced Bahá'í institutions of learning and entrust them to the care of Bahá'í instructors.

So too is the promotion and execution of the laws set forth in the Book of God.

6.26 Your short but impressive letter addressed to Shoghi Effendi was received. He perused it with deep interest and charged me to thank you on his behalf and to express his fondest hopes that you will pursue with an abiding zeal your academic studies. Being a Bahá'í you are certainly aware of the fact that Bahá'u'lláh considered education as one of the most fundamental factors of a true civilization. This education, however, in order to be adequate and fruitful, should be comprehensive in nature and should take into consideration not only the physical and the intellectual side of man but also his spiritual and ethical aspects. This should be the programme of the Bahá'í youth all over the world.

6.27 You ask him about the fear of God: perhaps the friends do not realize that the majority of human beings need the element of fear in order to discipline their conduct? Only a relatively very highly evolved soul would always be disciplined by love alone. Fear of punishment, fear of the anger of God if we do evil, are needed to keep people's feet on the right path. Of course we should love God—but we must fear Him in the sense of a child fearing the righteous anger and chastisement of a parent; not cringe before Him as before a tyrant, but know His mercy exceeds His justice!

FROM THE WRITINGS AND LETTERS WRITTEN BY, OR ON BEHALF OF, THE UNIVERSAL HOUSE OF JUSTICE

6.28 The cause of universal education, which has already enlisted in its service an army of dedicated people from every faith and nation, deserves the utmost support that the governments of the world can lend it. For ignorance is indisputably the principal reason for the decline and fall of peoples and the perpetuation of prejudice. No nation can achieve success unless education is accorded all its citizens. Lack of resources limits the ability of many nations to fulfil this necessity, imposing a certain ordering of priorities. The decision-making agencies involved would do well to consider giving first priority to the education of women and girls, since it is through educated mothers that the benefits of knowledge can be most effectively and rapidly diffused throughout society. In keeping with the requirements of the times, consideration should also be given to teaching the concept of world citizenship as part of the standard education of every child.

OTHER SOURCES

6.29 Education is seen by Bahá'ís as a continuous and creative process. Its aim is to develop the capacities latent in human nature and to coordinate their expression for the enrichment and progress of society. At certain moments in history, Bahá'ís believe, education may also act as a powerful instrument for profound societal transformation. Within this creative process, it is possible to achieve an essential harmony between faith and reason through an approach to education that encourages the free investigation of all reality and trains minds to recognize truth, irrespective of its origin. (Bahá'í International Community, 1989 Jan 02, *Position Statement on Education*)

6.30 An educational approach directed towards personal growth and societal transformation, and based on the belief that human beings are essentially spiritual, however, must go well beyond a mere statement of purpose. When words and actions are not directed by a moral force, scientific knowledge and technological know-how conduce as readily to misery as they do to prosperity and happiness. But moral values are not mere constructs of social processes. Rather, they are expressions of the inner forces that operate in the spiritual reality of every human being, and education must concern itself with these forces if it is to tap the roots of motivation and produce meaningful and lasting change. (Bahá'í International Community, 1989 Jan 02, *Position Statement on Education*)

6.31 Some of these principles can be expressed in terms of values and imperatives, such as the compulsory nature of education, the importance of the role of the family, the urgency of promoting an awareness of the fundamental unity of humanity, the necessity to free people from religious fanaticism, and the need to abolish all forms of prejudice. The compulsory nature of education is expressed as an element of individual belief, as an obligation of every family, and as the responsibility of the entire community, which must assign the necessary funds to ensure its fulfilment. The emphasis on the importance of the family as an educational environment makes parent education an integral element in the process of educating children. Commitment to the unity of mankind implies a balance between a study of one's own cultural heritage and an exploration of those universal qualities that distinguish the entire human race. Awareness of the necessity to free people from religious bigotry and fanaticism gives rise to a non-sectarian yet spiritual approach to moral education. The zeal to abolish all forms of prejudice leads to policies that favor groups who have suffered systematic discrimination, including women, entire races, and disadvantaged social classes, to help them overcome the obstacles most social systems have incorporated into their structures. In connection with this policy, the education of girls is given primary importance, with boys and girls following the same curriculum so that women may take their place alongside men in the sciences and arts, commerce and public administration, and every other field of human endeavor. (Bahá'í International Community, 1989 Jan 02, *Position Statement on Education*)

6.32 Other important principles relate directly to the content and the methods of educational programs. There is a strong tendency to encourage the initiation of educational endeavors at the grass roots, and then to support and enrich them from other levels. A basic principle of universal participation reinforces this inclination and strongly influences methods used in teaching-learning situations. For example, sharp distinctions between teacher and student often disappear after students reach a certain age, so that an individual may be a trainee in one aspect of a program and a teacher in a parallel aspect, allowing educational endeavors to empower a vast pool of human resources for change. The value placed on service, and the elevation of work to an act of worship when it is done in the spirit of service, helps programs achieve a balance between working with one's hands and acquiring abstract knowledge. The student's attention is focused from the beginning on needs and aspirations of the local community, and curricula seek to develop those skills and capacities that render acts of service meaningful and effective. (Bahá'í International Community, 1989 Jan 02, *Position Statement on Education*)

6.33 Bahá'ís see education in terms of the knowledge, qualities, skills, attitudes, and capacities that enable individuals to become conscious subjects of their own growth, and active, responsible participants in a systematic process of building a new world order. Ongoing education is at the very heart of any healthy Bahá'í community. Successful community action requires the development of each person's capacity for intellectual investigation. Through community consultation, members learn to analyze social conditions and discover the forces that have caused them. In order to contribute to consultation on community problems and generate plans, each person must develop the ability to express ideas and listen carefully to others. A well-educated community member is a determined yet humble participant who helps overcome conflict and division, thereby contributing to a spirit of unity and collaboration. (Bahá'í International Community, 1990 Mar 09, *New Delivery Systems for Basic Education*)

6.34 Bahá'í literacy projects promote not only the acquisition of reading and writing skills but also the spiritual empowerment of individuals and communities. In Guyana, for example, the "On the Wings of Words" project builds preliteracy and literacy skills in children and junior youth aged 4 to 16 years, while helping them to reflect on issues significant to their lives. The project has trained more than 7,200 facilitators and reached more than 13,000 young people in both urban and rural areas.

Bahá'í educational centers range from simple tutorial classes to schools at both elementary and secondary levels. While all aim at academic excellence and place special emphasis on service to the community based on moral values and spiritual principles, each strives to meet the particular needs of the society in which it operates. A few examples from various parts of the globe illustrate how Bahá'ís are putting this ideal into practice.

The Santitham Vidhayakhom School in Thailand, founded in 1967, provides government- accredited nursery, kindergarten, and primary education to over 700 children from the surrounding rural communities. The school's character development program helps to prepare students for service to humanity. On the opposite side of the globe, the Nancy Campbell Collegiate Institute in Canada, an accredited private international school for boys and girls in grades 7 to 12, fosters academic achievement within a clear moral framework that incorporates 19 specific leadership capabilities.

In Lilongwe, Malawi, the Bambino Private Schools reach some 1,100 students from nursery to secondary level. Students enrolled in the program aimed at the spiritual empowerment of junior youth participate in such service activities as planting trees in the neighborhood, looking after the children in the nursery, and visiting and assisting orphanages in the community. In neighboring Tanzania, the Ruaha Secondary School is providing instruction for grades 8 to 11, giving particular attention to the education of girls. In 2006, Ruaha began to offer a teacher-training program to a network of Bahá'í preschools in Tanzania in order to assist in meeting the educational needs of the country. (The Baha'i International Community, *For the Betterment of the World*)

CHAPTER 7:

PROMOTING THE EQUALITY OF MEN AND WOMEN

82 ❓ Making a Better World with the Bahá'í Faith: QUOTATIONS

FROM THE WRITINGS OF BAHÁ'U'LLÁH

7.1. Exalted, immensely exalted is He Who hath removed differences and established harmony. Glorified, infinitely glorified is He Who hath caused discord to cease, and decreed solidarity and unity. Praised be God, the Pen of the Most High hath lifted distinctions from between His servants and handmaidens, and, through His consummate favours and all-encompassing mercy, hath conferred upon all a station and rank of the same plane. He hath broken the back of vain imaginings with the sword of utterance and hath obliterated the perils of idle fancies through the pervasive power of His might

7.2. In this Day the Hand of divine grace hath removed all distinctions. The servants of God and His handmaidens are regarded on the same plane. Blessed is the servant who hath attained unto that which God hath decreed, and likewise the leaf moving in accordance with the breezes of His will. This favour is great and this station lofty. His bounties and bestowals are ever present and manifest. Who is able to offer befitting gratitude for His successive bestowals and continuous favours?

7.3. All should know, and in this regard attain the splendours of the sun of certitude, and be illumined thereby: Women and men have been and will always be equal in the sight of God. The Dawning-Place of the Light of God sheddeth its radiance upon all with the same effulgence. Verily God created women for men, and men for women. The most beloved of people before God are the most steadfast and those who have surpassed others in their love for God, exalted be His glory....

The friends of God must be adorned with the ornament of justice, equity, kindness and love. As they do not allow themselves to be the object of cruelty and transgression, in like manner they should not allow such tyranny to visit the handmaidens of God. He, verily, speaketh the truth and commandeth that which benefitteth His servants and handmaidens. He is the Protector of all in this world and the next.

7.4. Bless Thou, also, O Lord my God, Thy servants and Thy handmaidens who have attained unto Thee.

7.5. Thou seest Thy handmaiden, O my God, standing before the habitation of Thy mercy, and calling upon Thee by Thy name which Thou hast chosen above all other names and set up over all that are in heaven and on earth. Send down upon her the breaths of Thy mercy, that she may be carried away wholly from herself, and be drawn entirely towards the seat which, resplendent with the glory of Thy face, sheddeth afar the radiance of Thy sovereignty, and is established as Thy throne.

7.6. Unto every father hath been enjoined the instruction of his son and daughter in the art of reading and writing and in all that hath been laid down in the Holy Tablet.

7.7. I implore Thee, O Thou Fashioner of the nations and the King of eternity, to guard Thy handmaidens within the tabernacle of Thy chastity, and to cancel such of their deeds as are unworthy of Thy days. Purge out, then, from them, O my God, all doubts and idle fancies, and sanctify them from whatsoever becometh not their kinship with Thee, O Thou Who art the Lord of names, and the Source of utterance. Thou art He in Whose grasp are the reins of the entire creation.

7.8. Glory be to Thee, O Lord my God! I beg of Thee by Thy Name through which He Who is Thy Beauty hath been stablished upon the throne of Thy Cause, and by Thy Name through which Thou changest all things, and gatherest together all things, and callest to account all things, and rewardest all things, and preservest all things, and sustainest all things—I beg of Thee to guard this handmaiden who hath fled for refuge to Thee, and hath sought the shelter of Him in Whom Thou Thyself art manifest, and hath put her whole trust and confidence in Thee.

7.9. By the righteousness of God! The title 'O My handmaiden' far excelleth aught else that can be seen in the world.

7.10. O MY handmaiden, O My leaf! Render thou thanks unto the Best-Beloved of the world for having attained this boundless grace at a time when the world's learned and most distinguished men have remained deprived thereof. We have designated thee 'a leaf' that thou mayest, like unto leaves, be stirred by the gentle wind of the Will of God—exalted be His glory—even as the leaves of the trees are stirred by onrushing winds. Yield thou thanks unto thy Lord by virtue of this brilliant utterance. Wert thou to perceive the sweetness of the title 'O My handmaiden' thou wouldst find thyself detached from all mankind, devoutly engaged day and night in communion with Him Who is the sole Desire of the world.

In words of incomparable beauty We have made fitting mention of such leaves and handmaidens as have quaffed from the living waters of heavenly grace and have kept their eyes directed towards God. Happy and blessed are they indeed. Ere long shall God reveal their station whose loftiness no word can befittingly express nor any description adequately describe.

FROM THE WRITINGS AND UTTERANCES OF 'ABDU'L-BAHÁ

7.11. And among the teachings of Bahá'u'lláh is the equality of women and men. The world of humanity has two wings—one is women and the other men. Not until both wings are equally developed can the bird fly. Should one wing remain weak, flight is impossible. Not until the world of women becomes equal to the world of men in the acquisition of virtues and perfections, can success and prosperity be attained as they ought to be.

7.12. ...Bahá'u'lláh emphasized and established the equality of man and woman. Sex is not particularized to humanity; it exists throughout the animate kingdoms but without distinction or preference. In the vegetable kingdom there is complete equality between male and female of species. Likewise, in the animal plane equality exists; all are under the protection of God. Is it becoming to man that he, the noblest of creatures, should observe and insist upon such distinction? Woman's lack of progress and proficiency has been due to her need of equal education and opportunity. Had she been allowed this equality, there is no doubt she would be the counterpart of man in ability and capacity. The happiness of mankind will be realized when women and men coordinate and advance equally, for each is the complement and helpmeet of the other.

7.13. In the Orient women were degraded and considered subordinate to man. Bahá'u'lláh proclaimed equality of the sexes—that both man and woman are servants of God before Whom there is no distinction. Whosoever has a pure heart and renders good deeds is nearer to God and the object of His favor—whether man or woman. The sex distinction which exists in the human world is due to the lack of education for woman, who has been denied equal opportunity for development and advancement. Equality of the sexes will be established in proportion to the increased opportunities afforded woman in this age, for man and woman are equally the recipients of powers and endowments from God, the Creator. God has not ordained distinction between them in His consummate purpose.

7.14. To accept and observe a distinction which God has not intended in creation is ignorance and superstition. The fact which is to be considered, however, is that woman, having formerly been deprived, must now be allowed equal opportunities with man for education and training. There must be no difference in their education. Until the reality of equality between man and woman is fully established and attained, the highest social development of mankind is not possible. Even granted that woman is inferior to man in some degree of capacity or accomplishment, this or any other distinction would continue to be productive of discord and trouble. The only remedy is education, opportunity; for equality means equal qualification. In brief, the assumption of superiority by man will continue to be depressing to the ambition of woman, as if her attainment to equality was creationally impossible; woman's aspiration toward advancement will be checked by it, and she will gradually become hopeless. On the contrary, we must declare that her capacity is equal, even greater than man's. This will inspire her with hope and ambition, and her susceptibilities for advancement will continually increase. She must not be told and taught that she is weaker and inferior in capacity and qualification. If a pupil is told that his intelligence is less than his fellow pupils, it is a very great drawback and handicap to his progress. He must be encouraged to advance by the statement, "You are most capable, and if you endeavor, you will attain the highest degree."

It is my hope that the banner of equality may be raised throughout the five continents where as yet it is not fully recognized and established. In this enlightened world of the West woman has advanced an immeasurable degree beyond the women of the Orient. And let it be known once more that until woman and man recognize and realize equality, social and political progress here or anywhere will not be possible. For the world of humanity consists of two parts or members: one is woman; the other is man. Until these two members are equal in strength, the oneness of humanity cannot be established, and the happiness and felicity of mankind will not be a reality. God willing, this is to be so.

7.15. The sixth principle or teaching of Bahá'u'lláh concerns the equality of man and woman. He has declared that in the estimation of God there is no distinction of sex. The one whose heart is most pure, whose deeds and service in the Cause of God are greater and nobler, is most acceptable before the divine threshold—whether male or female. In the vegetable and animal kingdoms sex exists in perfect equality and without distinction or invidious estimate. The animal, although inferior to man in intelligence and reason, recognizes sex equality. Why should man, who is endowed with the sense of justice and sensibilities of conscience, be willing that one of the members of the human family should be rated and considered as subordinate? Such differentiation is neither intelligent nor conscientious; therefore, the principle of religion has been revealed by Bahá'u'lláh that woman must be given the privilege of equal education with man and full right to his prerogatives. That is to say, there must be no difference in the education of male and female in order that womankind may develop equal capacity and importance with man in the social and economic equation. Then the world will attain unity and harmony. In past ages humanity has been defective and inefficient because it has been incomplete. War and its ravages have blighted the world; the education of woman will be a mighty step toward its abolition and ending, for she will use her whole influence against war. Woman rears the child and educates the youth to maturity. She will refuse to give her sons for sacrifice upon the field of battle. In truth, she will be the greatest factor in establishing universal peace and international arbitration. Assuredly, woman will abolish warfare among mankind. Inasmuch as human society consists of two parts, the male and female, each the complement of the other, the happiness and stability of humanity cannot be assured unless both are perfected. Therefore, the standard and status of man and woman must become equalized.

7.16. One of these questions concerns the rights of woman and her equality with man. In past ages it was held that woman and man were not equal—that is to say, woman was considered inferior to man, even from the standpoint of her anatomy and creation. She was considered especially inferior in intelligence, and the idea prevailed universally that it was not allowable for her to step into the arena of important affairs. In some countries man went so far as to believe and teach that woman belonged to a sphere lower than human. But in this century, which is the century of light and the revelation of mysteries, God is proving to the satisfaction of humanity that all this is ignorance and error; nay, rather, it is well established that mankind and womankind as parts of composite humanity are coequal and that no difference in estimate is allowable, for all are human. The conditions in past centuries were due to woman's lack of opportunity. She was denied the right and privilege of education and left in her undeveloped state. Naturally, she could not and did not advance. In reality, God has created all mankind, and in the estimation of God there is no distinction as to male and female. The one whose heart is pure is acceptable in His sight, be that one man or woman. God does not inquire, "Art thou woman or art thou man?" He judges human actions. If these are acceptable in the threshold of the Glorious One, man and woman will be equally recognized and rewarded.

Furthermore, the education of woman is more necessary and important than that of man, for woman is the trainer of the child from its infancy. If she be defective and imperfect herself, the child will necessarily be deficient; therefore, imperfection of woman implies a condition of imperfection in all mankind, for it is the mother who rears, nurtures and guides the growth of the child. This is not the function of the father. If the educator be incompetent, the educated will be correspondingly lacking. This is evident and incontrovertible. Could the student be brilliant and accomplished if the teacher is illiterate and ignorant? The mothers are the first educators of mankind; if they be imperfect, alas for the condition and future of the race.

7.17. Man and woman both should be educated equally and equally regarded.

7.18. Upon another occasion 'Abdu'l-Bahá said to a group of friends around him: "Taken in general, women today have a stronger sense of religion than men. The woman's intuition is more correct; she is more receptive and her intelligence is quicker. The day is coming when woman will claim her superiority to man.

7.19. Woman has everywhere been commended for her faithfulness. After the Lord Christ suffered, the disciples wept, and gave way to their grief. They thought that their hopes were shattered, and that the Cause was utterly lost, till Mary Magdalene came to them and strengthened them saying: 'Do you mourn the body of Our Lord or His Spirit? If you mourn His Spirit, you are mistaken, for Jesus lives! His Spirit will never leave us!' Thus through her wisdom and encouragement the Cause of Christ was upheld for all the days to come. Her intuition enabled her to grasp the spiritual fact.

'Abdu'l-Bahá then added: "But in the sight of God sex makes no difference. He or she is greatest who is nearest to God."

FROM THE WRITINGS AND LETTERS WRITTEN BY, OR ON BEHALF OF, THE UNIVERSAL HOUSE OF JUSTICE

7.20. Concerning your questions about the equality of men and women, this, as 'Abdu'l-Bahá has often explained, is a fundamental principle of Bahá'u'lláh; therefore the Laws of the "Aqdas" should be studied in the light of it. Equality between men and women does not, indeed physiologically it cannot, mean identity of functions. In some things women excel men, for others men are better fitted than women, while in very many things the difference of sex is of no effect at all. The differences of function are most apparent in family life. The capacity for motherhood has many far-reaching implications which are recognized in Bahá'í Law. For example, when it is not possible to educate all one's children, daughters receive preference over sons, as mothers are the first educators of the next generation. Again, for physiological reasons, women are granted certain exemptions from fasting that are not applicable to men.

7.21. With regard to the status of women, the important point for Bahá'ís to remember is that in the face of the categorical pronouncements in Bahá'í Scripture establishing the equality of men and women, the ineligibility of women for membership on the Universal House of Justice does not constitute evidence of the superiority of men over women. It must also be borne in mind that women are not excluded from any other international institution of the Faith. They are found among the ranks of the Hands of the Cause. They serve as members of the International Teaching Center and as Continental Counsellors. And, there is nothing in the text to preclude the participation of women in such future international bodies as the Supreme Tribunal.

Though at the present time, it may be difficult for the believers to appreciate the reason for the circumscription of membership on the Universal House of Justice to men, we call upon the friends to remain assured by the Master's promise that clarity of understanding will be achieved in due course. The friends, both women and men, must accept this with faith that the Covenant of Bahá'u'lláh will aid them and the institutions of His World Order to see the realization of every principle ordained by His unerring Pen, including the equality of men and women, as expounded in the Writings of the Cause.

OTHER SOURCES

7.22. Today, in the Bahá'í world community, in over 200 nations and territories, women are joining with men in building a global society. Their full contribution toward the establishment of a world civilization is possible, Bahá'ís believe, because of the all-pervasive spiritual power released in this age by Bahá'u'lláh, Who has erased all limitations preventing the fulfillment of human potentialities. For in the Bahá'í view, since this is the century of light, it is evident that the Sun of Reality, the Word has revealed itself to all humankind. One of the potentialities hidden in the realm of humanity was the capability or capacity of womanhood. Through the effulgent rays of divine illumination, the capacity of woman has become so awakened and manifest in this age that equality of man and woman is an established fact. (Bahá'í International Community, 1993 Apr 05, *Equality of Men & Women A New Reality*)

7.23. The advancement of women is, in the Bahá'í view, essential for social progress. (Bahá'í International Community, 1989 Mar 30, *Women and Development*)

7.24. In Bahá'í communities, promoting the equality of the sexes is considered to be the task of both men and women, and one that can be achieved fully only if the goal is shared by everyone. Thus, one aspect of the Institute's programme is an effort to foster in male family members a desire for women's advancement. Bahá'í institutions lend crucial support. Members of the national Bahá'í council of India and other respected Bahá'í consultants speak to the men of the village about the principle of equality, and they urge husbands to take pride in their wives' accomplishments. Moreover, they discuss with the men how they, as husbands and fathers, should vigorously defend women's rights, protect women's interests, and promote the development of women's capacities. Local Bahá'í councils, composed of both women and men, also lend their support by helping select the trainees, monitoring the institute's programs, and offering suggestions for improvement. (Bahá'í International Community, 1989 Mar 30, *Women and Development*)

7.25. To prepare for a time when legal discrimination against women is eliminated, and the social and economic support structures are erected which will allow women a voice in public policy, women must not only be given experience in consultation, so that they will be ready to step forward and speak their minds and hearts, but they must also be given education to develop the full range of their capacities. (Bahá'í International Community, 1990 Feb 27, *Equality in Political Participation Decision-Making*)

7.26. The concept of sustainable development itself has emerged largely in response to a growing disillusionment with the prevalent development models and an increasing collaboration among three great forward-looking movements—peace, the environment and women's emancipation. A crucial element common to all three movements is the significant role played by women. For decades, development planners neglected the needs of women, paid scant attention to the deterioration of the environment, and failed to discern the connection between development and peace. As a result, development failed. The convergence of these movements has amplified women's voices and strengthened their call for a sustainable future for their children and their children's children. As women help to redefine development, planners are beginning to take a more holistic approach. (Bahá'í International Community, 1992 Mar 11, *Women and Development*)

7.27. Indeed, profound changes will be wrought as women move to take their place on decision-making bodies in every sphere around the world. This organic shift need not cause conflict. In the Bahá'í view, the material and spiritual progress of society depends on women's full participation in every arena of human activity. Thus the Bahá'í approach seeks a full and dynamic partnership with men for the advancement of civilization as a whole. Indeed, an important part of a larger program to educate girls must be the re-socialization of males for partnership. Boys and men must be given the opportunity to grasp, on the one hand, the harmful effects of attitudes and values which condone and even encourage violence, oppression, and war; and to see, on the other hand, the advantages to society, families and the girls themselves when girls are educated. (Bahá'í International Community, 1995 Aug 26, *Educating Girls - An Investment in Future*)

7.28. The effect of the persistent denial to women of full equality with men sharpens still further the challenge to science and religion in the economic life of humankind. To any objective observer the principle of the equality of the sexes is fundamental to all realistic thinking about the future well-being of the earth and its people. It represents a truth about human nature that has waited largely unrecognized throughout the long ages of the race's childhood and adolescence. "Women and men," is Bahá'u'lláh's emphatic assertion, "have been and will always be equal in the sight of God." The rational soul has no sex, and whatever social inequities may have been dictated by the survival requirements of the past, they clearly cannot be justified at a time when humanity stands at the threshold of maturity. A commitment to the establishment of full equality between men and women, in all departments of life and at every level of society, will be central to the success of efforts to conceive and implement a strategy of global development.

Indeed, in an important sense, progress in this area will itself be a measure of the success of any development program. Given the vital role of economic activity in the advancement of civilization, visible evidence of the pace at which development is progressing will be the extent to which women gain access to all avenues of economic endeavor. The challenge goes beyond ensuring an equitable distribution of opportunity, important as that is. It calls for a fundamental rethinking of economic issues in a manner that will invite the full participation of a range of human experience and insight hitherto largely excluded from the discourse. The classical economic models of impersonal markets in which human beings act as autonomous makers of self-regarding choices will not serve the needs of a world motivated by ideals of unity and justice. Society will find itself increasingly challenged to develop new economic models shaped by insights that arise from a sympathetic understanding of shared experience, from viewing human beings in relation to others, and from a recognition of the centrality to social well-being of the role of the family and the community. Such an intellectual breakthrough—strongly altruistic rather than self-centered in focus—must draw heavily on both the spiritual and scientific sensibilities of the race, and millennia of experience have prepared women to make crucial contributions to the common effort. (Bahá'í International Community, 1995 Mar 03, *The Prosperity of Humankind*)

7.29. The equality of men and women is a cardinal principle of the Bahá'í Faith. Central to every project undertaken by Bahá'ís is a commitment to the goal of ensuring that men and women are allowed to work shoulder to shoulder in all fields of human endeavor—scientific, political, economic, social, and cultural—with the same rewards and in equal conditions. Specific programs aim at eliminating prejudices against women, at establishing mechanisms to protect their interests, and at providing the education they need to take their rightful place in society.

An example is the Barli Development Institute for Rural Women, which offers six-month and one-year residential programs for tribal women at its facilities in the Indian state of Madhya Pradesh. The program combines practical skills training with consciousness raising and the development of spiritual qualities. Recognizing that attitudinal change on the part of husbands, parents, and children is equally essential, the Institute continues to work with the women after they return home and conducts conferences and meetings in their villages. A number of extension centers have also been established in order to make the educational program available to an increasing number of women. More than 2,500 women in some 300 villages have taken part in the program since the Institute's inception in 1985.

In a different context, the Tahirih Justice Center in the United States offers legal, medical, and social services to immigrant and refugee women seeking protection from gender-based human rights abuses. The Center provides pro bono legal representation to foreign-born women and girls fleeing abuse through the Gender-Based Asylum Project, the Battered Immigrant Women Project, and the Protection for Victims of Trafficking and Other Crimes Project. A referral program makes available a range of social and medical services that assist women and children to rebuild their lives. In the area of public policy advocacy, the Tahirih Justice Center counts among its successes a campaign launched to end exploitation of foreign women by international marriage brokers, which led to the signing into law of the International Marriage Broker Regulation Act that enables foreign women to access important information that can protect them from violent abuse by men through the mail-order bride industry. Since its founding in 1997, the Center has helped well over 5,500 women and children. (They Baha'i International Community, *For the Betterment of the World*)

CHAPTER 8:

ELIMINATING PREJUDICE FROM OUR HEARTS

FROM THE WRITINGS OF BAHÁ'U'LLÁH

8.1 The utterance of God is a lamp, whose light is these words: Ye are the fruits of one tree, and the leaves of one branch. Deal ye one with another with the utmost love and harmony, with friendliness and fellowship. He Who is the Day Star of Truth beareth Me witness! So powerful is the light of unity that it can illuminate the whole earth. The one true God, He Who knoweth all things, Himself testifieth to the truth of these words.

8.2 O CHILDREN OF MEN! Know ye not why We created you all from the same dust? That no one should exalt himself over the other. Ponder at all times in your hearts how ye were created. Since We have created you all from one same substance it is incumbent on you to be even as one soul, to walk with the same feet, eat with the same mouth and dwell in the same land, that from your inmost being, by your deeds and actions, the signs of oneness and the essence of detachment may be made manifest. Such is My counsel to you, O concourse of light! Heed ye this counsel that ye may obtain the fruit of holiness from the tree of wondrous glory.

8.3 Through the power of the words He hath uttered the whole of the human race can be illumined with the light of unity, and the remembrance of His Name is able to set on fire the hearts of all men, and burn away the veils that intervene between them and His glory. One righteous act is endowed with a potency that can so elevate the dust as to cause it to pass beyond the heaven of heavens. It can tear every bond sunder, and hath the power to restore the force that hath spent itself and vanished....

8.4 It beseemeth all men, in this Day, to take firm hold on the Most Great Name, and to establish the unity of all mankind.

8.5 They that are endued with sincerity and faithfulness should associate with all the peoples and kindreds of the earth with joy and radiance, inasmuch as consorting with people hath promoted and will continue to promote unity and concord, which in turn are conducive to the maintenance of order in the world and to the regeneration of nations. Blessed are such as hold fast to the cord of kindliness and tender mercy and are free from animosity and hatred.

8.6 The incomparable Creator hath created all men from one same substance, and hath exalted their reality above the rest of His creatures. Success or failure, gain or loss, must, therefore, depend upon man's own exertions. The more he striveth, the greater will be his progress.

8.7 And now, concerning thy question regarding the creation of man. Know thou that all men have been created in the nature made by God, the Guardian, the Self-Subsisting. Unto each one hath been prescribed a pre-ordained measure, as decreed in God's mighty and guarded Tablets. All that which ye potentially possess can, however, be manifested only as a result of your own volition. Your own acts testify to this truth.

FROM THE WRITINGS AND UTTERANCES OF 'ABDU'L-BAHÁ

8.8 Love ye all religions and all races with a love that is true and sincere and show that love through deeds and not through the tongue; for the latter hath no importance, as the majority of men are, in speech, well-wishers, while action is the best.

8.9 And among the teachings of Bahá'u'lláh is that religious, racial, political, economic and patriotic prejudices destroy the edifice of humanity. As long as these prejudices prevail, the world of humanity will not have rest. For a period of 6,000 years history informs us about the world of humanity. During these 6,000 years the world of humanity has not been free from war, strife, murder and bloodthirstiness. In every period war has been waged in one country or another and that war was due to either religious prejudice, racial prejudice, political prejudice or patriotic prejudice. It has therefore been ascertained and proved that all prejudices are destructive of the human edifice. As long as these prejudices persist, the struggle for existence must remain dominant, and bloodthirstiness and rapacity continue. Therefore, even as was the case in the past, the world of humanity cannot be saved from the darkness of nature and cannot attain illumination except through the abandonment of prejudices and the acquisition of the morals of the Kingdom.

8.10 Ye observe how the world is divided against itself, how many a land is red with blood and its very dust is caked with human gore. The fires of conflict have blazed so high that never in early times, not in the Middle Ages, not in recent centuries hath there ever been such a hideous war, a war that is even as millstones, taking for grain the skulls of men. Nay, even worse, for flourishing countries have been reduced to rubble, cities have been levelled with the ground, and many a once prosperous village hath been turned into ruin. Fathers have lost their sons, and sons their fathers. Mothers have wept away their hearts over dead children. Children have been orphaned, women left to wander, vagrants without a home. From every aspect, humankind hath sunken low. Loud are the piercing cries of fatherless children; loud the mothers' anguished voices, reaching to the skies.

And the breeding-ground of all these tragedies is prejudice: prejudice of race and nation, of religion, of political opinion; and the root cause of prejudice is blind imitation of the past—imitation in religion, in racial attitudes, in national bias, in politics. So long as this aping of the past persisteth, just so long will the foundations of the social order be blown to the four winds, just so long will humanity be continually exposed to direst peril.

Now, in such an illumined age as ours, when realities previously unknown to man have been laid bare, and the secrets of created things have been disclosed, and the Morn of Truth hath broken and lit up the world—is it admissible that men should be waging a frightful war that is bringing humanity down to ruin? No, by the Lord God!

8.11 Consider the flowers of a garden: though differing in kind, colour, form and shape, yet, inasmuch as they are refreshed by the waters of one spring, revived by the breath of one wind, invigorated by the rays of one sun, this diversity increaseth their charm, and addeth unto their beauty. Thus when that unifying force, the penetrating influence of the Word of God, taketh effect, the difference of customs, manners, habits, ideas, opinions and dispositions embellisheth the world of humanity. This diversity, this difference is like the naturally created dissimilarity and variety of the limbs and organs of the human body, for each one contributeth to the beauty, efficiency and perfection of the whole. When these different limbs and organs come under the influence of man's sovereign soul, and the soul's power pervadeth the limbs and members, veins and arteries of the body, then difference reinforceth harmony, diversity strengtheneth love, and multiplicity is the greatest factor for co-ordination.

How unpleasing to the eye if all the flowers and plants, the leaves and blossoms, the fruits, the branches and the trees of that garden were all of the same shape and colour! Diversity of hues, form and shape, enricheth and adorneth the garden, and heighteneth the effect thereof. In like manner, when divers shades of thought, temperament and character, are brought together under the power and influence of one central agency, the beauty and glory of human perfection will be revealed and made manifest. Naught but the celestial potency of the Word of God, which ruleth and transcendeth the realities of all things, is capable of harmonizing the divergent thoughts, sentiments, ideas, and convictions of the children of men. Verily, it is the penetrating power in all things, the mover of souls and the binder and regulator in the world of humanity.

8.12 Bahá'u'lláh also taught that prejudices—whether religious, racial, patriotic or political—are destructive to the foundations of human development. Prejudices of any kind are the destroyers of human happiness and welfare. Until they are dispelled, the advancement of the world of humanity is not possible; yet racial, religious and national biases are observed everywhere. For thousands of years the world of humanity has been agitated and disturbed by prejudices. As long as it prevails, warfare, animosity and hatred will continue. Therefore, if we seek to establish peace, we must cast aside this obstacle; for otherwise, agreement and composure are not to be attained.

8.13 …Bahá'u'lláh taught that an equal standard of human rights must be recognized and adopted. In the estimation of God all men are equal; there is no distinction or preferment for any soul in the dominion of His justice and equity.

8.14 When the racial elements of the American nation unite in actual fellowship and accord, the lights of the oneness of humanity will shine, the day of eternal glory and bliss will dawn, the spirit of God encompass, and the divine favors descend. Under the leadership and training of God, the real Shepherd, all will be protected and preserved. He will lead them in green pastures of happiness and sustenance, and they will attain to the real goal of existence. This is the blessing and benefit of unity; this is the outcome of love. This is the sign of the Most Great Peace; this is the star of the oneness of the human world. Consider how blessed this condition will be. I pray for you and ask the confirmation and assistance of God in your behalf

8.15 Bahá'u'lláh has proclaimed the promise of the oneness of humanity. Therefore, we must exercise the utmost love toward each other. We must be loving to all the people of the world. We must not consider any people the people of Satan, but know and recognize all as the servants of the one God. At most it is this: Some do not know; they must be guided and trained. They must be taught to love their fellow creatures and be encouraged in the acquisition of virtues. Some are ignorant; they must be informed. Some are as children, undeveloped; they must be helped to reach maturity. Some are ailing, their moral condition is unhealthy; they must be treated until their morals are purified. But the sick man is not to be hated because he is sick, the child must not be shunned because he is a child, the ignorant one is not to be despised because he lacks knowledge. They must all be treated, educated, trained and assisted in love. Everything must be done in order that humanity may live under the shadow of God in the utmost security, enjoying happiness in its highest degree.

8.16 We have already stated that science or the attribute of scientific penetration is supernatural and that all other blessings of God are within the boundary of nature. What is the proof of this? All created things except man are captives of nature. The stars and suns swinging through infinite space, all earthly forms of life and existence—whether mineral, vegetable or animal—come under the dominion and control of natural law. Man through scientific knowledge and power rules nature and utilizes her laws to do his bidding. According to natural limitations he is a creature of earth, restricted to life upon its surface, but through scientific utilization of material laws he soars in the sky, sails upon the ocean and dives beneath it. The products of his invention and discovery, so familiar to us in daily life, were once mysteries of nature. For instance, man has brought electricity out of the plane of the invisible into the plane of the visible, harnessed and imprisoned that mysterious natural agent and made it the servant of his needs and wishes. Similar instances are many, but we will not prolong this. Man, as it were, takes the sword out of nature's hand and with it for his scepter of authority dominates nature itself. Nature is without the crown of human faculties and attributes. Man possesses conscious intelligence and reflection; nature does not. This is an established fundamental among philosophers. Man is endowed with volition and memory; nature has neither. Man can seek out the mysteries latent in nature, whereas nature is not conscious of her own hidden phenomena. Man is progressive; nature is stationary, without the power of progression or retrogression. Man is endowed with ideal virtues—for example, intellection, volition, faith, confession and acknowledgment of God—while nature is devoid of all these. The ideal faculties of man, including the capacity for scientific acquisition, are beyond nature's ken. These are powers whereby man is differentiated and distinguished from all other forms of life. This is the bestowal of divine idealism, the crown adorning human heads. Notwithstanding the gift of this supernatural power, it is most amazing that materialists still consider themselves within the bonds and captivity of nature. The truth is that God has endowed man with virtues, powers and ideal faculties of which nature is entirely bereft and by which man is elevated, distinguished and superior. We must thank God for these bestowals, for these powers He has given us, for this crown He has placed upon our heads.

How shall we utilize these gifts and expend these bounties? By directing our efforts toward the unification of the human race. We must use these powers in establishing the oneness of the world of humanity, appreciate these virtues by accomplishing the unity of whites and blacks, devote this divine intelligence to the perfecting of amity and accord among all branches of the human family so that under the protection and providence of God the East and West may hold each other's hands and become as lovers. Then will mankind be as one nation, one race and kind—as waves of one ocean. Although these waves may differ in form and shape, they are waves of the same sea. Flowers may be variegated in colors, but they are all flowers of one garden. Trees differ though they grow in the same orchard. All are nourished and quickened into life by the bounty of the same rain, all grow and develop by the heat and light of the one sun, all are refreshed and exhilarated by the same breeze that they may bring forth varied fruits. This is according to the creative wisdom. If all trees bore the same kind of fruit, it would cease to be delicious. In their never-ending variety man finds enjoyment instead of monotony.

FROM THE WRITINGS AND LETTERS WRITTEN BY, OR ON BEHALF OF, SHOGHI EFFENDI

8.17 No less serious is the stress and strain imposed on the fabric of American society through the fundamental and persistent neglect, by the governed and governors alike, of the supreme, the inescapable and urgent duty—so repeatedly and graphically represented and stressed by 'Abdu'l-Bahá in His arraignment of the basic weaknesses in the social fabric of the nation—of remedying, while there is yet time, through a revolutionary change in the concept and attitude of the average white American toward his Negro fellow citizen, a situation which, if allowed to drift, will, in the words of 'Abdu'l-Bahá, cause the streets of American cities to run with blood, aggravating thereby the havoc which the fearful weapons of destruction, raining from the air, and amassed by a ruthless, a vigilant, a powerful and inveterate enemy, will wreak upon those same cities.

8.18 As to racial prejudice, the corrosion of which, for well-nigh a century, has bitten into the fiber, and attacked the whole social structure of American society, it should be regarded as constituting the most vital and challenging issue confronting the Bahá'í community at the present stage of its evolution. The ceaseless exertions which this issue of paramount importance calls for, the sacrifices it must impose, the care and vigilance it demands, the moral courage and fortitude it requires, the tact and sympathy it necessitates, invest this problem, which the American believers are still far from having satisfactorily resolved, with an urgency and importance that cannot be overestimated. White and Negro, high and low, young and old, whether newly converted to the Faith or not, all who stand identified with it must participate in, and lend their assistance, each according to his or her capacity, experience, and opportunities, to the common task of fulfilling the instructions, realizing the hopes, and following the example, of 'Abdu'l-Bahá. Whether colored or noncolored, neither race has the right, or can conscientiously claim, to be regarded as absolved from such an obligation, as having realized such hopes, or having faithfully followed such an example. A long and thorny road, beset with pitfalls, still remains untraveled, both by the white and the Negro exponents of the redeeming Faith of Bahá'u'lláh. On the distance they cover, and the manner in which they travel that road, must depend, to an extent which few among them can imagine, the operation of those intangible influences which are indispensable to the spiritual triumph of the American believers and the material success of their newly launched enterprise.

8.19 Freedom from racial prejudice, in any of its forms, should, at such a time as this when an increasingly large section of the human race is falling a victim to its devastating ferocity, be adopted as the watchword of the entire body of the American believers, in whichever state they reside, in whatever circles they move, whatever their age, traditions, tastes, and habits. It should be consistently demonstrated in every phase of their activity and life, whether in the Baháʼí community or outside it, in public or in private, formally as well as informally, individually as well as in their official capacity as organized groups, committees and Assemblies. It should be deliberately cultivated through the various and everyday opportunities, no matter how insignificant, that present themselves, whether in their homes, their business offices, their schools and colleges, their social parties and recreation grounds, their Baháʼí meetings, conferences, conventions, summer schools and Assemblies. It should, above all else, become the keynote of the policy of that august body which, in its capacity as the national representative, and the director and coordinator of the affairs of the community, must set the example, and facilitate the application of such a vital principle to the lives and activities of those whose interests it safeguards and represents.

8.20 A tremendous effort is required by both races if their outlook, their manners, and conduct are to reflect, in this darkened age, the spirit and teachings of the Faith of Baháʼuʼlláh. Casting away once and for all the fallacious doctrine of racial superiority, with all its attendant evils, confusion, and miseries, and welcoming and encouraging the intermixture of races, and tearing down the barriers that now divide them, they should each endeavor, day and night, to fulfill their particular responsibilities in the common task which so urgently faces them. Let them, while each is attempting to contribute its share to the solution of this perplexing problem, call to mind the warnings of ʻAbduʼl-Bahá, and visualize, while there is yet time, the dire consequences that must follow if this challenging and unhappy situation that faces the entire American nation is not definitely remedied.

Let the white make a supreme effort in their resolve to contribute their share to the solution of this problem, to abandon once for all their usually inherent and at times subconscious sense of superiority, to correct their tendency towards revealing a patronizing attitude towards the members of the other race, to persuade them through their intimate, spontaneous and informal association with them of the genuineness of their friendship and the sincerity of their intentions, and to master their impatience of any lack of responsiveness on the part of a people who have received, for so long a period, such grievous and slow-healing wounds. Let the Negroes, through a corresponding effort on their part, show by every means in their power the warmth of their response, their readiness to forget the past, and their ability to wipe out every trace of suspicion that may still linger in their hearts and minds. Let neither think that the solution of so vast a problem is a matter that exclusively concerns the other. Let neither think that such a problem can either easily or immediately be resolved. Let neither think that they can wait confidently for the solution of this problem until the initiative has been taken, and the favorable circumstances created, by agencies that stand outside the orbit of their Faith. Let neither think that anything short of genuine love, extreme patience, true humility, consummate tact, sound initiative, mature wisdom, and deliberate, persistent, and prayerful effort, can succeed in blotting out the stain which this patent evil has left on the fair name of their common country. Let them rather believe, and be firmly convinced, that on their mutual understanding, their amity, and sustained cooperation, must depend, more than on any other force or organization operating outside the circle of their Faith, the deflection of that dangerous course so greatly feared by 'Abdu'l-Bahá, and the materialization of the hopes He cherished for their joint contribution to the fulfillment of that country's glorious destiny.

8.21 I welcome with open arms the unexpectedly large number of the representatives of the pure-hearted and spiritually receptive Negro race, so dearly loved by 'Abdu'l-Bahá, for whose conversion to His Father's Faith He so deeply yearned and whose interests He so ardently championed in the course of His memorable visit to the North American continent. I am reminded on this historic occasion, of the significant words uttered by Bahá'u'lláh Himself Who as attested by the Center of the Covenant in His Writings, compared he coloured people to the black pupil of the eye', through which 'the light of the spirit shineth forth'.

8.22 The Negro believers must be just as active as their white brothers and sisters in spreading the Faith, both among their own race and members of other races. It has been a great steep forward in the Cause's development in America to have Negro pioneers go forth, and their work has been of the greatest help and very productive of results.

8.23 As we neither feel nor acknowledge any distinction between the duties and privileges of a Bahá'í, whoever he may be, it is incumbent upon the negro believers to rise above this great test which the attitude of some of their white brethren may present. They must prove their innate equality not by words but by deeds. They must accept the Cause of Bahá'u'lláh for the sake of the Cause, love it, and cling to it, and teach it, and fight for it as their own Cause, forgetful of the shortcoming of others. Any other attitude is unworthy of their faith.

Proud and happy in the praises which even Bahá'u'lláh Himself has bestowed upon them, they must feel He revealed Himself for them and every other down-trodden race, loves them, and will help them to attain their destiny.

The whole race question in America is a national one and of great importance. But the negro friends must not waste their precious opportunity to serve the Faith, in these momentous days, by dwelling on the admitted short-comings of the white friends. They must arise and serve and teach, confident of the future they are building, a future in which we know these barriers will have once and for all been overcome!

FROM THE WRITINGS AND LETTERS WRITTEN BY, OR ON BEHALF OF, THE UNIVERSAL HOUSE OF JUSTICE

8.24 Racism, one of the most baneful and persistent evils, is a major barrier to peace. Its practice perpetrates too outrageous a violation of the dignity of human beings to be countenanced under any pretext. Racism retards the unfoldment of the boundless potentialities of its victims, corrupts its perpetrators, and blights human progress. Recognition of the oneness of mankind, implemented by appropriate legal measures, must be universally upheld if this problem is to be overcome.

8.25 The words, the deeds, the attitudes, the lack of prejudice, the nobility of character, the high sense of service to others-in- a word, those qualities and actions which distinguish a Bahá'í must unfailingly characterize their inner life and outer behavior, and their interactions with friend or foe.

OTHER SOURCES

8.26 Accordingly, any campaign to eradicate racism must be concerned vitally with endeavors to change beliefs and attitudes. Political action alone cannot offer a permanent solution. In the absence of a change in human attitudes, and the development, among ordinary people and their leaders, of a firm conviction in the truth of racial equality, political advances can easily be reversed by those individuals and groups continuing to harbor racial animosities.

How can these racial prejudices be abolished? Fueled by a complex array of societal pressures, racial hatred are the fruits of ignorance, of stereotypic misconceptions, of the human tendency to elevate one's group to a position of superiority over others and of the absence of spiritual values. In the Bahá'í view, the blatantly false and misguided premises upon which racism rests must be countered by the truth: that all human beings belong to a single human family, the human race, a family united biologically, socially, and spiritually, while displaying, to the enrichment of the entire planet a limitless variety of secondary physical characteristics. If every person is led to perceive this truth and to welcome those of another skin color as members of his own spiritual family, racism will find a receptive home nowhere and will evaporate of its own accord. It is therefore essential to educate every individual, but especially young children, in the truth of the unity of the human race, a truth confirmed by all the human sciences. (Baha'i International Community, 1988 Aug 03, *Combating Racism*)

8.27 Since the founding of the Bahá'í Faith in 1844, Bahá'ís around the world have been staunchly committed to the goal of eliminating prejudice and fostering racial unity. We have witnessed the positive, unifying results of those efforts in our own communities.

Because of our experience in this field, we recognize that the road to the elimination of racial discrimination is long and rocky. But we are equally optimistic that humankind will, with the necessary resolve, reach the ultimate destination of racial unity and understanding. If individuals, non-governmental organizations, and governments can resolve to educate themselves, their communities and their children in the truth of human unity, we may well be able to look back upon the Second Decade as a turning point in the struggle against racism. (Baha'i International Community, 1988 Aug 03, *Combating Racism*)

8.28 Of all the factors which give rise to human rights violations throughout the world, prejudice—simple prejudice—is surely one of the most pervasive. And prejudice—whether of race, religion, nationality or sex—is notoriously difficult to eradicate simply because it has no basis in logic or reason. It cannot be legislated out of existence. Even though enlightened legislation may prevent the gross and overt victimization of individuals or groups, it has no power to remove the seeds of prejudice from men's hearts—and as long as those seeds of prejudice exist, the danger also exists that, sooner or later, they will produce the poisonous fruits of intolerance, discrimination, and even persecution.

In the view of the Bahá'í International Community, the only sure means of eradicating prejudice is through education, for education dispels ignorance, and blind ignorance is at the root of all prejudice. (Baha'i International Community, 1993 Feb 18, *Eliminating Religious Intolerance*)

8.29 The Bahá'í International Community has participated extensively in activities aimed at the eradication of racism and racial discrimination. It welcomed the proclamation of the Second Decade to Combat Racism and Racial Discrimination through, inter alia, the distribution of the text of the Programme of Action for the Second Decade to all its 148 national affiliates. In the intervening years, many of these communities have sponsored public meetings, conferences, summer schools, newspaper articles, radio programmes and exhibits in support of the objectives of the Second Decade. Moreover, drawing on the creative spirit of grassroots participation, Bahá'ís in a number of countries have established race unity committees, with multiracial membership, which have developed programmes to combat racial prejudice and to create bonds of mutual respect among peoples of different races in their local communities. These committees have attempted to assist Bahá'ís to free themselves of their own racial prejudices and, beyond that, to contribute to the elimination of racial prejudice in society at large through extensive collaboration with leaders in government, education and religion. Despite the inevitable obstacles encountered by the Bahá'ís in their ongoing process of eradicating racism from their communities, their experience has been a positive and unifying one.

The Bahá'í International Community holds firmly that the constructive forces present at this stage in the social evolution of humankind are manifesting themselves with increasing intensity. It is its earnest hope that the international community will seize upon these forces and take advantage of the opportunities afforded by them: thus to realize, in the second half of the Second Decade to Combat Racism and Racial Discrimination, unprecedented victories in the face of new challenges. (Baha'i International Community, 1990 Jan 26, *Combating Racism*)

8.30 The Bahá'í International Community, for example, has over a century of experience in building communities committed to the principle of the oneness of mankind. Since the mid-19th century, myriad religious, racial, ethnic, cultural, linguistic and national elements have come together to promote the concept of unity in diversity. Our programme for the realization of racial unity is at once social, spiritual and organic. Recognizing that commitment to a spiritual principle has social implications, the Bahá'í system of community organization employs practical measures to encourage the participation of minorities. The principle of racial equality is taught, and individuals are encouraged to identify and overcome old patterns of behaviour.

Thus, concerted effort on the part of ordinary people has brought about a unique form of racial integration in Bahá'í communities in every part of the world. If our experience can in any way contribute to the struggle against racism and racial discrimination, we are happy to offer it for study. (Baha'i International Community, 1989 Feb 08, *Eliminating Racism*)

CHAPTER 9:

ALIGNING THE WORLD'S FAITHS

114 ❓ Making a Better World with the Bahá'í Faith: QUOTATIONS

FROM THE WRITINGS OF BAHÁ'U'LLÁH

9.1 Consort with all religions with amity and concord, that they may inhale from you the sweet fragrance of God.

9.2 O ye that dwell on earth! The religion of God is for love and unity; make it not the cause of enmity or dissension.

9.3 The fundamental purpose animating the Faith of God and His Religion is to safeguard the interests and promote the unity of the human race, and to foster the spirit of love and fellowship amongst men. Suffer it not to become a source of dissension and discord, of hate and enmity.

9.4 That which the Lord hath ordained as the sovereign remedy and mightiest instrument for the healing of all the world is the union of all its peoples in one universal Cause, one common Faith. This can in no wise be achieved except through the power of a skilled, an all-powerful and inspired Physician.

9.5 Gird up the loins of your endeavor, O people of Baha, that haply the tumult of religious dissension and strife that agitateth the peoples of the earth may be stilled, that every trace of it may be completely obliterated. For the love of God, and them that serve Him, arise to aid this most sublime and momentous Revelation. Religious fanaticism and hatred are a world-devouring fire, whose violence none can quench. The Hand of Divine power can, alone, deliver mankind from this desolating affliction....

9.6 O CONCOURSE of priests! The Day of Reckoning hath appeared, the Day whereon He Who was in heaven hath come. He, verily, is the One Whom ye were promised in the Books of God, the Holy, the Almighty, the All-Praised. How long will ye wander in the wilderness of heedlessness and superstition? Turn with your hearts in the direction of your Lord, the Forgiving, the Generous.

9.7 O CONCOURSE of monks! Seclude not yourselves in churches and cloisters. Come forth by My leave, and occupy yourselves with that which will profit your souls and the souls of men. Thus biddeth you the King of the Day of Reckoning. Seclude yourselves in the stronghold of My love. This, verily, is a befitting seclusion, were ye of them that perceive it. He that shutteth himself up in a house is indeed as one dead. It behoveth man to show forth that which will profit all created things, and he that bringeth forth no fruit is fit for fire. Thus counselleth you your Lord, and He, verily, is the Almighty, the All-Bounteous. Enter ye into wedlock, that after you someone may fill your place. We have forbidden you perfidious acts, and not that which will demonstrate fidelity. Have ye clung to the standards fixed by your own selves, and cast the standards of God behind your backs? Fear God, and be not of the foolish. But for man, who would make mention of Me on My earth, and how could My attributes and My name have been revealed? Ponder ye, and be not of them that are veiled and fast asleep. He that wedded not (Jesus) found no place wherein to dwell or lay His head, by reason of that which the hands of the treacherous had wrought. His sanctity consisteth not in that which ye believe or fancy, but rather in the things We possess. Ask, that ye may apprehend His station which hath been exalted above the imaginings of all that dwell on earth. Blessed are they who perceive it.

9.8 This is the Day when the loved ones of God should keep their eyes directed towards His Manifestation, and fasten them upon whatsoever that Manifestation may be pleased to reveal. Certain traditions of bygone ages rest on no foundations whatever, while the notions entertained by past generations, and which they have recorded in their books, have, for the most part, been influenced by the desires of a corrupt inclination. Thou dost witness how most of the commentaries and interpretations of the words of God, now current amongst men, are devoid of truth. Their falsity hath, in some cases, been exposed when the intervening veils were rent asunder. They themselves have acknowledged their failure in apprehending the meaning of any of the words of God.

Our purpose is to show that should the loved ones of God sanctify their hearts and their ears from the vain sayings that were uttered aforetime, and turn with their inmost souls to Him Who is the Day Spring of His Revelation, and to whatsoever things He hath manifested, such behavior would be regarded as highly meritorious in the sight of God....

FROM THE WRITINGS AND UTTERANCES OF 'ABDU'L-BAHÁ

9.9 The divine religions must be the cause of oneness among men, and the means of unity and love; they must promulgate universal peace, free man from every prejudice, bestow joy and gladness, exercise kindness to all men and do away with every difference and distinction.

9.10 In every dispensation, there hath been the commandment of fellowship and love, but it was a commandment limited to the community of those in mutual agreement, not to the dissident foe. In this wondrous age, however, praised be God, the commandments of God are not delimited, not restricted to any one group of people, rather have all the friends been commanded to show forth fellowship and love, consideration and generosity and loving-kindness to every community on earth. Now must the lovers of God arise to carry out these instructions of His: let them be kindly fathers to the children of the human race, and compassionate brothers to the youth, and self-denying offspring to those bent with years. The meaning of this is that ye must show forth tenderness and love to every human being, even to your enemies, and welcome them all with unalloyed friendship, good cheer, and loving-kindness. When ye meet with cruelty and persecution at another's hands, keep faith with him; when malevolence is directed your way, respond with a friendly heart. To the spears and arrows rained upon you, expose your breasts for a target mirror-bright; and in return for curses, taunts and wounding words, show forth abounding love. Thus will all peoples witness the power of the Most

Great Name, and every nation acknowledge the might of the Ancient Beauty, and see how He hath toppled down the walls of discord, and how surely He hath guided all the peoples of the earth to oneness; how He hath lit man's world, and made this earth of dust to send forth streams of light.

These human creatures are even as children, they are brash and unconcerned. These children must be reared with infinite, loving care, and tenderly fostered in the embraces of mercy, so that they may taste the spiritual honey-sweetness of God's love; that they may become like unto candles shedding their beams across this darksome world, and may clearly perceive what blazing crowns of glory the Most Great Name, the Ancient Beauty, hath set on the brows of His beloved, what bounties He hath bestowed on the hearts of those He holdeth dear, what a love He hath cast into the breasts of humankind, and what treasures of friendship He hath made to appear amongst all men.

O God, my God! Aid Thou Thy trusted servants to have loving and tender hearts. Help them to spread, amongst all the nations of the earth, the light of guidance that cometh from the Company on high. Verily Thou art the Strong, the Powerful, the Mighty, the All-Subduing, the Ever-Giving. Verily Thou art the Generous, the Gentle, the Tender, the Most Bountiful.

9.11 I hope that the lights of the Sun of Reality will illumine the whole world so that no strife and warfare, no battles and bloodshed remain. May fanaticism and religious bigotry be unknown, all humanity enter the bond of brotherhood, souls consort in perfect agreement, the nations of earth at last hoist the banner of truth, and the religions of the world enter the divine temple of oneness, for the foundations of the heavenly religions are one reality. Reality is not divisible; it does not admit multiplicity. All the holy Manifestations of God have proclaimed and promulgated the same reality. They have summoned mankind to reality itself, and reality is one. The clouds and mists of imitations have obscured the Sun of Truth. We must forsake these imitations, dispel these clouds and mists and free the Sun from the darkness of superstition. Then will the Sun of Truth shine most gloriously; then all the inhabitants of the world will be united, the religions will be one, sects and denominations will reconcile, all nationalities will flow together in the recognition of one Fatherhood, and all degrees of humankind will gather in the shelter of the same tabernacle, under the same banner.

9.12   Therefore, we also must strive in this pathway of love and service, sacrificing life and possessions, passing our days in devotion, consecrating our efforts wholly to the Cause of God so that, God willing, the ensign of universal religion may be uplifted in the world of mankind and the oneness of the world of humanity be established.

9.13   May we endeavor with heart and soul to reconcile the religions of the earth, unify the peoples and races and blend the nations in a perfect solidarity.

9.14   ...The third teaching of Bahá'u'lláh is that religion must be the source of fellowship, the cause of unity and the nearness of God to man. If it rouses hatred and strife, it is evident that absence of religion is preferable and an irreligious man better than one who professes it. According to the divine Will and intention religion should be the cause of love and agreement, a bond to unify all mankind, for it is a message of peace and goodwill to man from God.

9.15   The divine religions were founded for the purpose of unifying humanity and establishing universal peace. Any movement which brings about peace and agreement in human society is truly a divine movement; any reform which causes people to come together under the shelter of the same tabernacle is surely animated by heavenly motives. At all times and in all ages of the world, religion has been a factor in cementing together the hearts of men and in uniting various and divergent creeds. It is the peace element in religion that blends mankind and makes for unity. Warfare has ever been the cause of separation, disunion and discord.

9.16   Fourth, that religion must be conducive to love and unity among mankind; for if it be the cause of enmity and strife, the absence of religion is preferable. When Moses appeared, the tribes of Israel were in a state of disunion as captives of the Pharaohs. Moses gathered them together, and the divine law established fellowship among them. They became as one people, united, consolidated, after which they were rescued from bondage. They passed into the promised land, advanced in all degrees, developed sciences and arts, progressed in material affairs, increased in divine or spiritual civilization until their nation rose to its zenith in the sovereignty of Solomon. It is evident, therefore, that religion is the cause of unity, fellowship and progress among mankind. The function of a shepherd is to gather the sheep together and not to scatter them. Then Christ appeared. He united varying and divergent creeds and warring people of His time. He brought together Greeks and Romans, reconciled Egyptians and Assyrians, Chaldeans and Phoenicians. Christ established unity and agreement among people of these hostile and warring nations. Therefore, it is again evident that the purpose of religion is peace and concord. Likewise, Muhammad appeared at a time when the peoples and tribes of Arabia were divergent and in a state of continual warfare. They killed each other, pillaged and took captive wives and children. Muhammad united these fierce tribes, established a foundation of fellowship among them so that they gave up warring against each other absolutely and established communities. The result was that the Arabian tribes freed themselves from the Persian yoke and Roman control, established an independent sovereignty which rose to a high degree of civilization, advanced in sciences and arts, extended the Saracen dominion as far west as Spain and Andalusia and became famous throughout the world. Therefore, it is proved once more that the religion of God is intended to be the cause of advancement and solidarity and not of enmity and dissolution. If it becomes the cause of hatred and strife, its absence is preferable. Its purpose is unity, and its foundations are one.

When Bahá'u'lláh appeared in Persia, violent strife and hatred separated the peoples and tribes of that country. They would not come together for any purpose except war; they would not partake of the same food, or drink of the same water; association and intercourse were impossible. Bahá'u'lláh founded the oneness of humanity among these people and bound their hearts together with such ties of love that they were completely united.

He reestablished the prophetic foundations, reformed and renewed the principles laid down by the Messengers of God who had preceded Him. And now it is hoped that through His life and teachings the East and West shall become so united that no trace of enmity, strife and discord shall remain.

9.17 As all mankind have been created by the one God, we are sheep under the care and protection of one Shepherd. Therefore, as His sheep we must associate in accord and agreement. If one single lamb becomes separated from the flock, the thoughts and efforts of all the others must be to bring it back again. Consequently, Bahá'u'lláh proclaimed that, inasmuch as God is the one heavenly Shepherd and all mankind are the sheep of His fold, the religion or guidance of God must be the means of love and fellowship in the world. If religion proves to be the source of hatred, enmity and contention, if it becomes the cause of warfare and strife and influences men to kill each other, its absence is preferable. For that which is productive of hatred amongst the people is rejected by God, and that which establishes fellowship is beloved and sanctioned by Him. Religion and divine teachings are like unto a remedy. A remedy must produce the condition of health. If it occasions sickness, it is wiser and better to have no remedy whatever. This is the significance of the statement that if religion becomes the cause of warfare and bloodshed, irreligion and the absence of religion are preferable among mankind.

9.18 Fundamentally, all warfare and bloodshed in the human world are due to the lack of unity between the religions, which through superstitions and adherence to theological dogmas have obscured the one reality which is the source and basis of them all.

9.19 Therefore, there is need of turning back to the original foundation. The fundamental principles of the Prophets are correct and true. The imitations and superstitions which have crept in are at wide variance with the original precepts and commands. Bahá'u'lláh has revoiced and reestablished the quintessence of the teachings of all the Prophets, setting aside the accessories and purifying religion from human interpretation. He has written a book entitled the Hidden Words. The preface announces that it contains the essences of the words of the Prophets of the past, clothed in the garment of brevity, for the teaching and spiritual guidance of the people of the world. Read it that you may understand the true foundations of religion and reflect upon the inspiration of the Messengers of God. It is light upon light

FROM THE WRITINGS AND LETTERS WRITTEN BY, OR ON BEHALF OF, SHOGHI EFFENDI

9.20 As the lights of liberty flicker and go out, as the din of discord grows louder and louder every day, as the fires of fanaticism flame with increasing fierceness in the breasts of men, as the chill of irreligion creeps relentlessly over the soul of mankind, the limbs and organs that constitute the body of the Faith of Bahá'u'lláh appear, in varying measure, to have become afflicted with the crippling influences that now hold in their grip the whole of the civilized world.

9.21 The light of religion is dimmed and moral authority disintegrating. The nations of the world have, for the most part, fallen a prey to battling ideologies that threaten to disrupt the very foundations of their dearly won political unity. Agitated multitudes in these countries seethe with discontent, are armed to the teeth, are stampeded with fear, and groan beneath the yoke of tribulations engendered by political strife, racial fanaticism, national hatreds, and religious animosities.

9.22 ... the Guardian would certainly advise, and even urge the friends to make a thorough study of the Qur'án as the knowledge of this Sacred Scripture is absolutely indispensable for every believer who wishes to adequately understand and intelligently read the Writings of Bahá'u'lláh. Although there are very few persons among our Western Bahá'ís who are capable of handling such a course in a scholarly way yet, the mere lack of such competent teachers should encourage and stimulate the believers to get better acquainted with the Sacred Scriptures of Islam. In this way, there will gradually appear some distinguished Bahá'ís who will be so well versed in the teachings of Islam as to be able to guide the believers in their study of that religion.

9.23 ... Although each believer realizes that he is a member of one great spiritual family, a member of the New World Order of Bahá'u'lláh, he does not often carry this thought through to its logical conclusion; which is that if the Bahá'ís all over the world each belong to some different kind of society or church or political party, the unity of the Faith will be destroyed; because inevitably they will become involved in doctrines and policies that are in some way against our Teachings, and often against another group of people in another part of the world, or another race, or another religious block.

Therefore, all the Bahá'ís everywhere have been urged to give up their old affiliations and withdraw from membership in the Masonic and other secret Societies in order to be entirely free to serve the Faith of Bahá'u'lláh as a united Body. Such groups as Masonry, however high the local standard may be, are in other countries gradually being influenced by the issues sundering the nations at present.

The Guardian wants the Bahá'ís to disentangle themselves from anything that may in any way now or in the future, compromise their independent status as Bahá'ís and the supranational nature of their Faith.

FROM THE WRITINGS AND LETTERS WRITTEN BY, OR ON BEHALF OF, THE UNIVERSAL HOUSE OF JUSTICE

9.24 Religious strife, throughout history, has been the cause of innumerable wars and conflicts, a major blight to progress, and is increasingly abhorrent to the people of all faiths and no faith. Followers of all religions must be willing to face the basic questions which this strife raises, and to arrive at clear answers. How are the differences between them to be resolved, both in theory and in practice? The challenge facing the religious leaders of mankind is to contemplate, with hearts filled with the spirit of compassion and a desire for truth, the plight of humanity, and to ask themselves whether they cannot, in humility before their Almighty Creator, submerge their theological differences in a great spirit of mutual forbearance that will enable them to work together for the advancement of human understanding and peace.

9.25 The time has come for the Bahá'í community to become more involved in the life of the society around it, without in the least supporting any of the world's moribund and divisive concepts, or slackening its direct teaching efforts, but rather, by association, exerting its influence towards unity, demonstrating its ability to settle differences by consultation rather than by confrontation, violence or schism, and declaring its faith in the divine purpose of human existence.

9.26 In no sense can Bahá'ís profess to have grasped at this early hour more than a minute portion of the truths inherent in the revelation on which their Faith is based. With reference, for example, to the evolution of the Cause, the Guardian said, "All we can reasonably venture to attempt is to strive to obtain a glimpse of the first streaks of the promised Dawn that must, in the fullness of time, chase away the gloom that has encircled humanity." Apart from encouraging humility, this fact should serve also as a constant reminder that Bahá'u'lláh has not brought into existence a new religion to stand beside the present multiplicity of sectarian organizations. Rather has He recast the whole conception of religion as the principal force impelling the development of consciousness. As the human race in all its diversity is a single species, so the intervention by which God cultivates the qualities of mind and heart latent in that species is a single process. Its heroes and saints are the heroes and saints of all stages in the struggle; its successes, the successes of all stages. This is the standard demonstrated in the life and work of the Master and exemplified today in a Bahá'í community that has become the inheritor of humanity's entire spiritual legacy, a legacy equally available to all the earth's peoples.

OTHER SOURCES

9.27   Bahá'ís believe that religious revelation is continuous and progressive and that, from the very beginning of human history, God has periodically sent divine educators to the world to guide mankind. The appearance of these divine educators—Krishna, Buddha, Zoroaster, Abraham, Moses, Christ, Muhammad and, in our own age, the Báb and Bahá'u'lláh—has signified the founding of a new religion, and yet none of these religions is really new; they are stages in the unfoldment of the same religious truth proceeding from the same God. They teach the same, unchanging spiritual principles, and they differ only in their social teachings, which vary according to the needs of the age in which they were revealed.

   Bahá'ís accordingly believe in the divine origin of all the major religions and honor and revere their founders as prophets of God. The reason that Bahá'ís are Bahá'ís is solely because they believe that Bahá'u'lláh, the founder of their Faith, is the latest—but not the last—of the divine educators sent by God, and that his teachings have been sent by God specifically to meet the needs of our own age. (Baha'i International Community, 1993 Feb 18, *Eliminating Religious Intolerance*)

9.28   Those interested in these ideas may well find great encouragement in the experience of the Bahá'í communities. In attempting to put these ideas into practice, the Bahá'í communities are as living laboratories for religious unity; people from every religious tradition meet with the shared intention of establishing and strengthening the ties of unity among them. They gather to worship, to deepen their understanding of spiritual truths, to discover the requirements for social progress, to solve common practical problems, to organize and carry out activities for the welfare of mankind, and, last but not least, simply to enjoy the pleasures of friendship. In these communities religious prejudice has given way to inter-religious brotherhood. They share a common goal: to demonstrate through deeds that the oneness of mankind is a reality and that its fruits are the material, intellectual and spiritual progress of all those who live in its light. (Bahá'í International Community, 1995 Jan 10, *Promoting Religious Tolerance*)

9.29 Many believers find it difficult to reconcile deep religious conviction with tolerance of other beliefs. It is tempting to insist that one has discovered the one and only truth and to relegate the remaining masses of humanity, adhering to other beliefs, to the status of apostates or unbelievers, spiritually doomed, deserving pity at best, or outright ridicule and persecution at worst. Throughout history too many sincere people in every part of the world have fallen victim to this thinking.

In the Bahá'í view, such attitudes are, in part, the product of ignorance. If other religions are shrouded in mystery, then they become an empty vessel into which the individual is tempted to pour fears and fantasies. Experience shows that ignorance breeds superstition and perpetuates religious prejudice and animosity.

The effectiveness of any individual grows as he is taught to appreciate through the exercise of his own faculties, the way in which diversity of faith enriches social life. Bahá'u'lláh urges the right of the individual to freely investigate truth for himself as a principle essential to the advancement of civilization. In order to exercise this capacity fully, however, one must be able to read. One great value of literacy, therefore, is the access it gives ordinary people to the scriptures of their own faith as well as to the sacred texts of other faiths.

The most powerful remedy for religious superstition and contention is an examination of the original teachings of the founders of the world's great faiths. No student of comparative religion can fail to be struck by the extraordinary degree of harmony to be found in these original scriptures. Certainly, a fair-minded examination of these principal sources for the civilizing of human nature will reveal nothing to support the animosities that pit one religious community against another.

Lamentably, some sectarian leaders discourage investigation of other beliefs and even dissuade their followers from fully investigating the truth of their own religious teachings. Such attitudes foster prejudice, and lead, all too often, to violent attacks on believers of other faiths. Indeed, one of the strangest and saddest features of the current outbreak of religious fanaticism is the extent to which, in each case, it is undermining not only the spiritual values which are conducive to the unity of mankind but also those unique moral victories won by the particular religion it purports to serve. (Baha'i International Community, 1993 Aug 03, *Ending Religious Intolerance*)

CHAPTER 10:

CHERISHING OUR ENVIRONMENT

Making a Better World with the Bahá'í Faith: QUOTATIONS

FROM THE WRITINGS OF BAHÁ'U'LLÁH

10.1 Every created thing in the whole universe is but a door leading into His knowledge, a sign of His sovereignty, a revelation of His names, a symbol of His majesty, a token of His power, a means of admittance into His straight Path....

10.2 Know thou that every created thing is a sign of the revelation of God.

10.3 Upon the inmost reality of each and every created thing He hath shed the light of one of His names, and made it a recipient of the glory of one of His attributes.

10.4 I yield Thee such thanks as can make every created thing to be a book that shall speak of Thee, and a scroll that shall unfold Thy praise.

10.5 Strange and astonishing things exist in the earth but they are hidden from the minds and the understanding of men. These things are capable of changing the whole atmosphere of the earth and their contamination would prove lethal.

10.6 He should show kindness to animals, how much more unto his fellow-man, to him who is endowed with the power of utterance.

10.7 As to thy question whether the physical world is subject to any limitations, know thou that the comprehension of this matter dependeth upon the observer himself. In one sense, it is limited; in another, it is exalted beyond all limitations. The one true God hath everlastingly existed, and will everlastingly continue to exist. His creation, likewise, hath had no beginning, and will have no end. All that is created, however, is preceded by a cause. This fact, in itself, establisheth, beyond the shadow of a doubt, the unity of the Creator.

10.8 He looketh on all things with the eye of oneness, and seeth the brilliant rays of the divine sun shining from the dawning-point of Essence alike on all created things, and the lights of singleness reflected over all creation.

10.9 It is incumbent upon them who are in authority to exercise moderation in all things. Whatsoever passeth beyond the limits of moderation will cease to exert a beneficial influence. Consider for instance such things as liberty, civilization and the like. However much men of understanding may favorably regard them, they will, if carried to excess, exercise a pernicious influence upon men.

10.10 Overstep not the bounds of moderation, and deal justly with them that serve thee.

FROM THE WRITINGS AND UTTERANCES OF 'ABDU'L-BAHÁ

10.11 My meaning is this, that in every aspect of life, purity and holiness, cleanliness and refinement, exalt the human condition and further the development of man's inner reality. Even in the physical realm, cleanliness will conduce to spirituality, as the Holy Writings clearly state. And although bodily cleanliness is a physical thing, it hath, nevertheless, a powerful influence on the life of the spirit. It is even as a voice wondrously sweet, or a melody played: although sounds are but vibrations in the air which affect the ear's auditory nerve, and these vibrations are but chance phenomena carried along through the air, even so, see how they move the heart. A wondrous melody is wings for the spirit, and maketh the soul to tremble for joy. The purport is that physical cleanliness doth also exert its effect upon the human soul.

10.12 For desire is a flame that has reduced to ashes uncounted lifetime harvests of the learned, a devouring fire that even the vast sea of their accumulated knowledge could never quench. How often has it happened that an individual who was graced with every attribute of humanity and wore the jewel of true understanding, nevertheless followed after his passions until his excellent qualities passed beyond moderation and he was forced into excess. His pure intentions changed to evil ones, his attributes were no longer put to uses worthy of them, and the power of his desires turned him aside from righteousness and its rewards into ways that were dangerous and dark. A good character is in the sight of God and His chosen ones and the possessors of insight, the most excellent and praiseworthy of all things, but always on condition that its center of emanation should be reason and knowledge and its base should be true moderation. Were the implications of this subject to be developed as they deserve the work would grow too long and our main theme would be lost to view.

10.13 Consequently, when thou lookest at the orderly pattern of kingdoms, cities and villages, with the attractiveness of their adornments, the freshness of their natural resources, the refinement of their appliances, the ease of their means of travel, the extent of knowledge available about the world of nature, the great inventions, the colossal enterprises, the noble discoveries and scientific researches, thou wouldst conclude that civilization conduceth to the happiness and the progress of the human world. Yet shouldst thou turn thine eye to the discovery of destructive and infernal machines, to the development of forces of demolition and the invention of fiery implements, which uproot the tree of life, it would become evident and manifest unto thee that civilization is conjoined with barbarism. Progress and barbarism go hand in hand, unless material civilization be confirmed by Divine Guidance, by the revelations of the All-Merciful and by godly virtues, and be reinforced by spiritual conduct, by the ideals of the Kingdom and by the outpourings of the Realm of Might.

10.14 And among the teachings of Bahá'u'lláh is that although material civilization is one of the means for the progress of the world of mankind, yet until it becomes combined with Divine civilization, the desired result, which is the felicity of mankind, will not be attained. Consider! These battleships that reduce a city to ruins within the space of an hour are the result of material civilization; likewise the Krupp guns, the Mauser rifles, dynamite, submarines, torpedo boats, armed aircraft and bombers—all these weapons of war are the malignant fruits of material civilization.

Had material civilization been combined with Divine civilization, these fiery weapons would never have been invented. Nay, rather, human energy would have been wholly devoted to useful inventions and would have been concentrated on praiseworthy discoveries. Material civilization is like a lamp-glass. Divine civilization is the lamp itself and the glass without the light is dark. Material civilization is like the body. No matter how infinitely graceful, elegant and beautiful it may be, it is dead. Divine civilization is like the spirit, and the body gets its life from the spirit, otherwise it becomes a corpse. It has thus been made evident that the world of mankind is in need of the breaths of the Holy Spirit. Without the spirit the world of mankind is lifeless, and without this light the world of mankind is in utter darkness. For the world of nature is an animal world.   Until man is born again from the world of nature, that is to say, becomes detached from the world of nature, he is essentially an animal, and it is the teachings of God which convert this animal into a human soul.

10.15 O Thou the Compassionate God. Bestow upon me a heart which, like unto glass, may be illumined with the light of Thy love, and confer upon me thoughts which may change this world into a rose garden through the outpourings of heavenly grace.

10.16 Is it not astonishing that although man has been created for the knowledge and love of God, for the virtues of the human world, for spirituality, heavenly illumination and eternal life, nevertheless, he continues ignorant and negligent of all this? Consider how he seeks knowledge of everything except knowledge of God. For instance, his utmost desire is to penetrate the mysteries of the lowest strata of the earth. Day by day he strives to know what can be found ten meters below the surface, what he can discover within the stone, what he can learn by archaeological research in the dust. He puts forth arduous labors to fathom terrestrial mysteries but is not at all concerned about knowing the mysteries of the Kingdom, traversing the illimitable fields of the eternal world, becoming informed of the divine realities, discovering the secrets of God, attaining the knowledge of God, witnessing the splendors of the Sun of Truth and realizing the glories of everlasting life. He is unmindful and thoughtless of these. How much he is attracted to the mysteries of matter, and how completely unaware he is of the mysteries of Divinity! Nay, he is utterly negligent and oblivious of the secrets of Divinity. How great his ignorance! How conducive to his degradation! It is as if a kind and loving father had provided a library of wonderful books for his son in order that he might be informed of the mysteries of creation, at the same time surrounding him with every means of comfort and enjoyment, but the son amuses himself with pebbles and playthings, neglectful of all his father's gifts and provision. How ignorant and heedless is man! The Father has willed for him eternal glory, and he is content with blindness and deprivation. The Father has built for him a royal palace, but he is playing with the dust; prepared for him garments of silk, but he prefers to remain unclothed; provided for him delicious foods and fruits, while he seeks sustenance in the grasses of the field.

10.17 Consider: Unity is necessary to existence. Love is the very cause of life; on the other hand, separation brings death. In the world of material creation, for instance, all things owe their actual life to unity. The elements which compose wood, mineral, or stone, are held together by the law of attraction. If this law should cease for one moment to operate these elements would not hold together, they would fall apart, and the object would in that particular form cease to exist. The law of attraction has brought together certain elements in the form of this beautiful flower, but when that attraction is withdrawn from this centre the flower will decompose, and, as a flower, cease to exist.

So it is with the great body of humanity. The wonderful Law of Attraction, Harmony and Unity, holds together this marvellous Creation.

As with the whole, so with the parts; whether a flower or a human body, when the attracting principle is withdrawn from it, the flower or the man dies. It is therefore clear that attraction, harmony, unity and Love, are the cause of life, whereas repulsion, discord, hatred and separation bring death.

FROM THE WRITINGS AND LETTERS WRITTEN BY, OR ON BEHALF OF, SHOGHI EFFENDI

10.18   It is quite natural for anyone, observing the present state of the world, to feel very depressed and apprehensive of the future. Any intelligent person must be wondering what you are wondering. It is indeed hard to see what lies ahead of us in the near future—but we, as Bahá'ís, unlike most people, have absolute assurance that the distant future is serene and bright.

FROM THE WRITINGS AND LETTERS WRITTEN BY, OR ON BEHALF OF, THE UNIVERSAL HOUSE OF JUSTICE

10.19   Similarly, assisting in endeavors to conserve the environment in ways which blend with the rhythm of life of our community must assume more importance in Bahá'í activities.

10.20   At the national level, the structure of Bahá'í communities is growing in complexity as the number of believers rises, and National Spiritual Assemblies are being increasingly invited by national governments and non-governmental organizations to offer advice and assistance in upholding human rights, in safeguarding the environment, in promoting moral education, and in overcoming the ravages of prejudice and the rising tide of lawlessness which are undermining the social structure. Internationally a parallel process is taking place.

10.21   The worsening state of the environment and of the health of huge populations is a source of alarm.

10.22   With great pleasure the House of Justice takes this opportunity to announce the establishment of an Office of the Environment, which will conduct the external relations of the Bahá'í International Community with regard to environmental matters. Thus it will foster relations with the World Wide

Fund for Nature and other like-minded non-governmental organizations and will work in collaboration with the Office of Social and Economic Development. The new Office operates alongside the other offices of the Bahá'í International Community in New York, namely, the United Nations Office and the Office of Public Information.

10.23 LET US ACKNOWLEDGE AT THE OUTSET the magnitude of the ruin that the human race has brought upon itself during the period of history under review. The loss of life alone has been beyond counting. The disintegration of basic institutions of social order, the violation—indeed, the abandonment—of standards of decency, the betrayal of the life of the mind through surrender to ideologies as squalid as they have been empty, the invention and deployment of monstrous weapons of mass annihilation, the bankrupting of entire nations and the reduction of masses of human beings to hopeless poverty, the reckless destruction of the environment of the planet—such are only the more obvious in a catalogue of horrors unknown to even the darkest of ages past.

10.24 To accept willingly the rupture of one after another strand of the moral fabric that guides and disciplines individual life in any social system, is a self-defeating approach to reality. If leaders of thought were to be candid in their assessment of the evidence readily available, it is here that one would find the root cause of such apparently unrelated problems as the pollution of the environment, economic dislocation, ethnic violence, spreading public apathy, the massive increase in crime, and epidemics that ravage whole populations. However important the application of legal, sociological or technological expertise to such issues undoubtedly is, it would be unrealistic to imagine that efforts of this kind will produce any significant recovery without a fundamental change of moral consciousness and behaviour.

OTHER SOURCES

10.25 The major issues facing the environmental movement today hinge on this point. The problems of ocean pollution, the extinction of species, acid rain and deforestation—not to mention the ultimate scourge of nuclear war—respect no boundaries. All require a transnational approach. (Bahá'í International Community, *The Bahá'í Statement on Nature*)

10.26 Our efforts now and in the future to safeguard our common habitat and to promote the well-being and development of all peoples must be characterized by a unified approach within an effective universal framework. The unity we envision is more than an academic matter of geography, climatology or oceanography. It is based on the concept of the fundamental unity of mankind living as one world community, in which the problems of economic relations and the use of natural resources must be addressed from a global perspective with due regard for the wide diversity of climates and cultures. The universal framework proposed by Bahá'u'lláh over one hundred years ago calls for universally agreed-upon and enforceable laws, the equitable sharing of resources, fundamental adjustments to present institutional and economic relations, and world-wide changes in the values, behavior, and consumption patterns of individuals and communities. (Bahá'í International Community, 1990 Aug 06, *Environment and Development*)

10.27 Long-term solutions will require a new and comprehensive vision of a global society, supported by new values. In the view of the Bahá'í International Community, acceptance of the oneness of humanity is the first fundamental prerequisite for this reorganization and administration of the world as one country, the home of humankind. Recognition of this principle does not imply abandonment of legitimate loyalties, the suppression of cultural diversity, or the abolition of national autonomy. It calls for a wider loyalty, for a far higher aspiration than has so far animated human efforts. It clearly requires the subordination of national impulses and interests to the imperative claims of a unified world. It is inconsistent not only with any attempt to impose uniformity, but with any tendency towards excessive centralization. Its goal is well captured in the concept of "unity in diversity." (Bahá'í International Community, 1991 Aug 13, *International Legislation for Environment Development*)

10.28 A challenge of similar nature faces economic thinking as a result of the environmental crisis. The fallacies in theories based on the belief that there is no limit to nature's capacity to fulfill any demand made on it by human beings have now been coldly exposed. A culture which attaches absolute value to expansion, to acquisition, and to the satisfaction of people's wants is being compelled to recognize that such goals are not, by themselves, realistic guides to policy. Inadequate, too, are approaches to economic issues whose decision-making tools cannot deal with the fact that most of the major challenges are global rather than particular in scope.

The earnest hope that this moral crisis can somehow be met by deifying nature itself is an evidence of the spiritual and intellectual desperation that the crisis has engendered. Recognition that creation is an organic whole and that humanity has the responsibility to care for this whole, welcome as it is, does not represent an influence which can by itself establish in the consciousness of people a new system of values. Only a breakthrough in understanding that is scientific and spiritual in the fullest sense of the terms will empower the human race to assume the trusteeship toward which history impels it.

All people will have sooner or later to recover, for example, the capacity for contentment, the welcoming of moral discipline, and the devotion to duty that, until relatively recently, were considered essential aspects of being human. Repeatedly throughout history, the teachings of the Founders of the great religions have been able to instill these qualities of character in the mass of people who responded to them. The qualities themselves are even more vital today, but their expression must now take a form consistent with humanity's coming-of-age. Here again, religion's challenge is to free itself from the obsessions of the past: contentment is not fatalism; morality has nothing in common with the life-denying Puritanism that has so often presumed to speak in its name; and a genuine devotion to duty brings feelings not of self-righteousness but of self-worth. (Bahá'í International Community, 1995 Mar 03, *The Prosperity of Humankind*)

10.29 In the field of environmental protection, Bahá'í projects generally take a community-based approach. An example is a program being offered in the Talamanca and Caribbean regions of Costa Rica among the Bribri and Cabecar indigenous peoples. "Community learning groups" study modules on environmental and moral leadership with the aid of a local tutor and initiate projects such as school and family gardens, fish farms, and poultry raising. Through their participation in the program, over 200 individuals, many associated with local organizations engaged in the conservation of natural resources, have been able to enhance their ability to contribute to the sustainable development of their communities.

Besides such community-based initiatives, the International Environmental Forum operating in Europe links environmental professionals and activists worldwide. The Forum, whose membership is drawn from 50 countries, hosts an annual conference, promotes networking, publishes monographs, sponsors online courses on sustainable development, and provides mentoring to students and young professionals. (Bahá'í International Community, *For the Betterment of the World*))

CHAPTER 11:

POWERING THE SPIRITUAL ECONOMY

FROM THE WRITINGS OF BAHÁ'U'LLÁH

11.1 …Man's merit lieth in service and virtue and not in the pageantry of wealth and riches. Take heed that your words be purged from idle fancies and worldly desires and your deeds be cleansed from craftiness and suspicion. Dissipate not the wealth of your precious lives in the pursuit of evil and corrupt affection, nor let your endeavours be spent in promoting your personal interest. Be generous in your days of plenty, and be patient in the hour of loss. Adversity is followed by success and rejoicings follow woe. Guard against idleness and sloth, and cling unto that which profiteth mankind, whether young or old, whether high or low. Beware lest ye sow tares of dissension among men or plant thorns of doubt in pure and radiant hearts.

11.2 The days of your life are far spent, O people, and your end is fast approaching. Put away, therefore, the things ye have devised and to which ye cleave, and take firm hold on the precepts of God, that haply ye may attain that which He hath purposed for you, and be of them that pursue a right course. Delight not yourselves in the things of the world and its vain ornaments, neither set your hopes on them. Let your reliance be on the remembrance of God, the Most Exalted, the Most Great. He will, erelong, bring to naught all the things ye possess. Let Him be your fear, and forget not His covenant with you, and be not of them that are shut out as by a veil from Him.

11.3 Allow not the abject to rule over and dominate them who are noble and worthy of honor, and suffer not the high-minded to be at the mercy of the contemptible and worthless, for this is what We observed upon Our arrival in the City (Constantinople), and to it We bear witness. We found among its inhabitants some who were possessed of an affluent fortune and lived in the midst of excessive riches, while others were in dire want and abject poverty. This ill beseemeth thy sovereignty, and is unworthy of thy rank.

11.4 O YE THAT PRIDE YOURSELVES ON MORTAL RICHES! Know ye in truth that wealth is a mighty barrier between the seeker and his desire, the lover and his beloved. The rich, but for a few, shall in no wise attain the court of His presence nor enter the city of content and resignation. Well is it then with him, who, being rich, is not hindered by his riches from the eternal kingdom, nor deprived by them of imperishable dominion. By the Most Great Name! The splendor of such a wealthy man shall illuminate the dwellers of heaven even as the sun enlightens the people of the earth!

11.5 Neither the pomp of the mighty, nor the wealth of the rich, nor even the ascendancy of the ungodly will endure. All will perish, at a word from Him. He, verily, is the All-Powerful, the All-Compelling, the Almighty. What advantage is there in the earthly things which men possess? That which shall profit them, they have utterly neglected. Erelong, they will awake from their slumber, and find themselves unable to obtain that which hath escaped them in the days of their Lord, the Almighty, the All-Praised. Did they but know it, they would renounce their all, that their names may be mentioned before His throne. They, verily, are accounted among the dead.

11.6 To give and to be generous are attributes of Mine; well is it with him that adorneth himself with My virtues.

11.7 O YE RICH ONES ON EARTH! The poor in your midst are My trust; guard ye My trust, and be not intent only on your own ease.

11.8 O SON OF MAN! Bestow My wealth upon My poor, that in heaven thou mayest draw from stores of unfading splendor and treasures of imperishable glory. But by My life! To offer up thy soul is a more glorious thing couldst thou but see with Mine eye.

11.9 Know ye that the poor are the trust of God in your midst. Watch that ye betray not His trust, that ye deal not unjustly with them and that ye walk not in the ways of the treacherous.

Ye will most certainly be called upon to answer for His trust on the day when the Balance of Justice shall be set, the day when unto everyone shall be rendered his due, when the doings of all men, be they rich or poor, shall be weighed.

11.10 If ye meet the abased or the down-trodden, turn not away disdainfully from them, for the King of Glory ever watcheth over them and surroundeth them with such tenderness as none can fathom except them that have suffered their wishes and desires to be merged in the Will of your Lord, the Gracious, the All-Wise. O ye rich ones of the earth! Flee not from the face of the poor that lieth in the dust, nay rather befriend him and suffer him to recount the tale of the woes with which God's inscrutable Decree hath caused him to be afflicted. By the righteousness of God! Whilst ye consort with him, the Concourse on high will be looking upon you, will be interceding for you, will be extolling your names and glorifying your action. Blessed are the learned that pride not themselves on their attainments; and well is it with the righteous that mock not the sinful, but rather conceal their misdeeds, so that their own shortcomings may remain veiled to men's eyes.

11.11 Fear the sighs of the poor and of the upright in heart who, at every break of day, bewail their plight, and be unto them a benignant sovereign. They, verily, are thy treasures on earth. It behoveth thee, therefore, to safeguard thy treasures from the assaults of them who wish to rob thee. Inquire into their affairs, and ascertain, every year, nay every month, their condition, and be not of them that are careless of their duty.

11.12 Therefore as a token of favour towards men We have prescribed that interest on money should be treated like other business transactions that are current amongst men. Thus, now that this lucid commandment hath descended from the heaven of the Will of God, it is lawful and proper to charge interest on money, that the people of the world may, in a spirit of amity and fellowship and with joy and gladness, devotedly engage themselves in magnifying the Name of Him Who is the Well-Beloved of all mankind. Verily He ordaineth according to His Own choosing. He hath now made interest on money lawful, even as He had made it unlawful in the past. Within His grasp He holdeth the kingdom of authority. He doeth and ordaineth. He is in truth the Ordainer, the All-Knowing.

FROM THE WRITINGS AND UTTERANCES OF 'ABDU'L-BAHÁ

11.13   Regarding the economic prejudice, it is apparent that whenever the ties between nations become strengthened and the exchange of commodities accelerated, and any economic principle is established in one country, it will ultimately affect the other countries and universal benefits will result…

11.14   But the principal cause of these difficulties lies in the laws of the present civilization; for they lead to a small number of individuals accumulating incomparable fortunes, beyond their needs, while the greater number remain destitute, stripped and in the greatest misery. This is contrary to justice, to humanity, to equity; it is the height of iniquity, the opposite to what causes divine satisfaction.

11.15   Every business company should be established on divine principles. Its foundations should be trustworthiness, piety and truthfulness in order to protect the rights of the people.

11.16   Then rules and laws should be established to regulate the excessive fortunes of certain private individuals and meet the needs of millions of the poor masses; thus a certain moderation would be obtained. However, absolute equality is just as impossible, for absolute equality in fortunes, honors, commerce, agriculture, industry would end in disorderliness, in chaos, in disorganization of the means of existence, and in universal disappointment: the order of the community would be quite destroyed. Thus difficulties will also arise when unjustified equality is imposed. It is, therefore, preferable for moderation to be established by means of laws and regulations to hinder the constitution of the excessive fortunes of certain individuals, and to protect the essential needs of the masses. For instance, the manufacturers and the industrialists heap up a treasure each day, and the poor artisans do not gain their daily sustenance: that is the height of iniquity, and no just man can accept it. Therefore, laws and regulations should be established which would permit the workmen to receive from the factory owner their wages and a share in the fourth or the fifth part of the profits, according to the capacity of the factory; or in some other way the body of workmen and the manufacturers should share equitably the profits and advantages. Indeed, the capital and management come from the owner of the factory, and the work and labor, from the body of the workmen. Either the workmen should receive wages which assure them an adequate support and, when they cease work, becoming feeble or helpless, they should have sufficient benefits from the income of the industry; or the wages should be high enough to satisfy the workmen with the amount they receive so that they may themselves be able to put a little aside for days of want and helplessness.

11.17 … Bahá'u'lláh set forth principles of guidance and teaching for economic readjustment. Regulations were revealed by Him which ensure the welfare of the commonwealth. As the rich man enjoys his life surrounded by ease and luxuries, so the poor man must, likewise, have a home and be provided with sustenance and comforts commensurate with his needs. This readjustment of the social economy is of the greatest importance inasmuch as it ensures the stability of the world of humanity; and until it is effected, happiness and prosperity are impossible.

11.18 For man two wings are necessary. One wing is physical power and material civilization; the other is spiritual power and divine civilization. With one wing only, flight is impossible. Two wings are essential. Therefore, no matter how much material civilization advances, it cannot attain to perfection except through the uplift of spiritual civilization.

11.19 All the Prophets have come to promote divine bestowals, to found the spiritual civilization and teach the principles of morality. Therefore, we must strive with all our powers so that spiritual influences may gain the victory. For material forces have attacked mankind. The world of humanity is submerged in a sea of materialism. The rays of the Sun of Reality are seen but dimly and darkly through opaque glasses. The penetrative power of the divine bounty is not fully manifest.

FROM THE WRITINGS AND LETTERS WRITTEN BY, OR ON BEHALF OF, SHOGHI EFFENDI

11.20 Humanity, whether viewed in the light of man's individual conduct or in the existing relationships between organized communities and nations, has, alas, strayed too far and suffered too great a decline to be redeemed through the unaided efforts of the best among its recognized rulers and statesmen—however disinterested their motives, however concerted their action, however unsparing in their zeal and devotion to its cause. No scheme which the calculations of the highest statesmanship may yet devise; no doctrine which the most distinguished exponents of economic theory may hope to advance; no principle which the most ardent of moralists may strive to inculcate, can provide, in the last resort, adequate foundations upon which the future of a distracted world can be built. No appeal for mutual tolerance which the worldly-wise might raise, however compelling and insistent, can calm its passions or help restore its vigor. Nor would any general scheme of mere organized international cooperation, in whatever sphere of human activity, however ingenious in conception, or extensive in scope, succeed in removing the root cause of the evil that has so rudely upset the equilibrium of present-day society. Not even, I venture to assert, would the very act of devising the machinery required for the political and economic unification of the world—a principle that has been increasingly advocated in recent times—provide in itself the antidote against the poison that is steadily undermining the vigor of organized peoples and nations. What else, might we not confidently affirm, but the unreserved acceptance of the Divine Program enunciated, with such simplicity and force as far back as sixty years ago, by Bahá'u'lláh, embodying in its essentials God's divinely appointed scheme for the unification of mankind in this age, coupled with an indomitable conviction in the unfailing efficacy of each and all of its provisions, is eventually capable of withstanding the forces of internal disintegration which, if unchecked, must needs continue to eat into the vitals of a despairing society. It is towards this goal—the goal of a new World Order, Divine in origin, all-embracing in scope, equitable in principle, challenging in its features—that a harassed humanity must strive.

11.21   ... Of course conditions in the East differ where the Countries are rarely industrial and mostly agricultural we should have to apply different laws from the West and that is why the principles of the Movement strike at the root which is common to them both. 'Abdu'l-Bahá has developed in various of His talks, which the Bahá'í economic system would be based. A system that prevents among others the gradual control of wealth in the hands of a few and the resulting state of both extremes, wealth and poverty.

11.22   Regarding your questions concerning the Bahá'í attitude on various economic problems, such as the problem of ownership, control and distribution of capital, and of other means of production, the problem of trusts and monopolies, and such economic experiments as social cooperatives; the Teachings of Bahá'u'lláh and 'Abdu'l-Bahá do not provide specific and detailed solutions to all such economic questions which mostly pertain to the domain of technical economics, and as such do not concern directly the Cause. True, there are certain guiding principles in Bahá'í Sacred Writings on the subject of economics, but these do by no means cover the whole field of theoretical and applied economics, and are mostly intended to guide further Bahá'í economic writers and technicians to evolve an economic system which would function in full conformity with the spirit and the exact provisions of the Cause on this and similar subjects. The International House of Justice will have, in consultation with economic experts, to assist in the formulation and evolution of the Bahá'í economic system of the future. One thing, however, is certain that the Cause neither accepts the theories of the Capitalistic economics in full, nor can it agree with the Marxists and Communists in their repudiation of the principle of private ownership and of the vital sacred rights of the individual.

11.23 No, Bahá'u'lláh did not bring a complete system of economics to the world. Profit-sharing is recommended as a solution to one form of economic problems. There is nothing in the teachings against some kind of capitalism; its present form, though, would require adjustments to be made.

11.24 ... There are practically no technical teachings on economics in the Cause, such as banking, the price system, and others. The Cause is not an economic system, nor can its Founders be considered as having been technical economists. The contribution of the Faith to this subject is essentially indirect, as it consists in the application of spiritual principles to our present-day economic system. Bahá'u'lláh has given us a few basic principles which should guide future Bahá'í economists in establishing such institutions which will adjust the economic relationships of the world.

FROM THE WRITINGS AND LETTERS WRITTEN BY, OR ON BEHALF OF, THE UNIVERSAL HOUSE OF JUSTICE

11.25 The inordinate disparity between rich and poor, a source of acute suffering, keeps the world in a state of instability, virtually on the brink of war. Few societies have dealt effectively with this situation. The solution calls for the combined application of spiritual, moral and practical approaches. A fresh look at the problem is required, entailing consultation with experts from a wide spectrum of disciplines, devoid of economic and ideological polemics, and involving the people directly affected in the decisions that must urgently be made. It is an issue that is bound up not only with the necessity for eliminating extremes of wealth and poverty but also with those spiritual verities the understanding of which can produce a new universal attitude. Fostering such an attitude is itself a major part of the solution

11.26 If the friends, however, are willing, spontaneously, to establish a profitable business in order to benefit themselves as well as the other friends it is meritorious anod there is no objection.'

Should such a business venture as you propose be undertaken—and there is nothing wrong with it in principle—it would be well to advise the Bahá'ís who participated to approach it on the basis of its viability as a business project and they should not underestimate the possibilities of financial loss.

OTHER SOURCES

11.27 Indeed, in an important sense, progress in this area will itself be a measure of the success of any development program. Given the vital role of economic activity in the advancement of civilization, visible evidence of the pace at which development is progressing will be the extent to which women gain access to all avenues of economic endeavor. The challenge goes beyond ensuring an equitable distribution of opportunity, important as that is. It calls for a fundamental rethinking of economic issues in a manner that will invite the full participation of a range of human experience and insight hitherto largely excluded from the discourse. The classical economic models of impersonal markets in which human beings act as autonomous makers of self-regarding choices will not serve the needs of a world motivated by ideals of unity and justice. Society will find itself increasingly challenged to develop new economic models shaped by insights that arise from a sympathetic understanding of shared experience, from viewing human beings in relation to others, and from a recognition of the centrality to social well-being of the role of the family and the community. Such an intellectual breakthrough—strongly altruistic rather than self-centered in focus—must draw heavily on both the spiritual and scientific sensibilities of the race, and millennia of experience have prepared women to make crucial contributions to the common effort. (Bahá'í International Community, 1995 Mar 03, *The Prosperity of Humankind*)

11.28 The problem of poverty is a case in point. Proposals aimed at addressing it are predicated on the conviction that material resources exist, or can be created by scientific and technological endeavor, which will alleviate and eventually entirely eradicate this age-old condition as a feature of human life. A major reason why such relief is not achieved is that the necessary scientific and technological advances respond to a set of priorities only tangentially related to the real interests of the generality of humankind. A radical reordering of these priorities will be required if the burden of poverty is finally to be lifted from the world. Such an achievement demands a determined quest for appropriate values, a quest that will test profoundly both the spiritual and scientific resources of humankind. Religion will be severely hampered in contributing to this joint undertaking so long as it is held prisoner by sectarian doctrines which cannot distinguish between contentment and mere passivity and which teach that poverty is an inherent feature of earthly life, escape from which lies only in the world beyond. To participate effectively in the struggle to bring material well-being to humanity, the religious spirit must find—in the Source of inspiration from which it flows—new spiritual concepts and principles relevant to an age that seeks to establish unity and justice in human affairs.

Unemployment raises similar issues. In most of contemporary thinking, the concept of work has been largely reduced to that of gainful employment aimed at acquiring the means for the consumption of available goods. The system is circular: acquisition and consumption resulting in the maintenance and expansion of the production of goods and, in consequence, in supporting paid employment. Taken individually, all of these activities are essential to the well-being of society. The inadequacy of the overall conception, however, can be read in both the apathy that social commentators discern among large numbers of the employed in every land and the demoralization of the growing armies of the unemployed.

Not surprisingly, therefore, there is increasing recognition that the world is in urgent need of a new "work ethic." Here again, nothing less than insights generated by the creative interaction of the scientific and religious systems of knowledge can produce so fundamental a reorientation of habits and attitudes. Unlike animals, which depend for their sustenance on whatever the environment readily affords, human beings are impelled to express the immense capacities latent within them through productive work designed to meet their own needs and those of others. In acting thus they become participants, at however modest a level, in the processes of the advancement of civilization. They fulfill purposes that unite them with others. To the extent that work is consciously undertaken in a spirit of service to humanity, Bahá'u'lláh says, it is a form of prayer, a means of worshipping God. Every individual has the capacity to see himself or herself in this light, and it is to this inalienable capacity of the self that development strategy must appeal, whatever the nature of the plans being pursued, whatever the rewards they promise. No narrower a perspective will ever call up from the people of the world the magnitude of effort and commitment that the economic tasks ahead will require. (Bahá'í International Community, 1995 Mar 03, *The Prosperity of Humankind*)

11.29 The Bahá'í approach to the problem of extreme poverty is based on the belief that economic problems can be solved only through the application of spiritual principles. This approach suggests that to adjust the economic relationships of society, man's character must first be transformed. Until the actions of humankind promote justice above the satisfaction of greed and readjusts the world's economies accordingly, the gap between the rich and the poor will continue to widen, and the dream of sustainable economic growth, peace, and prosperity must remain elusive. Sensitizing mankind to the vital role of spirituality in solving economic problems including the realization of universal equitable access to wealth and opportunity will, we are convinced, create a new impetus for change.

A new economic order can be founded only on an unshakable conviction of the oneness of mankind. Discussions aimed at solving problems related to extreme poverty based on the premise that we are one human family rapidly expand beyond the current vocabulary of economics. They demand a wider context, one which anticipates the emergence of a global system of relationships resting on the principles of equity and justice.

Although it will resemble the present system in many ways, the evolving economic system which Bahá'ís envision will have significant points of distinction. (Bahá'í International Community, 1993 Feb 12, *Human Rights and Extreme Poverty*)

11.30 At the same time, significant sections of the world community—including many social theorists, economists, and religious and secular leaders—cling to the view that human beings are incorrigibly selfish and aggressive and thus incapable of erecting a peaceful and progressive, world-embracing social order. Such a cynical view of human nature, with its attendant attitudes and behaviors, has contributed enormously to the ills plaguing society today, including poverty, unemployment, social strife, over-consumption, chauvinistic nationalism, war, and moral and spiritual apathy. (Bahá'í International Community, 1994 Jan 21, *Global Action Plan for Social Development*)

11.31 In our increasingly interdependent world, it is no longer possible for a people or a nation to achieve lasting prosperity at the expense of other peoples and nations. Thus, real progress on the Summit's core issues—achieving durable social integration, alleviating the root causes of poverty, and expanding sustainable productive employment—can only be achieved through those strategies and actions that foster unity both within and among the nations of the world. A strong commitment to the principle of the oneness of humanity will greatly assist the PREPCOM in crafting an effective "global strategy and action-plan" to address these core issues. (Bahá'í International Community, 1994 Jan 21, *Global Action Plan for Social Development*)

11.32 Microfinance programs generally involve credit, savings, and related services for the less prosperous segments of society, depending on an outside lending agency and outside capital in order to operate. However, Education, Curriculum, and Training Associates (ECTA), a Bahá'í-inspired nongovernmental organization in Nepal, has developed a program through which groups of between 10 and 30 men and women form and manage community banks capitalized from their own savings. Loans from these banks are small at first, but interest earned on them remains with the members, divided proportionally according to the amount of savings each has on deposit. Further, a portion of the profits is put into a social and economic development fund for the benefit of the community at large. The banks provide their members with the opportunity to learn skills of sound financial management and encourage them to establish or expand their own businesses. More than just a savings and credit program, these community banks also serve to develop in their members attitudes and qualities vital to the task of managing financial resources—such as trustworthiness, cooperation, and a spirit of service—fostering consultation, solidarity, and unity within the group. ECTA's program began in 2002 with five banks in the Morang district of Nepal and has since grown to include 60 banks operating in different parts of the country. (Bahá'í International Community, *For the Betterment of the World*)

PART II: ORGANIZING FOR SUSTAINABLE CHANGE

CHAPTER 12:

CULTIVATING EFFECTIVE COMMUNITIES

158 ❷ Making a Better World with the Bahá'í Faith: QUOTATIONS

FROM THE WRITINGS OF BAHÁ'U'LLÁH

12.1 O contending peoples and kindreds of the earth! Set your faces towards unity, and let the radiance of its light shine upon you. Gather ye together, and for the sake of God resolve to root out whatever is the source of contention amongst you.

12.2 In one of the Tablets these words have been revealed: O people of God! Do not busy yourselves in your own concerns; let your thoughts be fixed upon that which will rehabilitate the fortunes of mankind and sanctify the hearts and souls of men. This can best be achieved through pure and holy deeds, through a virtuous life and a goodly behavior. Valiant acts will ensure the triumph of this Cause, and a saintly character will reinforce its power. Cleave unto righteousness, O people of Baha! This, verily, is the commandment which this wronged One hath given unto you, and the first choice of His unrestrained Will for every one of you.

12.3 The brightness of the fire of your love will no doubt fuse and unify the contending peoples and kindreds of the earth, whilst the fierceness of the flame of enmity and hatred cannot but result in strife and ruin.

12.4 They who are the beloved of God, in whatever place they gather and whomsoever they may meet, must evince, in their attitude towards God, and in the manner of their celebration of His praise and glory, such humility and submissiveness that every atom of the dust beneath their feet may attest the depth of their devotion. The conversation carried by these holy souls should be informed with such power that these same atoms of dust will be thrilled by its influence. They should conduct themselves in such manner that the earth upon which they tread may never be allowed to address to them such words as these: "I am to be preferred above you. For witness, how patient I am in bearing the burden which the husbandman layeth upon me. I am the instrument that continually imparteth unto all beings the blessings with which He Who is the Source of all grace hath entrusted me. Notwithstanding the honor conferred upon me, and the unnumbered evidences of my wealth—a wealth that supplieth the needs of all creation—behold the measure of my humility, witness with what absolute submissiveness I allow myself to be trodden beneath the feet of men....

12.5 It is Our wish and desire that every one of you may become a source of all goodness unto men, and an example of uprightness to mankind. Beware lest ye prefer yourselves above your neighbors. Fix your gaze upon Him Who is the Temple of God amongst men. He, in truth, hath offered up His life as a ransom for the redemption of the world. He, verily, is the All-Bountiful, the Gracious, the Most High. If any differences arise amongst you, behold Me standing before your face, and overlook the faults of one another for My name's sake and as a token of your love for My manifest and resplendent Cause. We love to see you at all times consorting in amity and concord within the paradise of My good-pleasure, and to inhale from your acts the fragrance of friendliness and unity, of loving-kindness and fellowship. Thus counselleth you the All-Knowing, the Faithful. We shall always be with you; if We inhale the perfume of your fellowship, Our heart will assuredly rejoice, for naught else can satisfy Us. To this beareth witness every man of true understanding.

12.6 Every eye, in this Day, should seek what will best promote the Cause of God. He, Who is the Eternal Truth, beareth Me witness! Nothing whatsoever can, in this Day, inflict a greater harm upon this Cause than dissension and strife, contention, estrangement and apathy, among the loved ones of God. Flee them, through the power of God and His sovereign aid, and strive ye to knit together the hearts of men, in His Name, the Unifier, the All-Knowing, the All-Wise

12.7 Say: He Who is the Unconditioned is come, in the clouds of light, that He may quicken all created things with the breezes of His Name, the Most Merciful, and unify the world, and gather all men around this Table which hath been sent down from heaven

12.8 O SON OF MAN! Deny not My servant should he ask anything from thee, for his face is My face; be then abashed before Me.

12.9 Show forbearance and benevolence and love to one another.

12.10 How vast is the tabernacle of the Cause of God! It hath overshadowed all the peoples and kindreds of the earth, and will, erelong, gather together the whole of mankind beneath its shelter. Thy day of service is now come. Countless Tablets bear the testimony of the bounties vouchsafed unto thee. Arise for the triumph of My Cause, and, through the power of thine utterance, subdue the hearts of men. Thou must show forth that which will ensure the peace and the well-being of the miserable and the down-trodden. Gird up the loins of thine endeavor, that perchance thou mayest release the captive from his chains, and enable him to attain unto true liberty.

12.11 Through the movement of Our Pen of glory We have, at the bidding of the omnipotent Ordainer, breathed a new life into every human frame, and instilled into every word a fresh potency. All created things proclaim the evidences of this world-wide regeneration. This is the most great, the most joyful tidings imparted by the Pen of this wronged One to mankind. Wherefore fear ye, O My well-beloved ones? Who is it that can dismay you? A touch of moisture sufficeth to dissolve the hardened clay out of which this perverse generation is molded. The mere act of your gathering together is enough to scatter the forces of these vain and worthless people...

12.12 This is the Day whereon He Who is the Revealer of the names of God hath stepped out of the Tabernacle of glory, and proclaimed unto all who are in the heavens and all who are on the earth: "Put away the cups of Paradise and all the life-giving waters they contain, for lo, the people of Baha have entered the blissful abode of the Divine Presence, and quaffed the wine of reunion, from the chalice of the beauty of their Lord, the All-Possessing, the Most High.

12.13 Rejoice with exceeding gladness, O people of Baha, as ye call to remembrance the Day of supreme felicity, the Day whereon the Tongue of the Ancient of Days hath spoken, as He departed from His House, proceeding to the Spot from which He shed upon the whole of creation the splendors of His name, the All-Merciful. God is Our witness. Were We to reveal the hidden secrets of that Day, all they that dwell on earth and in the heavens would swoon away and die, except such as will be preserved by God, the Almighty, the All-Knowing, the All-Wise.

12.14 Drink with healthy relish, O people of Baha. Ye are indeed they with whom it shall be well. This is what they who have near access to God have attained.

12.15 O friends! It behoveth you to refresh and revive your souls through the gracious favors which in this Divine, this soul-stirring Springtime are being showered upon you. The Day Star of His great glory hath shed its radiance upon you, and the clouds of His limitless grace have overshadowed you. How high the reward of him that hath not deprived himself of so great a bounty, nor failed to recognize the beauty of his Best-Beloved in this, His new attire. Watch over yourselves, for the Evil One is lying in wait, ready to entrap you. Gird yourselves against his wicked devices, and, led by the light of the name of the All-Seeing God, make your escape from the darkness that surroundeth you. Let your vision be world-embracing, rather than confined to your own self. The Evil One is he that hindereth the rise and obstructeth the spiritual progress of the children of men.

12.16 Verily this is the Day in which both land and sea rejoice at this announcement, the Day for which have been laid up those things which God, through a bounty beyond the ken of mortal mind or heart, hath destined for revelation. Ere long will God sail His Ark upon thee, and will manifest the people of Baha who have been mentioned in the Book of Names.

12.17 I beseech Thee, by Thy Most Great Name, to raise in every city a new creation that shall turn towards Thee, and shall remember Thee amidst Thy servants, and shall unfurl by virtue of their utterances and wisdom the ensigns of Thy victory, and shall detach themselves from all created things.

FROM THE WRITINGS AND UTTERANCES OF 'ABDU'L-BAHÁ

12.18   Ye have written as to the meetings of the friends, and how filled they are with peace and joy. Of course this is so; for wherever the spiritually minded are gathered together, there in His beauty reigneth Bahá'u'lláh. Thus it is certain that such reunions will yield boundless happiness and peace.

Today it behoveth one and all to forgo the mention of all else, and to disregard all things. Let their speaking, let their inner state be summed up thus: 'Keep all my words of prayer and praise confined to one refrain; make all my life but servitude to Thee.' That is, let them concentrate all their thoughts, all their words, on teaching the Cause of God and spreading the Faith of God, and inspiring all to characterize themselves with the characteristics of God; on loving mankind; on being pure and holy in all things, and spotless in their public and private life; on being upright and detached, and fervent, and afire. All is to be yielded up, save only the remembrance of God; all is to be dispraised, except His praise. Today, to this melody of the Company on high, the world will leap and dance: 'Glory be to my Lord, the All-Glorious!' But know ye this: save for this song of God, no song will stir the world, and save for this nightingale-cry of truth from the Garden of God, no melody will lure away the heart. 'Whence cometh this Singer Who speaketh the Beloved's name?'

12.19   It befitteth the friends to hold a gathering, a meeting, where they shall glorify God and fix their hearts upon Him, and read and recite the Holy Writings of the Blessed Beauty—may my soul be the ransom of His lovers!

12.20   Whensoever a company of people shall gather in a meeting place, shall engage in glorifying God, and shall speak with one another of the mysteries of God, beyond any doubt the breathings of the Holy Spirit will blow gently over them, and each shall receive a share thereof.

12.21 We hear that thou hast in mind to embellish thy house from time to time with a meeting of Bahá'ís, where some among them will engage in glorifying the All-Glorious Lord... Know that shouldst thou bring this about, that house of earth will become a house of heaven, and that fabric of stone a congress of the spirit.

12.22 May our purposes centralize in the earnest desire of attaining the good pleasure of God, and may our supreme energies be directed to welding together the human household. Let us not regard our own respective capacities; nay, rather, let us regard forever the favors and bounties of God. The drop must not estimate its own limited capacity; it must realize the volume and sufficiency of the ocean, which ever glorifieth the drop. The tender and simple seed, solitary though it may be, must not look upon its own lack of power. Nay, rather, its attention must ever be directed to the sun, in the rays of which it finds life and quickening; and it must ever consider the downpour of the cloud of mercy. For the bounty of the cloud, the effulgence and heat of the sun and the breath of the vernal zephyrs can transform the tiny seed and develop it into a mighty tree. And may you remember that a single infinitesimal atom in the ray of the sun through a shining beam of the solar energy becomes glorified and radiant.

FROM THE WRITINGS AND LETTERS WRITTEN BY, OR ON BEHALF OF, SHOGHI EFFENDI

12.23 Who knows but that triumphs, unsurpassed in splendour, are not in store for the mass of Bahá'u'lláh's toiling followers? Surely, we stand too near the colossal edifice His hand has reared to be able, at the present stage of the evolution of His Revelation, to claim to be able even to conceive the full measure of its promised glory. Its past history, stained by the blood of countless martyrs, may well inspire us with the thought that, whatever may yet befall this Cause, however formidable the forces that may still assail it, however numerous the reverses it will inevitably suffer, its onward march can never be stayed, and that it will continue to advance until the very last promise, enshrined within the words of Bahá'u'lláh, shall have been completely redeemed.

12.24 Dearly beloved friends! A rectitude of conduct which, in all its manifestations, offers a striking contrast to the deceitfulness and corruption that characterize the political life of the nation and of the parties and factions that compose it; a holiness and chastity that are diametrically opposed to the moral laxity and licentiousness which defile the character of a not inconsiderable proportion of its citizens; an interracial fellowship completely purged from the curse of racial prejudice which stigmatizes the vast majority of its people—these are the weapons which the American believers can and must wield in their double crusade, first to regenerate the inward life of their own community, and next to assail the long-standing evils that have entrenched themselves in the life of their nation. The perfection of such weapons, the wise and effective utilization of every one of them, more than the furtherance of any particular plan, or the devising of any special scheme, or the accumulation of any amount of material resources, can prepare them for the time when the Hand of Destiny will have directed them to assist in creating and in bringing into operation that World Order which is now incubating within the worldwide administrative institutions of their Faith.

12.25 We must bear with one another. It is only through suffering that the nobility of character can make itself manifest. The energy we expend in enduring the intolerance of some individuals of our community is not lost. It is transformed into fortitude, steadfastness and magnanimity. The lives of Bahá'u'lláh and 'Abdu'l-Bahá are the best examples for this. Sacrifices in the path of one's religion produce always immortal results, 'Out of the ashes rises the phoenix'.

12.26 Regarding your own condition: He strongly urges you not to dwell on yourself. Each one of us, if we look into our failures, is sure to feel unworthy and despondent, and this feeling only frustrates our constructive efforts and wastes time. The thing for us to focus on is the glory of the Cause and the Power of Bahá'u'lláh which can make of a mere drop a surging sea! You certainly have no right to feel negative; you have embraced this glorious Faith and arisen with devotion to serve it, and your labours are greatly appreciated by both the Guardian and your fellow-Bahá'ís. With something as positive as the Faith and all it teaches behind you, you should be a veritable lion of confidence, and he will pray that you may become so.

There is, unfortunately, no way that one can force his own good upon a man. The element of free will is there, and all we believers—and even the Manifestation of God Himself—can do is to offer the truth to mankind. If the people of the world persist, as they seem to be doing, in their blind materialism, they must bear the consequences in a prolongation of their present condition, and even a worsening of it. Our duty as Bahá'ís is to build up such a love and unity within our own ranks that the people will be attracted by this example to the Cause. We also must teach all we can and strengthen the Bahá'í Community in the administration. But more we cannot do to avert the great sufferings which seemingly still lie ahead of the world in its present evil state.

12.27 The people of the world not only need the laws and principles of the Bahá'í Faith—they desperately need to see the love that is engendered by it in the hearts of its followers, and to partake of that atmosphere of tolerance, understanding, forbearance and active kindness which should be the hall-mark of a Bahá'í Community.

12.28 Let every believer, desirous to witness the swift and healthy progress of the Cause of God, realize the twofold nature of his task. Let him first turn his eyes inwardly and search his own heart and satisfy himself that in his relations with his fellow-believers, irrespective of color and class, he is proving himself increasingly loyal to the spirit of his beloved Faith. Assured and content that he is exerting his utmost in a conscious effort to approach nearer every day the lofty station to which his gracious Master summons him, let him turn to his second task, and, with befitting confidence and vigor, assail the devastating power of those forces which in his own heart he has already succeeded in subduing. Fully alive to the unfailing efficacy of the power of Bahá'u'lláh, and armed with the essential weapons of wise restraint and inflexible resolve, let him wage a constant fight against the inherited tendencies, the corruptive instincts, the fluctuating fashions, the false pretences of the society in which he lives and moves.

In their relations amongst themselves as fellow-believers, let them not be content with the mere exchange of cold and empty formalities often connected with the organizing of banquets, receptions, consultative assemblies, and lecture-halls. Let them rather, as equal co-sharers in the spiritual benefits conferred upon them by Bahá'u'lláh, arise and, with the aid and counsel of their local and national representatives, supplement these official functions with those opportunities which only a close and intimate social intercourse can adequately provide. In their homes, in their hours of relaxation and leisure, in the daily contact of business transactions, in the association of their children, whether in their study-classes, their playgrounds, and club-rooms, in short under all possible circumstances, however insignificant they appear, the community of the followers of Bahá'u'lláh should satisfy themselves that in the eyes of the world at large and in the sight of their vigilant Master they are the living witnesses of those truths which He fondly cherished and tirelessly championed to the very end of His days. If we relax in our purpose, if we falter in our faith, if we neglect the varied opportunities given us from time to time by an all-wise and gracious Master, we are not merely failing in what is our most vital and conspicuous obligation, but are thereby insensibly retarding the flow of those quickening energies which can alone insure the vigorous and speedy development of God's struggling Faith.

FROM THE WRITINGS AND LETTERS WRITTEN BY, OR ON BEHALF OF, THE UNIVERSAL HOUSE OF JUSTICE

12.29 In the human body, every cell, every organ, every nerve has its part to play. When all do so the body is healthy, vigorous, radiant, ready for very call made upon it. No cell, however humble, lives apart from the body, whether in serving it or receiving from it. This is true of the body of mankind in which God has endowed each humble being with ability and talent', and is supremely true of the body of the Bahá'í World Community, for this body is already an organism, united in its aspirations, unified in its methods, seeking assistance and confirmation from the same Source, and illumined with the conscious knowledge of its unity... The Bahá'í World community, growing like a healthy new body, develops new cells, new organs, new functions and powers as it presses on to its maturity, when every soul, living for the Cause of God, will receive from that Cause, health, assurance, and the overflowing bounties of Bahá'u'lláh which are diffused through His Divinely-ordained Order.

12.30 As humanity plunges deeper into the condition of which Bahá'u'lláh wrote, 'to disclose it now would not be meet and seemly', so must the believers increasingly stand out as assured, oriented, and fundamentally happy beings, conforming to a standard which, in direct contrast to the ignoble and amoral attitudes of modern society, is the source of their honour, strength, and maturity. It is this marked contrast between the vigour, unity, and discipline of the Bahá'í community on the one hand, and the increasing confusion, despair and feverish tempo of a doomed society on the other, which during the turbulent years ahead will draw the eyes of humanity to the sanctuary of Bahá'u'lláh's world-redeeming Faith.

12.31 The experience of the Bahá'í community may be seen as an example of this enlarging unity. It is a community of some three to four million people drawn from many nations, cultures, classes and creeds, engaged in a wide range of activities serving the spiritual, social and economic needs of the peoples of many lands. It is a single social organism, representative of the diversity of the human family, conducting its affairs through a system of commonly accepted consultative principles, and cherishing equally all the great outpourings of divine guidance in human history. Its existence is yet another convincing proof of the practicality of its Founder's vision of a united world, another evidence that humanity can live as one global society, equal to whatever challenges its coming of age may entail. If the Bahá'í experience can contribute in whatever measure to reinforcing hope in the unity of the human race, we are happy to offer it as a model for study.

12.32 You are quite correct in your understanding of the importance of avoiding backbiting; such conduct strikes at the very unity of the Bahá'í community. In a letter written to an individual believer on behalf of the Guardian it is stated: "If we are better, if we show love, patience, and understanding of the weakness of others, if we seek to never criticize but rather encourage, others will do likewise, and we can really help the Cause through our example and spiritual strength.

OTHER SOURCES

12.33 Certainly the well-being of mankind depends on the development of the potential virtues and abilities of every individual, regardless of race, nationality, class, religion, or sex. For this reason prejudices, which cause division and oppression, are systematically abolished in Bahá'í community life. (Bahá'í International Community, 1993 Apr 05, *Equality of Men & Women A New Reality*)

12.34 TO FACILITATE LEARNING about development theory and practice within the Bahá'í community, the Office of Social and Economic Development (OSED) has been established at the Faith's world headquarters in Haifa, Israel. The agency helps to strengthen institutional capacity in every country to promote Bahá'í development efforts. It ensures that material resources become increasingly available to such efforts, coordinating the international flow of such resources and administering some of the funds intended for this purpose. OSED also offers general advice, technical and otherwise, in response to questions that arise.

The functions OSED performs provide it with the perspective needed to gather and systematize the learning about development taking place in Bahá'í communities around the world. When it identifies certain approaches and methodologies that are achieving particularly good results in some area of action, OSED arranges for pilot projects to be launched in different continents, the aim being to refine the content and methods and assemble them in a tested program. The program is then disseminated worldwide, so that national Bahá'í communities can adapt it to their specific needs. Four examples will help illustrate how the process unfolds. (Bahá'í International Community, *For the Betterment of the World*)

CHAPTER 13:

ENCOURAGING CONSULTATIVE LEADERSHIP

FROM THE WRITINGS OF BAHÁ'U'LLÁH

13.1 Please God, the peoples of the world may be led, as the result of the high endeavors exerted by their rulers and the wise and learned amongst men, to recognize their best interests. How long will humanity persist in its waywardness? How long will injustice continue? How long is chaos and confusion to reign amongst men? How long will discord agitate the face of society?... The winds of despair are, alas, blowing from every direction, and the strife that divideth and afflicteth the human race is daily increasing. The signs of impending convulsions and chaos can now be discerned, inasmuch as the prevailing order appeareth to be lamentably defective. I beseech God, exalted be His glory, that He may graciously awaken the peoples of the earth, may grant that the end of their conduct may be profitable unto them, and aid them to accomplish that which beseemeth their station.

13.2 O friends! Be not careless of the virtues with which ye have been endowed, neither be neglectful of your high destiny. Suffer not your labors to be wasted through the vain imaginations which certain hearts have devised. Ye are the stars of the heaven of understanding, the breeze that stirreth at the break of day, the soft-flowing waters upon which must depend the very life of all men, the letters inscribed upon His sacred scroll. With the utmost unity, and in a spirit of perfect fellowship, exert yourselves, that ye may be enabled to achieve that which beseemeth this Day of God. Verily I say, strife and dissension, and whatsoever the mind of man abhorreth are entirely unworthy of his station.

13.3 They who are the people of God have no ambition except to revive the world, to ennoble its life, and regenerate its peoples.

13.4 With the utmost friendliness and in a spirit of perfect fellowship take ye counsel together, and dedicate the precious days of your lives to the betterment of the world and the promotion of the Cause of Him Who is the Ancient and Sovereign Lord of all. He, verily, enjoineth upon all men what is right, and forbiddeth whatsoever degradeth their station.

13.5 The Great Being saith: The heaven of divine wisdom is illumined with the two luminaries of consultation and compassion. Take ye counsel together in all matters, inasmuch as consultation is the lamp of guidance which leadeth the way, and is the bestower of understanding.

13.6 Let My counsel be acceptable to thee, and strive thou to rule with equity among men, that God may exalt thy name and spread abroad the fame of thy justice in all the world. Beware lest thou aggrandize thy ministers at the expense of thy subjects. Fear the sighs of the poor and of the upright in heart who, at every break of day, bewail their plight, and be unto them a benignant sovereign. They, verily, are thy treasures on earth. It behoveth thee, therefore, to safeguard thy treasures from the assaults of them who wish to rob thee. Inquire into their affairs, and ascertain, every year, nay every month, their condition, and be not of them that are careless of their duty.

13.7 The system of government which the British people have adopted in London appeareth to be good, for it is adorned with the light of both kingship and of the consultation of the people.

13.8 Set before thine eyes God's unerring Balance and, as one standing in His Presence, weigh in that Balance thine actions every day, every moment of thy life. Bring thyself to account ere thou art summoned to a reckoning, on the Day when no man shall have strength to stand for fear of God, the Day when the hearts of the heedless ones shall be made to tremble.

It behoveth every king to be as bountiful as the sun, which fostereth the growth of all beings, and giveth to each its due, whose benefits are not inherent in itself, but are ordained by Him Who is the Most Powerful, the Almighty. The king should be as generous, as liberal in his mercy as the clouds, the outpourings of whose bounty are showered upon every land, by the behest of Him Who is the Supreme Ordainer, the All-Knowing.

Have a care not to entrust thine affairs of state entirely into another's hands. None can discharge thy functions better than thine own self. Thus do We make clear unto thee Our words of wisdom, and send down upon thee that which can enable thee to pass over from the left hand of oppression to the right hand of justice, and approach the resplendent ocean of His favours. Such is the path which the kings that were before thee have trodden, they that acted equitably towards their subjects, and walked in the ways of undeviating justice.

Thou art God's shadow on earth. Strive, therefore, to act in such a manner as befitteth so eminent, so august a station. If thou dost depart from following the things We have caused to descend upon thee and taught thee, thou wilt, assuredly, be derogating from that great and priceless honour. Return, then, and cleave wholly unto God, and cleanse thine heart from the world and all its vanities, and suffer not the love of any stranger to enter and dwell therein. Not until thou dost purify thine heart from every trace of such love can the brightness of the light of God shed its radiance upon it, for to none hath God given more than one heart. This, verily, hath been decreed and written down in His ancient Book. And as the human heart, as fashioned by God, is one and undivided, it behoveth thee to take heed that its affections be, also, one and undivided. Cleave thou, therefore, with the whole affection of thine heart, unto His love, and withdraw it from the love of any one besides Him, that He may aid thee to immerse thyself in the ocean of His unity, and enable thee to become a true upholder of His oneness. God is My witness. My sole purpose in revealing to thee these words is to sanctify thee from the transitory things of the earth, and aid thee to enter the realm of everlasting glory, that thou mayest, by the leave of God, be of them that abide and rule therein....

13.9   Although a republican form of government profiteth all the peoples of the world, yet the majesty of kingship is one of the signs of God. We do not wish that the countries of the world should remain deprived thereof. If the sagacious combine the two forms into one, great will be their reward in the presence of God.

13.10 Behold the disturbances which, for many a long year, have afflicted the earth, and the perturbation that hath seized its peoples. It hath either been ravaged by war, or tormented by sudden and unforeseen calamities. Though the world is encompassed with misery and distress, yet no man hath paused to reflect what the cause or source of that may be. Whenever the True Counsellor uttered a word in admonishment, lo, they all denounced Him as a mover of mischief and rejected His claim. How bewildering, how confusing is such behavior! No two men can be found who may be said to be outwardly and inwardly united. The evidences of discord and malice are apparent everywhere, though all were made for harmony and union. The Great Being saith: O well-beloved ones! The tabernacle of unity hath been raised; regard ye not one another as strangers. Ye are the fruits of one tree, and the leaves of one branch. We cherish the hope that the light of justice may shine upon the world and sanctify it from tyranny. If the rulers and kings of the earth, the symbols of the power of God, exalted be His glory, arise and resolve to dedicate themselves to whatever will promote the highest interests of the whole of humanity, the reign of justice will assuredly be established amongst the children of men, and the effulgence of its light will envelop the whole earth. The Great Being saith: The structure of world stability and order hath been reared upon, and will continue to be sustained by, the twin pillars of reward and punishment.... In another passage He hath written: Take heed, O concourse of the rulers of the world! There is no force on earth that can equal in its conquering power the force of justice and wisdom.... Blessed is the king who marcheth with the ensign of wisdom unfurled before him, and the battalions of justice massed in his rear. He verily is the ornament that adorneth the brow of peace and the countenance of security. There can be no doubt whatever that if the day star of justice, which the clouds of tyranny have obscured, were to shed its light upon men, the face of the earth would be completely transformed.

13.11   HEARKEN ye, O Rulers of America and the Presidents of the Republics therein, unto that which the Dove is warbling on the Branch of Eternity: There is none other God but Me, the Ever-Abiding, the Forgiving, the All-Bountiful. Adorn ye the temple of dominion with the ornament of justice and of the fear of God, and its head with the crown of the remembrance of your Lord, the Creator of the heavens. Thus counselleth you He Who is the Dayspring of Names, as bidden by Him Who is the All-Knowing, the All-Wise. The Promised One hath appeared in this glorified Station, whereat all beings, both seen and unseen, have rejoiced. Take ye advantage of the Day of God. Verily, to meet Him is better for you than all that whereon the sun shineth, could ye but know it. O concourse of rulers! Give ear unto that which hath been raised from the Dayspring of Grandeur: Verily, there is none other God but Me, the Lord of Utterance, the All-Knowing. Bind ye the broken with the hands of justice, and crush the oppressor who flourisheth with the rod of the commandments of your Lord, the Ordainer, the All-Wise

13.12   Consider the former generations. Witness how every time the Day Star of Divine bounty hath shed the light of His Revelation upon the world, the people of His Day have arisen against Him, and repudiated His truth. They who were regarded as the leaders of men have invariably striven to hinder their followers from turning unto Him Who is the Ocean of God's limitless bounty.

Behold how the people, as a result of the verdict pronounced by the divines of His age, have cast Abraham, the Friend of God, into fire; how Moses, He Who held converse with the Almighty, was denounced as liar and slanderer. Reflect how Jesus, the Spirit of God, was, notwithstanding His extreme meekness and perfect tender-heartedness, treated by His enemies. So fierce was the opposition which He, the Essence of Being and Lord of the visible and invisible, had to face, that He had nowhere to lay His head. He wandered continually from place to place, deprived of a permanent abode. Ponder that which befell Muhammad, the Seal of the Prophets, may the life of all else be a sacrifice unto Him. How severe the afflictions which the leaders of the Jewish people and of the idol-worshipers caused to rain upon Him, Who is the sovereign Lord of all, in consequence of His proclamation of the unity of God and of the truth of His Message! By the righteousness of My Cause! My Pen groaneth, and all created things weep with a great weeping, as a result of the woes He suffered at the hands of them that have broken the Covenant of God, violated His Testament, rejected His proofs, and disputed His signs. Thus recount We unto thee the tale of that which happened in days past, haply thou mayest comprehend.

13.13 Is it fair to reject the testimony of these detached and exalted beings to the truth of this pre-eminent and Glorious Revelation, and to regard as acceptable the denunciations which have been uttered against this resplendent Light by this faithless people, who for gold have forsaken their faith, and who for the sake of leadership have repudiated Him Who is the First Leader of all mankind?

13.14 Suffer not yourselves to be wrapt in the dense veils of your selfish desires, inasmuch as I have perfected in every one of you My creation, so that the excellence of My handiwork may be fully revealed unto men.

13.15 Be united in counsel, be one in thought.

FROM THE WRITINGS AND UTTERANCES OF 'ABDU'L-BAHÁ

13.16 Consequently, that which is conducive to association and attraction and unity among the sons of men is the means of the life of the world of humanity, and whatever causeth division, repulsion and remoteness leadeth to the death of humankind.

13.17 Let them willingly subject themselves to every just king, and to every generous ruler be good citizens. Let them obey the government and not meddle in political affairs, but devote themselves to the betterment of character and behaviour, and fix their gaze upon the Light of the world.

13.18 Glory be to God! What an extraordinary situation now obtains, when no one, hearing a claim advanced, asks himself what the speaker's real motive might be, and what selfish purpose he might not have hidden behind the mask of words. You find, for example, that an individual seeking to further his own petty and personal concerns, will block the advancement of an entire people. To turn his own water mill, he will let the farms and fields of all the others parch and wither. To maintain his own leadership, he will everlastingly direct the masses toward that prejudice and fanaticism which subvert the very base of civilization.

13.19 This physical world of man is subject to the power of the lusts, and sin is the consequence of this power of the lusts, for it is not subject to the laws of justice and holiness. The body of man is a captive of nature; it will act in accordance with whatever nature orders. It is, therefore, certain that sins such as anger, jealousy, dispute, covetousness, avarice, ignorance, prejudice, hatred, pride and tyranny exist in the physical world. All these brutal qualities exist in the nature of man. A man who has not had a spiritual education is a brute.

13.20 Man must sever himself from the influences of the world of matter, from the world of nature and its laws; for the material world is the world of corruption and death. It is the world of evil and darkness, of animalism and ferocity, bloodthirstiness, ambition and avarice, of self-worship, egotism and passion; it is the world of nature. Man must strip himself of all these imperfections, must sacrifice these tendencies which are peculiar to the outer and material world of existence.

FROM THE WRITINGS AND LETTERS WRITTEN BY, OR ON BEHALF OF, SHOGHI EFFENDI

13.21 The success of your past endeavours should encourage you all and the Community whom you represent, to forge ahead, unmindful of obstacles, and forgetful of personal differences of opinion in one united and unanimous effort to carry out all the work you have set for yourselves and achieve all your goals.

13.22 In view of this he feels your Assembly should constantly exhort the friends to be more conscious of their duties, and to be very careful of having differences of opinion which are so strong as to lead to disputes and thus humiliate our beloved Faith in the eyes of non-Bahá'ís. The public is beginning to observe them, and they must therefore conduct themselves at all times as befits those who bear the glorious Name of Baha. They must be forgetful of self, but ever mindful of the Cause of God!

13.23 Consultation, frank and unfettered, is the bedrock of this unique order. Authority is concentrated in the hands of the elected members of the National Assembly. Power and initiative are primarily vested in the entire body of the believers acting through their local representatives.

13.24 The questions you ask in your letter about individual guidance have two aspects, one might say. It is good that people should turn to God and beseech His aid in solving their problems and guiding their acts, indeed every day of their lives, if they feel the desire to do so. But they cannot possibly impose what they feel to be their guidance on anyone else, let alone on Assemblies or Committees, as Bahá'u'lláh has expressly laid down the law of consultation and never indicated that anything else superseded it.

13.25 ... Their functions is not to dictate, but to consult, and consult not only among themselves, but as much as possible with the friends whom they represent. They must regard themselves in no other light but that of chosen instrument for a more efficient and dignified presentation of the Cause of God. They should never be led to suppose that they are the central ornaments of the body of the Cause, intrinsically superior to others in capacity or merit, and sole promoters of its teachings and principles. They should approach their task with extreme humility, and endeavor by their open-mindedness, their high sense of justice and duty, their candour, their modesty, their entire devotion to the welfare and interest of the friends, the Cause, and humanity, to win not only the confidence and the genuine support and respect of those who they should serve, but also their esteem and real affection. They must at all times avoid the spirit of exclusiveness, the atmosphere of secrecy, free themselves from a domineering attitude, and banish all forms of prejudice and passion from their deliberations.

13.26 Let us also bear in mind that the keynote of the Cause of God is not dictatorial authority, but humble fellowship, not arbitrary power, but the spirit of frank and loving consultation.

Nothing short of the spirit of a true Bahá'í can hope to reconcile the principles of mercy and justice, of freedom and submission, of the sanctity of the right of the individual and of self-surrender, of vigilance, discretion and prudence on the one hand and fellowship, candour and courage on the other.

13.27 The first quality for leadership, both among individuals and Assemblies, is the capacity to use the energy and competence that exists in the rank and file of its followers. Otherwise the more competent members of the group will go at a tangent and try to find elsewhere a field of work and where they could use their energy.

Shoghi Effendi hopes that the Assemblies will do their utmost in planning such teaching activities that every single soul will be kept busy.

FROM THE WRITINGS AND LETTERS WRITTEN BY, OR ON BEHALF OF, THE UNIVERSAL HOUSE OF JUSTICE

13.28 The courage, the resolution, the pure motive, the selfless love of one people for another—all the spiritual and moral qualities required for effecting this momentous step towards peace are focused on the will to act. And it is towards arousing the necessary volition that earnest consideration must be given to the reality of man, namely, his thought. To understand the relevance of this potent reality is also to appreciate the social necessity of actualizing its unique value through candid, dispassionate and cordial consultation, and of acting upon the results of this process. Bahá'u'lláh insistently drew attention to the virtues and indispensability of consultation for ordering human affairs. He said: "Consultation bestows greater awareness and transmutes conjecture into certitude. It is a shining light which, in a dark world, leads the way and guides. For everything there is and will continue to be a station of perfection and maturity. The maturity of the gift of understanding is made manifest through consultation." The very attempt to achieve peace through the consultative action he proposed can release such a salutary spirit among the peoples of the earth that no power could resist the final, triumphal outcome.

13.29 Courtesy, reverence, dignity, respect for the rank and achievements of others are virtues which contribute to the harmony and well-being of every community, but pride and self-aggrandisement are among the most deadly of sins.

The House of Justice hopes that all the friends will remember that the ultimate aim in life of every soul should be to attain spiritual excellence-to win the good pleasure of God. The true spiritual station of any soul is known only to God. It is quite a different thing from the ranks and stations that men and women occupy in the various sectors of society. Whoever has his eyes fixed on the goal of attaining the good pleasure of God will accept with joy and radiant acquiescence whatever work or station is assigned to him in the Cause of God, and will rejoice to serve Him under all conditions.

There are many passages on this theme in the Holy Writing, and the Universal House of Justice hopes that these remarks will help the friends to turn to them and understand their purport."

13.30 It is important to realize that the spirit of Bahá'í consultation is very different from that current in the decision-making processes of non-Bahá'í bodies.

The ideal of Bahá'í consultation is to arrive at a unanimous decision. When this is not possible a vote must be taken. In the words of the beloved Guardian: ' ... when they are called upon to arrive at a certain decision, they should, after dispassionate, anxious and cordial consultation, turn to God in prayer, and with earnestness and conviction and courage record their vote and abide by the voice of majority, which we are told by the Master to be the voice of truth, never to be challenged, and always to be whole-heartedly enforced.'

As soon as a decision is reached it becomes the decision of the whole Assembly, not merely of those members who happened to be among the majority.

When it its proposed to put a matter to the vote, a member of the Assembly may feel that there are additional facts or views which must be sought before he can make up his mind and intelligently vote on the proposition. He should express this feeling to the Assembly, and it is for the Assembly to decide whether or not further consultation is needed before voting.

Whenever it is decided to vote on a proposition all that is required is to ascertain how many of the members are in favour of it; if this is a majority of those present, the motion is carried; if it is a minority, the motion is defeated. Thus the whole question of 'abstaining' does not arise in Bahá'í voting. A member who does not vote in favour of a proposition is, in effect, voting against it, even if at that moment he himself feels that he has been unable to make up his mind on a matter."

OTHER SOURCES

13.31 The institutions of society will succeed in eliciting and directing the potentialities latent in the consciousness of the world's peoples to the extent that the exercise of authority is governed by principles that are in harmony with the evolving interests of a rapidly maturing human race. Such principles include the obligation of those in authority to win the confidence, respect, and genuine support of those whose actions they seek to govern; to consult openly and to the fullest extent possible with all whose interests are affected by decisions being arrived at; to assess in an objective manner both the real needs and the aspirations of the communities they serve; to benefit from scientific and moral advancement in order to make appropriate use of the community's resources, including the energies of its members. No single principle of effective authority is so important as giving priority to building and maintaining unity among the members of a society and the members of its administrative institutions. Reference has already been made to the intimately associated issue of commitment to the search for justice in al0cting those who are to take collective decisions on its behalf, society does not need and is not well served by the political theater of nominations, candidature, electioneering, and solicitation. It lies within the capacity of all people, as they become progressively educated and convinced that their real development interests are being served by programs proposed to them, to adopt electoral procedures that will gradually refine the selection of their decision-making bodies.

As the integration of humanity gains momentum, those who are thus selected will increasingly have to see all their efforts in a global perspective. Not only at the national, but also at the local level, the elected governors of human affairs should, in Bahá'u'lláh's view, consider themselves responsible for the welfare of all of humankind. (Bahá'í International Community, 1995 Mar 03, *The Prosperity of Humankind*)

CHAPTER 14:

SERVING OUR SPIRITUAL ASSEMBLIES

FROM THE WRITINGS OF BAHÁ'U'LLÁH

14.1 The Lord hath ordained that in every city a House of Justice be established wherein shall gather counsellors to the number of Baha, and should it exceed this number it does not matter... It behoveth them to be the trusted ones of the Merciful among men and to regard themselves as the guardians appointed of God for all that dwell on earth. It is incumbent upon them to take counsel together and to have regard for the interests of the servants of God, for His sake, even as they regard their own interests, and to choose that which is meet and seemly. Thus hath the Lord your God, the Gracious, the Pardoner, commanded you. Beware lest ye put away that which is clearly revealed in His Tablet. Fear God, O ye that perceive.

14.2 Addressing the nations, the Ancient Beauty ordaineth that in every city in the world a house be established in the name of justice wherein shall gather pure and steadfast souls to the number of the most Great Name (9). At this meeting they should feel as if they were entering the presence of God, inasmuch as this binding command hath flowed from the Pen of Him Who is the Ancient of Days. The glances of God are directed towards this Assembly.

FROM THE WRITINGS AND UTTERANCES OF 'ABDU'L-BAHÁ

14.3 The Spiritual Assemblies are collectively the most effective of all instruments for establishing unity and harmony. This matter is of the utmost importance; this is the magnet that draweth down the confirmations of God. If once the beauty of the unity of the friends—this Divine Beloved—be decked in the adornments of the Abha Kingdom, it is certain that within a very short time those countries will become the Paradise of the All-Glorious, and that out of the west the splendours of unity will cast their bright rays over all the earth.

14.4 The first condition is absolute love and harmony amongst the members of the assembly. They must be wholly free from estrangement and must manifest in themselves the Unity of God, for they are the waves of one sea, the drops of one river, the stars of one heaven, the rays of one sun, the trees of one orchard, the flowers of one garden. Should harmony of thought and absolute unity be nonexistent, that gathering shall be dispersed and that assembly be brought to naught. The second condition is that the members of the assembly should unitedly elect a chairman and lay down guide-lines and by-laws for their meetings and discussions. The chairman should have charge of such rules and regulations and protect and enforce them; the other members should be submissive, and refrain from conversing on superfluous and extraneous matters. They must, when coming together, turn their faces to the Kingdom on high and ask aid from the Realm of Glory. They must then proceed with the utmost devotion, courtesy, dignity, care and moderation to express their views. They must in every matter search out the truth and not insist upon their own opinion, for stubbornness and persistence in one's views will lead ultimately to discord and wrangling and the truth will remain hidden. The honoured members must with all freedom express their own thoughts, and it is in no wise permissible for one to belittle the thought of another, nay, he must with moderation set forth the truth, and should differences of opinion arise a majority of voices must prevail, and all must obey and submit to the majority. It is again not permitted that any one of the honoured members object to or censure, whether in or out of the meeting, any decision arrived at previously, though that decision be not right, for such criticism would prevent any decision from being enforced. In short, whatsoever thing is arranged in harmony and with love and purity of motive, its result is light, and should the least trace of estrangement prevail the result shall be darkness upon darkness.... If this be so regarded, that assembly shall be of God, but otherwise it shall lead to coolness and alienation that proceed from the Evil One.... Should they endeavour to fulfill these conditions the Grace of the Holy Spirit shall be vouchsafed unto them, and that assembly shall become the centre of the Divine blessings, the hosts of Divine confirmation shall come to their aid, and they shall day by day receive a new effusion of Spirit.

14.5   The prime requisites for them that take counsel together are purity of motive, radiance of spirit, detachment from all else save God, attraction to His Divine Fragrances, humility and lowliness amongst His loved ones, patience and long-suffering in difficulties and servitude to His exalted Threshold. Should they be graciously aided to acquire these attributes, victory from the unseen Kingdom of Baha shall be vouchsafed to them

14.6   The members thereof [1] must take counsel together in such wise that no occasion for ill-feeling or discord may arise. This can be attained when every member expresseth with absolute freedom his own opinion and setteth forth his argument. Should anyone oppose, he must on no account feel hurt for not until matters are fully discussed can the right way be revealed. The shining spark of truth cometh forth only after the clash of differing opinions. If after discussion, a decision be carried unanimously well and good; but if, the Lord forbid, differences of opinion should arise, a majority of voices must prevail.
[1 Of a Spiritual Assembly]

14.7   These Spiritual Assemblies are aided by the Spirit of God. Their defender is 'Abdu'l-Bahá. Over them He spreadeth His wings. What bounty is there greater than this? These Spiritual Assemblies are shining lamps and heavenly gardens, from which the fragrances of holiness are diffused over all regions, and the lights of knowledge are shed abroad over all created things. From them the spirit of life streameth in every direction. They, indeed, are the potent sources of the progress of man, at all times and under all conditions. What bounty is there greater than this?

FROM THE WRITINGS AND LETTERS WRITTEN BY, OR ON BEHALF OF, SHOGHI EFFENDI

14.8   Shoghi Effendi feels that in any locality where the number of adult believers reaches nine, a Local Assembly should be established. He feels this to be an obligation rather than a purely voluntary act. Only in exceptional cases has the National Spiritual Assembly the right to postpone the formation of an Assembly if it feels that the situation does not warrant such a formation. This right, however, should be exercised if the situation absolutely demands it. As to the principle according to which the area of jurisdiction of a Local Assembly is to be determined, he feels, this to be the function of the National Spiritual Assembly; whatever principle they uphold should be fairly applied to all localities without any distinction whatever.

14.9   It is surely very important to give the local Spiritual Assemblies some legal standing, for as the Cause progresses and its adherents increase, they will be confronted with duties they cannot even imagine at present. Not only will they have to make contracts for acquiring halls for their meeting place, but also they will be obliged to create new institutions to care for their sick, poor, and aged people. We hope that before long the Bahá'ís will even [be able to] afford to have schools that would provide the children in the intellectual and spiritual education as prescribed in the writings of Bahá'u'lláh and the Master.

For such duties that will naturally devolve upon the local Spiritual Assemblies there will be an increasing need for a legal standing. They will have to be considered as a legal person with the power of making binding contracts.

In small centres where the Friends are still few, the taking of such steps is rather premature and may add to the complexity of Bahá'í administration.

14.10   In order to avoid division and disruption, that the Cause may not fall a prey to conflicting interpretations, and lose thereby its purity and pristine vigour, that its affairs may be conducted with efficiency and promptness, it is necessary that every one should conscientiously take an active part in the election of these Assemblies, abide by their decision, enforce their decree, and co-operate with them wholeheartedly in their task of stimulating the growth of the Movement throughout all regions. The members of these Assemblies, on their part, must disregard utterly their own likes and dislikes, their personal interests and inclinations, and concentrate their minds upon those measures that will conduce to the welfare and happiness of the Bahá'í Community and promote the common weal.

14.11　With reference to your next question concerning the qualifications of the members of the Spiritual Assembly: there is a distinction of fundamental importance which should be always remembered in this connection, and this is between the Spiritual Assembly as an institution, and the persons who compose it. These are by no means supposed to be perfect, nor can they be considered as being inherently superior to the rest of their fellow-believers. It is precisely because they are subject to the same human limitations that characterize the other members of the community that they have to be elected every year. The existence of elections is a sufficient indication that Assembly members, though forming part of an institution that is divine and perfect, are nevertheless themselves imperfect. But this does not necessarily imply that their judgement is defective. For as 'Abdu'l-Bahá has repeatedly emphasized Bahá'í Assemblies are under the guidance and protection of God. The elections, especially when annual, give the community a good opportunity to remedy any defect or imperfection from which the Assembly may suffer as a result of the actions of its members. Thus a safe method has been established whereby the quality of membership in Bahá'í Assemblies can be continually raised and improved. But, as already stated, the institution of the Spiritual Assembly should under no circumstances be identified with, or be estimated merely through, the personal qualifications of the members that compose it.

14.12　...I feel that reference to personalities before the election would give rise to misunderstanding and differences. What the friends should do is to get thoroughly acquainted with one another, to exchange views, to mix freely and discuss among themselves the requirements and qualifications for such a membership without reference or application, however indirect, to particular individuals. We should refrain from influencing the opinion of others, of canvassing for any particular individual, but should stress the necessity of getting fully acquainted with the qualifications of membership referred to in our Beloved's Tablets and of learning more about one another through direct, personal experience rather than through the reports and opinions of our friends.

14.13 Bahá'ís are not required to vote on an Assembly against their consciences. It is better if they submit to the majority view and make it unanimous. But they are not forced to. What they must do, however, is to abide by the majority decision, as this is what becomes effective. They must not go around undermining the Assembly by saying they disagreed with the majority. In other words, they must put the Cause first and not their own opinions. He (a Spiritual Assembly member) can ask the Assembly to reconsider a matter, but he has no right to force them or create inharmony because they won't change. Unanimous votes are preferable, but certainly cannot be forced upon Assembly members by artificial methods such as are used by other societies.

14.14 But before the majority of the Assembly comes to a decision, it is not only the right but the sacred obligation of every member to express freely and openly his views, without being afraid of displeasing or alienating any of his fellow-members. In view of this important administrative principle of frank and open consultation, the Guardian would advise you to give up the method of asking other members to voice your opinion and suggestions. This indirect way of expressing your views to the Assembly not only creates an atmosphere of secrecy which is most alien to the spirit of the Cause, but would also lead to many misunderstandings and complications. The Assembly members must have the courage of their convictions, but must also express whole-hearted and unqualified obedience to the well-considered judgement and directions of the majority of their fellow-members.

14.15 The Bahá'ís must learn to forget personalities and to overcome the desire—so natural in people—to take sides and fight about it. They must also learn to really make use of the great principle of consultation. There is a time set aside at the Nineteen Day Feasts for the Community to express its views and make suggestions to its Assembly; the Assembly and the believers should look forward to this happy period of discussion, and neither fear it nor suppress it. Likewise the Assembly members should fully consult, and in their decisions put the interests of the Cause first and not personalities, the will of the majority prevailing.

One of the healing remedies Bahá'u'lláh has given to a sick world is the Assembly (which in future will become a House of Justice); its members have very sacred and heavy responsibilities, its power to steer the Community, to protect and assist its members is likewise very great.

14.16 The duties of those whom the friends have freely and conscientiously elected as their representatives are no less vital and binding than the obligations of those who have chosen them. Their function is not to dictate, but to consult, and consult not only among themselves, but as much as possible with the friends whom they represent. They must regard themselves in no other light but that of chosen instruments for a more efficient and dignified presentation of the Cause of God. They should never be led to suppose that they are the central ornaments of the body of the Cause, intrinsically superior to others in capacity or merit, and sole promoters of its teachings and principles. They should approach their task with extreme humility, and endeavour by their open-mindedness, their high sense of justice and duty, their candour, their modesty, their entire devotion to the welfare and interests of the friends, the Cause, and humanity, to win not only the confidence and the genuine support and respect of those whom they should serve, but also their esteem and real affection. They must at all times avoid the spirit of exclusiveness, the atmosphere of secrecy, free themselves from a domineering attitude, and banish all forms of prejudice and passion from their deliberations. They should, within the limits of wise discretion, take the friends into their confidence, acquaint them with their plans, share with them their problems and anxieties, and seek their advice and counsel....

14.17 Regarding consultation: Any person can refer a matter to the Assembly for consultation whether the other party wishes to or not. In matters which affect the Cause the Assembly should, if it deems it necessary, intervene even if both sides don't want it to, because the whole purpose of the Assemblies is to protect the Faith, the Communities and the individual Bahá'ís as well.

14.18 What the Master desired to protect the friends against was continual bickering and opinionatedness. A believer can ask the Assembly why they made a certain decision and politely request them to reconsider. But then he must leave it at that, and not go on disrupting local affairs through insisting on his own views. This applies to an Assembly member as well. We all have a right to our opinions, we are bound to think differently; but a Bahá'í must accept the majority decision of his Assembly, realizing that acceptance and harmony—even if a mistake has been made—are the really important things, and when we serve the Cause properly, in the Bahá'í way, God will right any wrongs done in the end.

14.19 The administrators of the Faith of God must be like unto shepherds. Their aim should be to dispel all the doubts, misunderstandings and harmful differences which may arise in the community of the believers. And this they can adequately achieve provided they are motivated by a true sense of love for their fellow-brethren coupled with a firm determination to act with justice in all the cases which are submitted to them for their consideration.

FROM THE WRITINGS AND LETTERS WRITTEN BY, OR ON BEHALF OF, THE UNIVERSAL HOUSE OF JUSTICE

14.20 The institution of the House of Justice consists of elected councils which operate at the local, national and international levels of society. Bahá'u'lláh ordains both the Universal House of Justice and the Local Houses of Justice in the Kitáb-i-Aqdas. 'Abdu'l-Bahá, in His Will and Testament, provides for the Secondary (National or Regional) Houses of Justice and outlines the method to be pursued for the election of the Universal House of Justice.

In the verse cited above, the reference is to the Local House of Justice, an institution which is to be elected in a locality whenever there are nine or more resident adult Bahá'ís. For this purpose, the definition of adult was temporarily fixed at the age of 21 years by the Guardian, who indicated it was open to change by the Universal House of Justice in the future.

Local and Secondary Houses of Justice are, for the present, known as Local Spiritual Assemblies and National Spiritual Assemblies. Shoghi Effendi has indicated that this is a "temporary appellation" which, ...as the position and aims of the Bahá'í Faith are better understood and more fully recognized, will gradually be superseded by the permanent and more appropriate designation of House of Justice. Not only will the present-day Spiritual Assemblies be styled differently in future, but they will be enabled also to add to their present functions those powers, duties, and prerogatives necessitated by the recognition of the Faith of Bahá'u'lláh, not merely as one of the recognized religious systems of the world, but as the State Religion of an independent and Sovereign Power.

14.21 The divinely ordained institution of the Local Spiritual Assembly operates at the first levels of human society and is the basic administrative unit of Bahá'u'lláh's World Order. It is concerned with individuals and families whom it must constantly encourage to unite in a distinctive Bahá'í society, vitalized and guarded by the laws, ordinances and principles of Bahá'u'lláh's Revelation. It protects the Cause of God; it acts as the loving shepherd of the Bahá'í flock.

> Strengthening and development of Local Spiritual Assemblies is a vital objective... Success in this one goal will greatly enrich the quality of Bahá'í life, will heighten the capacity of the Faith to deal with entry by troops which is even now taking place and, above all, will demonstrate the solidarity and ever-growing distinctiveness of the Bahá'í community, thereby attracting more and more thoughtful souls to the Faith and offering a refuge to the leaderless and hapless millions of the spiritually bankrupt, moribund present order.
>
> The friends are called upon to give their whole-hearted support and cooperation to the Local Spiritual Assembly, first by voting for the membership and then by energetically pursuing its plans and programmes, by turning to it in time of trouble or difficulty, by praying for its success and taking delight in its rise to influence and honour. This great prize, this gift of God within each community must be cherished, nurtured, loved, assisted, obeyed and prayed for.
>
> Such a firmly founded, busy and happy community life as is envisioned when Local Spiritual Assemblies are truly effective, will provide a firm home foundation from which the friends may derive courage and strength and loving support in bearing the Divine Message to their fellow-men and conforming their lives to its benevolent rule.

14.22 The institution of the Local Spiritual Assembly is of primary importance in the firm establishment of the Faith, and we hope that you will give particular attention to ensuring that as many as possible, and in increasing numbers, are, in the words of the beloved Guardian,'broadly based, securely grounded' and 'efficiently functioning'.

14.23 What we find expounded in the writings of our Faith is the lofty station Local Spiritual Assemblies must attain in their gradual and at times painful development.... "Among the more salient objectives to be attained by the Local Spiritual Assembly in its process of development to full maturity are to act as a loving shepherd to the Bahá'í flock, promote unity and concord among the friends, direct the teaching work, protect the Cause of God, arrange for Feasts, Anniversaries and regular meetings of the community, familiarize the Bahá'ís with its plans, invite the community to offer its recommendations, promote the welfare of youth and children, and participate, as circumstances permit, in humanitarian activities. In its relationship to the individual believer, the Assembly should continuously invite and encourage him to study the Faith, to deliver its glorious message, to live in accordance with its teachings, to contribute freely and regularly to the Fund, to participate in community activities, and to seek refuge in the Assembly for advice and help, when needed. "In its own meetings it must endeavour to develop skill in the difficult but highly rewarding art of Bahá'í consultation, a process which will require great self-discipline on the part of all members and complete reliance on the power of Bahá'u'lláh. It should hold regular meetings and ensure that all its members are currently informed of the activities of the Assembly, that its Secretary carries out his duties, and its Treasurer holds and disburses the funds of the Faith to its satisfaction, keeping proper accounts and issuing receipts for all contributions. Many Assemblies find that some of their activities such as teaching, observance of Feasts and Anniversaries, solution of personal problems, and other duties are best dealt with by committees appointed by the Assembly and responsible to it.

14.24 And since the primary purpose for which Local Spiritual Assemblies are established is to promote the teaching work, it is clear that every National Spiritual Assembly must give careful consideration to ways and means to encourage each Local Assembly under its jurisdiction to fulfil its principal obligation... it is important that Local Assemblies share with the local friends stories of successes achieved by some of them, descriptions of effective presentations found useful by them, examples of various ways that a Bahá'í subject could be introduced to inquirers, or illustrations of methods which would enable the believer to relate the needs of society to our teachings. Such information and suggestions should be offered to the friends at Nineteen Day Feasts, through a local newsletter, or by any means open to each Local Assembly. In all these contacts with the believers, each Local Spiritual Assembly should impress upon the friends the unique and irreplaceable role the individual plays in the prosecution of any Bahá'í undertaking...

14.25 Great attention should be paid to the strengthening of local Spiritual Assemblies which must act as the nerve centres of the Bahá'í communities in the towns and villages, promote Bahá'í education of the youth and children, and increase cooperation and participation of the believers in Bahá'í community life. Travelling teachers and all who are actively engaged in spreading the Message should rededicate themselves to their vital work and set out with renewed enthusiasm. They should aim at assisting as large a number as possible of Bahá'í communities to stand on their own feet and become capable of carrying out the thrilling tasks which they are called upon to discharge in the Vineyard of God in this Day.

14.26 Unity within the Assembly itself is, of course, of immediate importance to the wider unity your actions are intended to foster and sustain. At no time can any member of your Assembly afford to be unmindful of this basic requirement nor neglect to work towards upholding it. Of particular relevance is the attitude that the members adopt towards their membership on that exalted body. There needs to be a recognition on their part of the Assembly's spiritual character and a feeling in their hearts of respect for the institution based upon a perception of it as something beyond or apart from themselves, as a sacred entity whose powers they have the privilege to engage and canalize by coming together in harmony and acting in accordance with divinely revealed principles. With such a perspective the members will be able better to acquire an appropriate posture in relation to the Assembly itself, to appreciate their role as Trustees of the Merciful and to counteract any impression that they have assumed ownership and control of the institution in the manner of major stockholders of a business enterprise.

Also relevant to effecting unity is the attitude of the friends, whether serving on any Assembly or not, towards the exercise of authority in the Bahá'í community. People generally tend to be suspicious of those in authority. The reason is not difficult to understand, since human history is replete with examples of the disastrous misuse of authority and power. A reversal of this tendency is not easily achievable, but the Bahá'í friends must be freed of suspicion toward their institutions if the wheels of progress are to turn with uninterrupted speed. A rigorous discipline of thought and action on the part of both the friends and the National Assembly will succeed in meeting this challenge; both must live up to their responsibilities in this regard by recognizing some fundamental realities.

14.27 When an application for divorce is made to a Spiritual Assembly its first thought and action should be to reconcile the couple and to ensure that they know the Bahá'í teachings on the matter. God willing, the Assembly will be successful and no year of waiting need be started. However, if the Assembly finds that it is unable to persuade the party concerned to withdraw the application for divorce, it must conclude that, from its point of view, there appears to be an irreconcilable antipathy, and it has no alternative to setting the date for the beginning of the year of waiting. During the year the couple have the responsibility of attempting to reconcile their difference, and the Assembly has the duty to help them and encourage them. But if the year of waiting comes to an end without reconciliation the Bahá'í divorce must be granted as at the date of the granting of the civil divorce if this has not already taken place.

14.28 It is clear that while Local Spiritual Assemblies must supervise all Bahá'í matters in their areas, including arrangements for the Nineteen Day Feast, the observance of the Holy Days, the election of the members of the Assembly, promoting the teaching work, caring for the spiritual welfare and Bahá'í education of the friends and children, etc., they and the friends themselves must at the same time be good citizens and loyal to the civil government, whether it be a Tribal council, a Cacique or a municipal authority.

14.29 ...Any information which comes to the notice of an Assembly member, solely by reason of his membership on that Assembly must not be divulged by that member, even though the Assembly itself may later decide to share it.
...The Assembly must itself carefully consider which information should rightly fall in the category of confidential

information and which should not be shared with others, and which information may be divulged under special circumstances, and how such information may be divulged. Should confidential matters regarding personal problems be freely shared with others, upon application, the confidence of the believers in the Assembly and its members will obviously be destroyed.

...It must be remembered that individuals can reform, and a reprehensible past does not necessarily disqualify a believer from a better future.

14.30 Every institution in the Faith has certain matters which it considers should be kept confidential, and any member who is privy to such confidential information is obliged to preserve the confidentiality within the institution where he learned it. Such matters, however, are but a small portion of the business of any Bahá'í institution. Most subjects dealt with are of common interest and can be discussed openly with anyone. Where no confidentiality is involved the institutions must strive to avoid the stifling atmosphere of secrecy; on the other hand, every believer must know that he can confide a personal problem to an institution of the Faith, with the assurance that knowledge of the matter will remain confidential.

14.31 As we have said in an earlier message, the flourishing of the community, especially at the local level, demands a significant enhancement in patterns of behavior: those patterns by which the collective expression of the virtues of the individual members and the functioning of the Spiritual Assembly is manifest in the unity and fellowship of the community and the dynamism of its activity and growth. This calls for the integration of the component elements—adults, youth and children—in spiritual, social, educational and administrative activities; and their engagement in local plans of teaching and development. It implies a collective will and sense of purpose to perpetuate the Spiritual Assembly through annual elections. It involves the practice of collective worship of God. Hence, it is essential to the spiritual life of the community that the friends hold regular devotional meetings in local Bahá'í centers, where available, or elsewhere, including the homes of believers.

14.32 In your letter of 4 April you enquire further about the principles governing the presence of a member of the National Assembly when a matter concerning him or her personally is being discussed.

The first principle to bear in mind is that every member of an Assembly has an absolute and incontrovertible right to be present at every meeting of that body and to be fully informed of every matter coming before it.

The second principle is that of detachment in consultation. The members of an Assembly must learn to express their views frankly, calmly, without passion or rancour. They must also learn to listen to the opinions of their fellow members without taking offence or belittling the views of another. Bahá'í consultation is not an easy process. It requires love, kindliness, moral courage and humility. Thus no member should ever allow himself to be prevented from expressing frankly his view because it may offend a fellow member; and, realizing this, no member should take offence at another member's statements.

The Third principle is that if a believer feels that he has been done an injustice by the Assembly, he should appeal the decision in the normal way.

OTHER SOURCES

14.33 A unique administrative system, rooted in the concept of unity in diversity, both insists on education for all members of the community and allows for the immediate assimilation of all those who in the past have been deprived of their rights. The Bahá'í electoral system, operating by secret ballot, with no nominations or electioneering, encourages universal participation: every adult Bahá'í is eligible for election to local and national administrative bodies responsible for decision in the conduct of Bahá'í affairs. The ease with which women, long deprived of equal opportunities, can now be integrated into the life of society, is vividly evidenced by the participation of women in all areas of Bahá'í community life. (Bahá'í International Community, 1993 Apr 05, *Equality of Men & Women A New Reality*)

Making a Better World with the Bahá'í Faith: QUOTATIONS

CHAPTER 15:

CHERISHING THE UNIVERSAL HOUSE OF JUSTICE

FROM THE WRITINGS OF BAHÁ'U'LLÁH

15.1 The essence of all that We have revealed for thee is Justice, is for man to free himself from idle fancy and imitation, discern with the eye of oneness His glorious handiwork, and look into all things with a searching eye.

15.2 It is incumbent upon the Trustees of the House of Justice to take counsel together regarding those things which have not outwardly been revealed in the Book, and to enforce that which is agreeable to them. God will verily inspire them with whatsoever He willeth, and He, verily, is the Provider, the Omniscient.

15.3 O people of God! That which traineth the world is Justice, for it is upheld by two pillars, reward and punishment. These two pillars are the sources of life to the world. Inasmuch as for each day there is a new problem and for every problem an expedient solution, such affairs should be referred to the Ministers of the House of Justice that they may act according to the needs and requirements of the time. They that, for the sake of God, arise to serve His Cause, are the recipients of divine inspiration from the unseen Kingdom. It is incumbent upon all to be obedient unto them. All matters of State should be referred to the House of Justice, but acts of worship must be observed according to that which God hath revealed in His Book.

15.4 O SON OF SPIRIT! The best beloved of all things in My sight is Justice; turn not away therefrom if thou desirest Me, and neglect it not that I may confide in thee. By its aid thou shalt see with thine own eyes and not through the eyes of others, and shalt know of thine own knowledge and not through the knowledge of thy neighbor. Ponder this in thy heart; how it behooveth thee to be. Verily justice is My gift to thee and the sign of My lovingkindness. Set it then before thine eyes.

15.5 Know verily that the essence of justice and the source thereof are both embodied in the ordinances prescribed by Him Who is the Manifestation of the Self of God amongst men, if ye be of them that recognize this truth.

15.6 According to the fundamental laws which We have formerly revealed in the Kitáb-i-Aqdas and other Tablets, all affairs are committed to the care of just kings and presidents and of the Trustees of the House of Justice. Having pondered on that which We have enunciated, every man of equity and discernment will readily perceive, with his inner and outer eyes, the splendours of the day-star of justice which radiate therefrom.

15.7 We exhort the men of the House of Justice and command them to ensure the protection and safeguarding of men, women and children. It is incumbent upon them to have the utmost regard for the interests of the people at all times and under all conditions. Blessed is the ruler who succoureth the captive, and the rich one who careth for the poor, and the just one who secureth from the wrong doer the rights of the downtrodden, and happy the trustee who observeth that which the Ordainer, the Ancient of Days hath prescribed unto him.

15.8 It is incumbent upon the men of God's House of Justice to fix their gaze by day and by night upon that which hath shone forth from the Pen of Glory for the training of peoples, the upbuilding of nations, the protection of man and the safeguarding of his honour.

15.9 This passage, now written by the Pen of Glory, is accounted as part of the Most Holy Book: The men of God's House of Justice have been charged with the affairs of the people. They, in truth, are the Trustees of God among His servants and the daysprings of authority in His countries.

FROM THE WRITINGS AND UTTERANCES OF 'ABDU'L-BAHÁ

15.10 Praise be to God, all such doors are closed in the Cause of Bahá'u'lláh for a special authoritative Centre hath been appointed—a Centre that solveth all difficulties and wardeth off all differences.

15.11   The House of Justice, however, according to the explicit text of the Law of God, is confined to men; this for a wisdom of the Lord God's, which will erelong be made manifest as clearly as the sun at high noon.

15.12   To epitomize: essential infallibility belongs especially to the supreme Manifestations, and acquired infallibility is granted to every holy soul. For instance, the Universal House of Justice, if it be established under the necessary conditions—with members elected from all the people—that House of Justice will be under the protection and the unerring guidance of God. If that House of Justice shall decide unanimously, or by a majority, upon any question not mentioned in the Book, that decision and command will be guarded from mistake. Now the members of the House of Justice have not, individually, essential infallibility; but the body of the House of Justice is under the protection and unerring guidance of God: this is called conferred infallibility.

15.13   Should the father fail in his duty he must be compelled to discharge his responsibility, and should he be unable to comply, let the House of Justice take over the education of the children; in no case is a child to be left without an education.

15.14   As to the difference between that material civilization now prevailing, and the divine civilization which will be one of the benefits to derive from the House of Justice, it is this: material civilization, through the power of punitive and retaliatory laws, restraineth the people from criminal acts; and notwithstanding this, while laws to retaliate against and punish a man are continually proliferating, as ye can see, no laws exist to reward him. In all the cities of Europe and America, vast buildings have been erected to serve as jails for the criminals.

Divine civilization, however, so traineth every member of society that no one, with the exception of a negligible few, will undertake to commit a crime. There is thus a great difference between the prevention of crime through measures that are violent and retaliatory, and so training the people, and enlightening them, and spiritualizing them, that without any fear of punishment or vengeance to come, they will shun all criminal acts. They will, indeed, look upon the very commission of a crime as a great disgrace and in itself the harshest of punishments. They will become enamoured of human perfections, and will consecrate their lives to whatever will bring light to the world and will further those qualities which are acceptable at the Holy Threshold of God.

15.15 He has ordained and established the House of Justice, which is endowed with a political as well as a religious function, the consummate union and blending of church and state. This institution is under the protecting power of Bahá'u'lláh Himself. A universal, or international, House of Justice shall also be organized. Its rulings shall be in accordance with the commands and teachings of Bahá'u'lláh, and that which the Universal House of Justice ordains shall be obeyed by all mankind. This international House of Justice shall be appointed and organized from the Houses of Justice of the whole world, and all the world shall come under its administration.

15.16 As regards the constitution of the House of Justice, Bahá'u'lláh addresses the men. He says: 'O ye men of the House of Justice!'
But when its members are to be elected, the right which belongs to women, so far as their voting and their voice is concerned, is indisputable. When the women attain to the ultimate degree of progress, then, according to the exigency of the time and place and their great capacity, they shall obtain extraordinary privileges. Be ye confident on these accounts. His Holiness Bahá'u'lláh has greatly strengthened the cause of women, and the rights and privileges of women is one of the greatest principles of 'Abdu'l-Bahá. Rest ye assured! Ere long the days shall come when the men addressing the women, shall say: 'Blessed are ye! Blessed are ye! Verily ye are worthy of every gift. Verily ye deserve to adorn your heads with the crown of everlasting glory, because in sciences and arts, in virtues and perfections ye shall become equal to man, and as regards tenderness of heart and the abundance of mercy and sympathy ye are superior'.

FROM THE WRITINGS AND LETTERS WRITTEN BY, OR ON BEHALF OF, SHOGHI EFFENDI

15.17 Having established the structure of their local Assemblies—the base of the edifice which the Architect of the Administrative Order of the Faith of Bahá'u'lláh had directed them to erect—His disciples, in both the East and the West, unhesitatingly embarked on the next and more difficult stage, of their high enterprise. In countries where the local Bahá'í communities had sufficiently advanced in number and in influence measures were taken for the initiation of National Assemblies, the pivots round which all national undertakings must revolve. Designated by 'Abdu'l-Bahá in His Will as the "Secondary Houses of Justice," they constitute the electoral bodies in the formation of the International House of Justice, and are empowered to direct, unify, coordinate and stimulate the activities of individuals as well as local Assemblies within their jurisdiction.

15.18 It must be pointed out, however, in this connection that, contrary to what has been confidently asserted, the establishment of the Supreme House of Justice is in no way dependent upon the adoption of the Bahá'í Faith by the mass of the peoples of the world, nor does it presuppose its acceptance by the majority of the inhabitants of any one country. In fact, 'Abdu'l-Bahá, Himself, in one of His earliest Tablets, contemplated the possibility of the formation of the Universal House of Justice in His own lifetime, and but for the unfavorable circumstances prevailing under the Turkish regime, would have, in all probability, taken the preliminary steps for its establishment. It will be evident, therefore, that given favorable circumstances, under which the Bahá'ís of Persia and of the adjoining countries under Soviet rule, may be enabled to elect their national representatives, in accordance with the guiding principles laid down in 'Abdu'l-Bahá's writings, the only remaining obstacle in the way of the definite formation of the International House of Justice will have been removed. For upon the National Houses of Justice of the East and the

West devolves the task, in conformity with the explicit provisions of the Will, of electing directly the members of the International House of Justice. Not until they are themselves fully representative of the rank and file of the believers in their respective countries, not until they have acquired the weight and the experience that will enable them to function vigorously in the organic life of the Cause, can they approach their sacred task, and provide the spiritual basis for the constitution of so august a body in the Bahá'í world. The Institution of Guardianship

15.19 It must be also clearly understood by every believer that the institution of Guardianship does not under any circumstances abrogate, or even in the slightest degree detract from, the powers granted to the Universal House of Justice by Bahá'u'lláh in the Kitáb-i-Aqdas, and repeatedly and solemnly confirmed by 'Abdu'l-Bahá in His Will. It does not constitute in any manner a contradiction to the Will and Writings of Bahá'u'lláh, nor does it nullify any of His revealed instructions. It enhances the prestige of that exalted assembly, stabilizes its supreme position, safeguards its unity, assures the continuity of its labors, without presuming in the slightest to infringe upon the inviolability of its clearly-defined sphere of jurisdiction. We stand indeed too close to so monumental a document to claim for ourselves a complete understanding of all its implications, or to presume to have grasped the manifold mysteries it undoubtedly contains. Only future generations can comprehend the value and the significance attached to this Divine Masterpiece, which the hand of the Master-builder of the world has designed for the unification and the triumph of the world-wide Faith of Bahá'u'lláh. Only those who come after us will be in a position to realize the value of the surprisingly strong emphasis that has been placed on the institution of the House of Justice and of the Guardianship. They only will appreciate the significance of the vigorous language employed by 'Abdu'l-Bahá with reference to the band of Covenant-breakers that has opposed Him in His days. To them alone will be revealed the suitability of the institutions initiated by 'Abdu'l-Bahá to the character of the future society which is to emerge out of the chaos and confusion of the present age.

15.20 And now, it behooves us to reflect on the animating purpose and the primary functions of these divinely-established institutions, the sacred character and the universal efficacy of which can be demonstrated only by the spirit they diffuse and the work they actually achieve. I need not dwell upon what I have already reiterated and emphasized that the administration of the Cause is to be conceived as an instrument and not a substitute for the Faith of Bahá'u'lláh, that it should be regarded as a channel through which His promised blessings may flow, that it should guard against such rigidity as would clog and fetter the liberating forces released by His Revelation. I need not enlarge at the present moment upon what I have stated in the past, that contributions to the local and national Funds are of a purely voluntary character; that no coercion or solicitation of funds is to be tolerated in the Cause; that general appeals addressed to the communities as a body should be the only form in which the financial requirements of the Faith are to be met; that the financial support accorded to a very few workers in the teaching and administrative fields is of a temporary nature; that the present restrictions imposed on the publication of Bahá'í literature will be definitely abolished; that the World Unity activity is being carried out as an experiment to test the efficacy of the indirect method of teaching; that the whole machinery of assemblies, of committees and conventions is to be regarded as a means, and not an end in itself; that they will rise or fall according to their capacity to further the interests, to coordinate the activities, to apply the principles, to embody the ideals and execute the purpose of the Bahá'í Faith. Who, I may ask, when viewing the international character of the Cause, its far-flung ramifications, the increasing complexity of its affairs, the diversity of its adherents, and the state of confusion that assails on every side the infant Faith of God, can for a moment question the necessity of some sort of administrative machinery that will insure, amid the storm and stress of a struggling civilization, the unity of the Faith, the preservation of its identity, and the protection of its interests? To repudiate the validity of the assemblies of the elected ministers of the Faith of Bahá'u'lláh would be to reject those countless Tablets of Bahá'u'lláh and

'Abdu'l-Bahá wherein They have extolled the station of the "trustees of the Merciful," enumerated their privileges and duties, emphasized the glory of their mission, revealed the immensity of their task, and warned them of the attacks they must needs expect from the unwisdom of their friends as well as from the malice of their enemies. It is surely for those to whose hands so priceless a heritage has been committed to prayerfully watch lest the tool should supersede the Faith itself, lest undue concern for the minute details arising from the administration of the Cause obscure the vision of its promoters, lest partiality, ambition, and worldliness tend in the course of time to becloud the radiance, stain the purity, and impair the effectiveness of the Faith of Bahá'u'lláh.

15.21 The Administrative Order of the Faith of Bahá'u'lláh must in no wise be regarded as purely democratic in character inasmuch as the basic assumption which requires all democracies to depend fundamentally upon getting their mandate from the people is altogether lacking in this Dispensation. In the conduct of the administrative affairs of the Faith, in the enactment of the legislation necessary to supplement the laws of the Kitáb-i-Aqdas, the members of the Universal House of Justice, it should be borne in mind, are not, as Bahá'u'lláh's utterances clearly imply, responsible to those whom they represent, nor are they allowed to be governed by the feelings, the general opinion, and even the convictions of the mass of the faithful, or of those who directly elect them. They are to follow, in a prayerful attitude, the dictates and promptings of their conscience. They may, indeed they must, acquaint themselves with the conditions prevailing among the community, must weigh dispassionately in their minds the merits of any case presented for their consideration, but must reserve for themselves the right of an unfettered decision. "God will verily inspire them with whatsoever He willeth," is Bahá'u'lláh's incontrovertible assurance. They, and not the body of those who either directly or indirectly elect them, have thus been made the recipients of the divine guidance which is at once the life-blood and ultimate safeguard of this Revelation. Moreover, he who symbolizes the hereditary principle in this Dispensation has been made the interpreter of the words of its Author, and ceases consequently, by virtue of the actual authority vested in him, to be the figurehead invariably associated with the prevailing systems of constitutional monarchies.

15.22 The vitality which the organic institutions of this great, this ever-expanding Order so strongly exhibit; the obstacles which the high courage, the undaunted resolution of its administrators have already surmounted; the fire of an unquenchable enthusiasm that glows with undiminished fervor in the hearts of its itinerant teachers; the heights of self-sacrifice which its champion-builders are now attaining; the breadth of vision, the confident hope, the creative joy, the inward peace, the uncompromising integrity, the exemplary discipline, the unyielding unity and solidarity which its stalwart defenders manifest; the degree to which its moving Spirit has shown itself capable of assimilating the diversified elements within its pale, of cleansing them of all forms of prejudice and of fusing them with its own structure—these are evidences of a power which a disillusioned and sadly shaken society can ill afford to ignore.

15.23 Let no one, while this System is still in its infancy, misconceive its character, belittle its significance or misrepresent its purpose. The bedrock on which this Administrative Order is founded is God's immutable Purpose for mankind in this day. The Source from which it derives its inspiration is no one less than Bahá'u'lláh Himself. Its shield and defender are the embattled hosts of the Abhá Kingdom. Its seed is the blood of no less than twenty thousand martyrs who have offered up their lives that it may be born and flourish. The axis round which its institutions revolve are the authentic provisions of the Will and Testament of 'Abdu'l-Bahá. Its guiding principles are the truths which He Who is the unerring Interpreter of the teachings of our Faith has so clearly enunciated in His public addresses throughout the West. The laws that govern its operation and limit its functions are those which have been expressly ordained in the Kitáb-i-Aqdas. The seat round which its spiritual, its humanitarian and administrative activities will cluster are the Mashriqu'l-Adhkár and its Dependencies. The pillars that sustain its authority and buttress its structure are the twin institutions of the Guardianship and of the Universal House of Justice. The central, the underlying aim which animates it is the establishment of the New World Order as adumbrated by Bahá'u'lláh. The methods it employs, the standard it inculcates, incline it to neither East nor West, neither Jew nor Gentile, neither rich nor poor, neither white nor colored. Its watchword is the unification of the human race; its standard the "Most Great Peace"; its consummation the advent of that golden millennium—the Day when the kingdoms of this world shall have become the Kingdom of God Himself, the Kingdom of Bahá'u'lláh.

FROM THE WRITINGS AND LETTERS WRITTEN BY, OR ON BEHALF OF, THE UNIVERSAL HOUSE OF JUSTICE

15.24 The members of the Universal House of Justice shall be elected by secret ballot by the members of all National Spiritual Assemblies at a meeting to be known as the International Bahá'í Convention.

(a) An election of the Universal House of Justice shall be held once every five years unless otherwise decided by the Universal House of Justice, and those elected shall continue in office until such time as their successors shall be elected and the first meeting of these successors is duly held.

(b) Upon receiving the call to Convention each National Spiritual Assembly shall submit to the Universal House of Justice a list of the names of its members. The recognition and seating of the delegates to the International Convention shall be vested in the Universal House of Justice.

(c) The principal business of the International Convention shall be to elect the members of the Universal House of

Justice, to deliberate on the affairs of the Bahá'í Cause throughout the world, and to make recommendations and suggestions for the consideration of the Universal House of Justice.

(d) The sessions of the International Convention shall be conducted in such manner as the Universal House of Justice shall from time to time decide.

(e) The Universal House of Justice shall provide a procedure whereby those delegates who are unable to be present in person at the International Convention shall cast their ballots for the election of the members of the Universal House of Justice.

(f) If at the time of an election the Universal House of Justice shall consider that it is impracticable or unwise to hold the International Convention it shall determine how the election shall take place.

(g) On the day of the election the ballots of all voters shall be scrutinized and counted and the result certified by tellers appointed in accordance with the instructions of the Universal House of Justice.

(h) If a member of a National Spiritual Assembly who has voted by mail ceases to be a member of that National Spiritual Assembly between the time of casting his ballot and the date of the counting of the ballots, his ballot shall nevertheless remain valid unless in the interval his successor shall have been elected and the ballot of such successor shall have been received by the tellers.

(i) In case by reason of a tie vote or votes the full membership of the Universal House of Justice is not determined on the first ballot, then one or more additional ballots shall be held on the persons tied until all members are elected. The electors in the case of additional ballots shall be the members of National Spiritual Assemblies in office at the time each subsequent vote is taken.

15.25   The Universal House of Justice has no officers. It shall provide for the conduct of its meetings and shall organize its activities in such manner as it shall from time to time decide.

15.26   The Universal House of Justice has the right to review any decision or action of any Spiritual Assembly, National or Local, and to approve, modify or reverse such decision or action. The Universal House of Justice also has the right to intervene in any matter in which a Spiritual Assembly is failing to take action or to reach a decision and, at its discretion, to require that action be taken, or itself to take action directly in the matter.

15.27   Any Bahá'í may appeal from a decision of his National Spiritual Assembly to the Universal House of Justice which shall determine whether it shall take jurisdiction of the matter or leave it within the final jurisdiction of the National Spiritual Assembly.

15.28   Bahá'u'lláh, the Revealer of God's Word in this Day, the Source of Authority, the Fountainhead of Justice, the Creator of a new World Order, the Establisher of the Most Great Peace, the Inspirer and Founder of a world civilization, the Judge, the Lawgiver, the Unifier and Redeemer of all mankind, has proclaimed the advent of God's Kingdom on earth, has formulated its laws and ordinances, enunciated its principles, and ordained its institutions. To direct and canalize the forces released by His Revelation He instituted His Covenant, whose power has preserved the integrity of His Faith, maintained its unity and stimulated its world-wide expansion throughout the successive ministries of 'Abdu'l-Bahá and Shoghi Effendi. It continues to fulfil its life-giving purpose through the agency of the Universal House of Justice whose fundamental object, as one of the twin successors of Bahá'u'lláh and 'Abdu'l-Bahá, is to ensure the continuity of that divinely-appointed authority which flows from the Source of the Faith, to safeguard the unity of its followers, and to maintain the integrity and flexibility of its teachings.

15.29 The provenance, the authority, the duties, the sphere of action of the Universal House of Justice all derive from the revealed Word of Bahá'u'lláh which, together with the interpretations and expositions of the Centre of the Covenant and of the Guardian of the Cause - who, after 'Abdu'l-Bahá, is the sole authority in the interpretation of Bahá'í Scripture - constitute the binding terms of reference of the Universal House of Justice and are its bedrock foundation. The authority of these Texts is absolute and immutable until such time as Almighty God shall reveal His new Manifestation to Whom will belong all authority and power.

There being no successor to Shoghi Effendi as Guardian of the Cause of God, the Universal House of Justice is the Head of the Faith and its supreme institution, to which all must turn, and on it rests the ultimate responsibility for ensuring the unity and progress of the Cause of God.

15.30 Among the powers and duties with which the Universal House of Justice has been invested are:

To ensure the preservation of the Sacred Texts and to safeguard their inviolability; to analyse, classify, and coordinate the Writings; and to defend and protect the Cause of God and emancipate it from the fetters of repression and persecution;

To advance the interests of the Faith of God; to proclaim, propagate and teach its Message; to expand and consolidate the institutions of its Administrative Order; to usher in the World Order of Bahá'u'lláh; to promote the attainment of those spiritual qualities which should characterize Bahá'í life individually and collectively; to do its utmost for the realization of greater cordiality and comity amongst the nations and for the attainment of universal peace; and to foster that which is conducive to the enlightenment and illumination of the souls of men and the advancement and betterment of the world;

To enact laws and ordinances not expressly recorded in the Sacred Texts; to abrogate, according to the changes and requirements of the time, its own enactments; to deliberate and decide upon all problems which have caused difference; to elucidate questions that are obscure; to safeguard the personal rights, freedom and initiative of individuals; and to give attention to the preservation of human honour, to the development of countries and the stability of states;

To promulgate and apply the laws and principles of the Faith; to safeguard and enforce that rectitude of conduct which the Law of God enjoins; to preserve and develop the Spiritual and Administrative Centre of the Bahá'í Faith, permanently fixed in the twin cities of 'Akká and Haifa; to administer the affairs of the Bahá'í community throughout the world; to guide, organize, coordinate and unify its activities; to found institutions; to be responsible for ensuring that no body or institution within the Cause abuse its privileges or decline in the exercise of its rights and prerogatives; and to provide for the receipt, disposition, administration and safeguarding of the funds, endowments and other properties that are entrusted to its care;

To adjudicate disputes falling within its purview; to give judgement in cases of violation of the laws of the Faith and to pronounce sanctions for such violations; to provide for the enforcement of its decisions; to provide for the arbitration and settlement of disputes arising between peoples; and to be the exponent and guardian of that Divine Justice which can alone ensure the security of, and establish the reign of law and order in, the world.

15.31 The Universal House of Justice is the supreme institution of an Administrative Order whose salient features, whose authority and whose principles of operation are clearly enunciated in the Sacred Writings of the Bahá'í Faith and their authorized interpretations. This Administrative Order consists, on the one hand, of a series of elected councils, universal, secondary and local, in which are vested legislative, executive and judicial powers over the Bahá'í community and, on the other, of eminent and devoted believers appointed for the specific purposes of protecting and propagating the Faith of Bahá'u'lláh under the guidance of the Head of that Faith.

This Administrative Order is the nucleus and pattern of the World Order adumbrated by Bahá'u'lláh. In the course of its divinely propelled organic growth its institutions will expand, putting forth auxiliary branches and developing subordinate agencies, multiplying their activities and diversifying their functions, in consonance with the principles and purposes revealed by Bahá'u'lláh for the progress of the human race.

15.32 This Constitution may be amended by decision of the Universal House of Justice when the full membership is present.

15.33 The Universal House of Justice, which the Guardian said would be regarded by posterity as 'the last refuge of a tottering civilization' is now, in the absence of the Guardian, the sole infallibly guided institution in the world to which all must turn, and on it rests the responsibility for ensuring the unity and progress of the Cause of God in accordance with the revealed Word. There are statements from the Master and the Guardian indicating that the Universal House of Justice, in addition to being the Highest Legislative Body of the Faith, is also the body to which all must turn, and is the 'apex' of the Bahá'í Administrative Order, as well as the 'supreme organ of the Bahá'í Commonwealth '. The Guardian has in his writings specified for the House of Justice such fundamental functions as the formulation of future worldwide teaching plans, the conduct of the administrative affairs of the Faith, and the guidance, organisation and unification of the affairs of the Cause throughout the world. Furthermore in 'God Passes By' the Guardian makes the following statement: 'The Kitáb-i-Aqdas ... not only preserves for posterity the basic laws and ordinances on which the fabric of His future World Order must rest, but ordain, in addition to the function of interpretation which it confers upon His Successor, the necessary institutions through which the integrity and unity of His Faith can alone safeguard.' He has also, in 'The Dispensation of Bahá'u'lláh ' written that the members of the Universal House of Justice 'and not the body of those who either directly or indirectly elect them, have thus been made the recipients of the divine guidance which is at once the lifeblood and ultimate safeguard of this Revelation'.

CHAPTER 16:

LEARNING THROUGH COLLECTIVE DISCOVERY

FROM THE WRITINGS OF BAHÁ'U'LLÁH

16.1 We cherish the hope that through the loving-kindness of the All-Wise, the All-Knowing, obscuring dust may be dispelled and the power of perception enhanced, that the people may discover the purpose for which they have been called into being. In this Day whatsoever serveth to reduce blindness and to increase vision is worthy of consideration. This vision acteth as the agent and guide for true knowledge. Indeed in the estimation of men of wisdom keenness of understanding is due to keenness of vision. The people of Baha must under all circumstances observe that which is meet and seemly and exhort the people accordingly.

16.2 Through the power of the words He hath uttered the whole of the human race can be illumined with the light of unity, and the remembrance of His Name is able to set on fire the hearts of all men, and burn away the veils that intervene between them and His glory.

16.3 He that riseth to serve My Cause should manifest My wisdom, and bend every effort to banish ignorance from the earth.

16.4 Happy are ye, O ye the learned ones in Baha. By the Lord! Ye are the billows of the Most Mighty Ocean, the stars of the firmament of Glory, the standards of triumph waving betwixt earth and heaven. Ye are the manifestations of steadfastness amidst men and the day-springs of Divine Utterance to all that dwell on earth. Well is it with him that turneth unto you, and woe betide the froward.

16.5 Abase not the station of the learned in Baha and belittle not the rank of such rulers as administer justice amidst you. Set your reliance on the army of justice, put on the armour of wisdom, let your adorning be forgiveness and mercy and that which cheereth the hearts of the well-favoured of God.

16.6 We have decreed, O people, that the highest and last end of all learning be the recognition of Him Who is the Object of all knowledge; and yet, behold how ye have allowed your learning to shut you out, as by a veil, from Him Who is the Dayspring of this Light, through Whom every hidden thing hath been revealed. Could ye but discover the source whence the splendour of this utterance is diffused, ye would cast away the peoples of the world and all that they possess, and would draw nigh unto this most blessed Seat of glory.

16.7 Know thou that he is truly learned who hath acknowledged My Revelation, and drunk from the Ocean of My knowledge, and soared in the atmosphere of My love, and cast away all else besides Me, and taken firm hold on that which hath been sent down from the Kingdom of My wondrous utterance. He, verily, is even as an eye unto mankind, and as the spirit of life unto the body of all creation. Glorified be the All-Merciful Who hath enlightened him, and caused him to arise and serve His great and mighty Cause. Verily, such a man is blessed by the Concourse on high, and by them who dwell within the Tabernacle of Grandeur, who have quaffed My sealed Wine in My Name, the Omnipotent, the All-Powerful.

16.8 O SON OF DUST! Blind thine eyes, that thou mayest behold My beauty; stop thine ears, that thou mayest hearken unto the sweet melody of My voice; empty thyself of all learning, that thou mayest partake of My knowledge; and sanctify thyself from riches, that thou mayest obtain a lasting share from the ocean of My eternal wealth. Blind thine eyes, that is, to all save My beauty; stop thine ears to all save My word; empty thyself of all learning save the knowledge of Me; that with a clear vision, a pure heart and an attentive ear thou mayest enter the court of My holiness.

16.9 O SON OF DUST! The wise are they that speak not unless they obtain a hearing, even as the cup-bearer, who proffereth not his cup till he findeth a seeker, and the lover who crieth not out from the depths of his heart until he gazeth upon the beauty of his beloved. Wherefore sow the seeds of wisdom and knowledge in the pure soil of the heart, and keep them hidden, till the hyacinths of divine wisdom spring from the heart and not from mire and clay. In the first line of the Tablet it is recorded and written, and within the sanctuary of the tabernacle of God is hidden:

16.10 O people of God! Righteous men of learning who dedicate themselves to the guidance of others and are freed and well guarded from the promptings of a base and covetous nature are, in the sight of Him Who is the Desire of the world, stars of the heaven of true knowledge. It is essential to treat them with deference. They are indeed fountains of soft-flowing water, stars that shine resplendent, fruits of the blessed Tree, exponents of celestial power, and oceans of heavenly wisdom. Happy is he that followeth them. Verily such a soul is numbered in the Book of God, the Lord of the mighty Throne, among those with whom it shall be well.

16.11 The Prophets of God should be regarded as physicians whose task is to foster the well-being of the world and its peoples, that, through the spirit of oneness, they may heal the sickness of a divided humanity. To none is given the right to question their words or disparage their conduct, for they are the only ones who can claim to have understood the patient and to have correctly diagnosed its ailments. No man, however acute his perception, can ever hope to reach the heights which the wisdom and understanding of the Divine Physician have attained. Little wonder, then, if the treatment prescribed by the physician in this day should not be found to be identical with that which he prescribed before. How could it be otherwise when the ills affecting the sufferer necessitate at every stage of his sickness a special remedy? In like manner, every time the Prophets of God have illumined the world with the resplendent radiance of the Day Star of Divine knowledge, they have invariably summoned its peoples to embrace the light of God through such means as best befitted the exigencies of the age in which they appeared. They were thus able to scatter the darkness of ignorance, and to shed upon the world the glory of their own knowledge. It is towards the inmost essence of these Prophets, therefore, that the eye of every man of discernment must be directed, inasmuch as their one and only purpose hath always been to guide the erring, and give peace to the afflicted.... These are not days of prosperity and triumph. The whole of mankind is in the grip of manifold ills. Strive, therefore, to save its life through the wholesome medicine which the almighty hand of the unerring Physician hath prepared.

16.12 We can well perceive how the whole human race is encompassed with great, with incalculable afflictions. We see it languishing on its bed of sickness, sore-tried and disillusioned. They that are intoxicated by self-conceit have interposed themselves between it and the Divine and infallible Physician. Witness how they have entangled all men, themselves included, in the mesh of their devices. They can neither discover the cause of the disease, nor have they any knowledge of the remedy. They have conceived the straight to be crooked, and have imagined their friend an enemy.

16.13 Consider this wronged One. Though the clearest proofs attest the truth of His Cause; though the prophecies He, in an unmistakable language, hath made have been fulfilled; though, in spite of His not being accounted among the learned, His being unschooled and inexperienced in the disputations current among the divines, He hath rained upon men the showers of His manifold and Divinely-inspired knowledge; yet, behold how this generation hath rejected His authority, and rebelled against Him! He hath, during the greater part of His life, been sore-tried in the clutches of His enemies. His sufferings have now reached their culmination in this afflictive Prison, into which His oppressors have so unjustly thrown Him. God grant that, with a penetrating vision and radiant heart, thou mayest observe the things that have come to pass and are now happening, and, pondering them in thine heart, mayest recognize that which most men have, in this Day, failed to perceive. Please God, He may enable thee to inhale the sweet fragrance of His Day, to partake of the limitless effusions of His grace, to quaff thy fill, through His gracious favor, from the most great Ocean that surgeth in this Day in the name of the Ancient King, and to remain firm and immovable as the mountain in His Cause.

16.14 The most grievous of all veils is the veil of knowledge.

FROM THE WRITINGS AND UTTERANCES OF 'ABDU'L-BAHÁ

16.15   Although to acquire the sciences and arts is the greatest glory of mankind, this is so only on condition that man's river flow into the mighty sea, and draw from God's ancient source His inspiration. When this cometh to pass, then every teacher is as a shoreless ocean, every pupil a prodigal fountain of knowledge. If, then, the pursuit of knowledge lead to the beauty of Him Who is the Object of all Knowledge, how excellent that goal; but if not, a mere drop will perhaps shut a man off from flooding grace, for with learning cometh arrogance and pride, and it bringeth on error and indifference to God.

The sciences of today are bridges to reality; if then they lead not to reality, naught remains but fruitless illusion. By the one true God! If learning be not a means of access to Him, the Most Manifest, it is nothing but evident loss.

It is incumbent upon thee to acquire the various branches of knowledge, and to turn thy face toward the beauty of the Manifest Beauty, that thou mayest be a sign of saving guidance amongst the peoples of the world, and a focal centre of understanding in this sphere from which the wise and their wisdom are shut out, except for those who set foot in the Kingdom of lights and become informed of the veiled and hidden mystery, the well-guarded secret.

16.16   Rest assured that the breathings of the Holy Spirit will loosen thy tongue. Speak, therefore; speak out with great courage at every meeting. When thou art about to begin thine address, turn first to Bahá'u'lláh, and ask for the confirmations of the Holy Spirit, then open thy lips and say whatever is suggested to thy heart; this, however, with the utmost courage, dignity and conviction. It is my hope that from day to day your gatherings will grow and flourish, and that those who are seeking after truth will hearken therein to reasoned arguments and conclusive proofs. I am with you heart and soul at every meeting; be sure of this.

16.17   Again, there are those famed and accomplished men of learning, possessed of praiseworthy qualities and vast erudition, who lay hold on the strong handle of the fear of God and keep to the ways of salvation. In the mirror of their minds the forms of transcendent realities are reflected, and the lamp of their inner vision derives its light from the sun of universal knowledge. They are busy by night and by day with meticulous research into such sciences as are profitable to mankind, and they devote themselves to the training of students of capacity. It is certain that to their discerning taste, the proffered treasures of kings would not compare with a single drop of the waters of knowledge, and mountains of gold and silver could not outweigh the successful solution of a difficult problem. To them, the delights that lie outside their work are only toys for children, and the cumbersome load of unnecessary possessions is only good for the ignorant and base. Content, like the birds, they give thanks for a handful of seeds, and the song of their wisdom dazzles the minds of the world's most wise.

Again, there are sagacious leaders among the people and influential personalities throughout the country, who constitute the pillars of state. Their rank and station and success depend on their being the well-wishers of the people and in their seeking out such means as will improve the nation and will increase the wealth and comfort of the citizens.

16.18 ... I most urgently request the friends of God to make every effort, as much as lieth within their competence, along these lines. The harder they strive to widen the scope of their knowledge, the better and more gratifying will be the result. Let the loved ones of God, whether young or old, whether male or female, each according to his capabilities, bestir themselves and spare no efforts to acquire the various current branches of knowledge, both spiritual and secular, and of the arts.

16.19 O nightingale of the rose-garden of God! Singing melodies will bring animation and happiness to the world of humanity, the hearers will be delighted and joyful and their deeper emotions stirred. But this gladness, this sense of emotion is transitory and will be forgotten within a short time. However, praise be to God, thou hast blended thy tunes with the melodies of the Kingdom, wilt impart solace to the world of the spirit and wilt everlastingly stimulate spiritual feelings. This will last forever and endure the revolution of ages and centuries.

16.20 Endeavour your utmost to compose beautiful poems to be chanted with heavenly music; thus may their beauty affect the minds and impress the hearts of those who listen.

16.21 There are certain pillars which have been established as the unshakable supports of the Faith of God. The mightiest of these is learning and the use of the mind, the expansion of consciousness, and insight into the realities of the universe and the hidden mysteries of Almighty God.

To promote knowledge is thus an inescapable duty imposed on every one of the friends of God. It is incumbent upon that Spiritual Assembly, that assemblage of God, to exert every effort to educate the children, so that from infancy they will be trained in Bahá'í conduct and the ways of God, and will, even as young plants, thrive and flourish in the soft-flowing waters that are the counsels and admonitions of the Blessed Beauty.

16.22 An actor mentioned the drama, and its influence. "The drama is of the utmost importance." said 'Abdu'l-Bahá. "It has been a great educational power in the past; it will be so again." He described how as a young boy he witnessed the Mystery Play of 'Ali's Betrayal and Passion, and how it affected him so deeply that he wept and could not sleep for many nights.

16.23 Is it not astonishing that although man has been created for the knowledge and love of God, for the virtues of the human world, for spirituality, heavenly illumination and eternal life, nevertheless, he continues ignorant and negligent of all this? Consider how he seeks knowledge of everything except knowledge of God. For instance, his utmost desire is to penetrate the mysteries of the lowest strata of the earth. Day by day he strives to know what can be found ten meters below the surface, what he can discover within the stone, what he can learn by archaeological research in the dust. He puts forth arduous labors to fathom terrestrial mysteries but is not at all concerned about knowing the mysteries of the Kingdom, traversing the illimitable fields of the eternal world, becoming informed of the divine realities, discovering the secrets of God, attaining the knowledge of God, witnessing the splendors of the Sun of Truth and realizing the glories of everlasting life. He is unmindful and thoughtless of these. How much he is attracted to the mysteries of matter, and how completely unaware he is of the mysteries of Divinity! Nay, he is utterly negligent and oblivious of the secrets of Divinity. How great his ignorance! How conducive to his degradation! It is as if a kind and loving father had provided a library of wonderful books for his son in order that he might be informed of the mysteries of creation, at the same time surrounding him with every means of comfort and enjoyment, but the son amuses himself with pebbles and playthings, neglectful of all his father's gifts and provision. How ignorant and heedless is man! The Father has willed for him eternal glory, and he is content with blindness and deprivation. The Father has built for him a royal palace, but he is playing with the dust; prepared for him garments of silk, but he prefers to remain unclothed; provided for him delicious foods and fruits, while he seeks sustenance in the grasses of the field.

16.24 You must come into the knowledge of the divine Manifestations and Their teachings through proofs and evidences. You must unseal the mysteries of the supreme Kingdom and become capable of discovering the inner realities of things. Then shall you be the manifestations of the mercy of God and true believers, firm and steadfast in the Cause of God.

16.25 As material and physical sciences are taught here and are constantly unfolding in wider vistas of attainment, I am hopeful that spiritual development may also follow and keep pace with these outer advantages. As material knowledge is illuminating those within the walls of this great temple of learning, so also may the light of the spirit, the inner and divine light of the real philosophy glorify this institution. The most important principle of divine philosophy is the oneness of the world of humanity, the unity of mankind, the bond conjoining East and West, the tie of love which blends human hearts.

16.26 Furthermore, He proclaims that religion must be in harmony with science and reason. If it does not conform to science and reconcile with reason, it is superstition. Down to the present day it has been customary for man to accept a religious teaching, even though it was not in accord with human reason and judgment. The harmony of religious belief with reason is a new vista which Bahá'u'lláh has opened for the soul of man.

16.27 All blessings are divine in origin, but none can be compared with this power of intellectual investigation and research, which is an eternal gift producing fruits of unending delight. Man is ever partaking of these fruits. All other blessings are temporary; this is an everlasting possession. Even sovereignty has its limitations and overthrow; this is a kingship and dominion which none may usurp or destroy. Briefly, it is an eternal blessing and divine bestowal, the supreme gift of God to man. Therefore, you should put forward your most earnest efforts toward the acquisition of science and arts. The greater your attainment, the higher your standard in the divine purpose. The man of science is perceiving and endowed with vision, whereas he who is ignorant and neglectful of this development is blind. The investigating mind is attentive, alive; the callous and indifferent mind is deaf and dead. A scientific man is a true index and representative of humanity, for through processes of inductive reasoning and research he is informed of all that appertains to humanity, its status, conditions and happenings. He studies the human body politic, understands social problems and weaves the web and texture of civilization. In fact, science may be likened to a mirror wherein the infinite forms and images of existing things are revealed and reflected. It is the very foundation of all individual and national development. Without this basis of investigation, development is impossible. Therefore, seek with diligent endeavor the knowledge and attainment of all that lies within the power of this wonderful bestowal.

16.28 Another cause of dissension and disagreement is the fact that religion has been pronounced at variance with science. Between scientists and the followers of religion there has always been controversy and strife for the reason that the latter have proclaimed religion superior in authority to science and considered scientific announcement opposed to the teachings of religion. Bahá'u'lláh declared that religion is in complete harmony with science and reason. If religious belief and doctrine is at variance with reason, it proceeds from the limited mind of man and not from God; therefore, it is unworthy of belief and not deserving of attention; the heart finds no rest in it, and real faith is impossible. How can man believe that which he knows to be opposed to reason? Is this possible? Can the heart accept that which reason denies? Reason is the first faculty of man, and the religion of God is in harmony with it. Bahá'u'lláh has removed this form of dissension and discord from among mankind and reconciled science with religion by revealing the pure teachings of the divine reality. This accomplishment is specialized to Him in this Day.

16.29 Music is one of the important arts. It has great effect upon human spirit. Musical melodies are a certain something which prove to be accidental upon etheric vibrations, for voice is nothing but the expression of vibrations, which reaching the tympanum, effect the nerves of hearing. Musical melodies are, therefore, those peculiar effects produced by, or from, vibration. However, they have the keenest effect upon the spirit. In sooth, although music is a material affair, yet its tremendous effect is spiritual, and its greatest attachment is to the realm of the spirit. If a person desires to deliver a discourse, it will prove more effectual after musical melodies. The ancient Greeks, as well as Persian philosophers, were in the habit of delivering their discourses in the following manner: first, playing a few musical melodies, and when their audience attained a certain receptivity thereby they would leave their instruments at once and begin their discourse. Among the most renowned musicians of Persia was one named Barbod, who, whenever a great question had been pleaded for at the court of the King, and the Ministry had failed to persuade the King, they would at once refer the matter to Barbod, whereupon he would go with his instrument to the court and play the most appropriate and touching music, the end being at once attained because the king was immediately affected by the touching musical melodies, certain feelings of generosity would swell up in his heart, and he would give way. You may try this: if you have a great desire and wish to attain your end, try to do so on a large audience after a great solo has been rendered, but it must be on an audience on which music is effective, for there are some people who are like stones, and music cannot affect stones.

It was for this reason that His Holiness David sang the psalms in the Holy of Holies at Jerusalem with sweet melodies. In this Cause the art of music is of paramount importance. The Blessed Perfection, when He first came to the barracks (Akká) repeated this statement: 'If among the immediate followers there had been those who could have played some musical instrument. i.e., flute or harp, or could have sung, it would have charmed every one.' In short, musical melodies form an important role in the associations, or outward and inward characteristics, or qualities of man, for it is the inspirer or motive power of both the material and spiritual susceptibilities. What a motive power it is in all feelings of love! When man is attached to the love of God, Music has great effect upon him.

FROM THE WRITINGS AND LETTERS WRITTEN BY, OR ON BEHALF OF, SHOGHI EFFENDI

16.30 The Guardian values the hymns that you are so beautifully composing. They certainly contain the realities of the Faith, and will indeed help you to give the Message to the young ones. It is the music which assists us to affect the human spirit; it is an important means which helps us to communicate with the soul. The Guardian hopes that through this assistance you will give the Message to the people, and will attract their hearts.

16.31 What Bahá'u'lláh meant primarily with "sciences that begin and end in words" are those theological treatises and commentaries that encumber the human mind rather than help it to attain the truth. The students would devote their life to their study but still attain no where. Bahá'u'lláh surely never meant to include story-writing under such a category; and shorthand and typewriting are both most useful talents, very necessary in our present social and economic life.

What you could do, and should do, is to use your stories to become a source of inspiration and guidance for those who read them. With such a means at your disposal you can spread the spirit and teachings of the Cause; you can show the evils that exist in society, as well as the way they can be remedied. If you possess a real talent in writing you should consider it as given by God and exert your efforts to use it for the betterment of society.

16.32   There is an answer in the teachings for everything; unfortunately the majority of the Bahá'ís, however intensely devoted and sincere they may be, lack for the most part the necessary scholarship and wisdom to reply to and refute the claims and attacks of people with some education and standing.

16.33   To deepen in the Cause means to read the Writings of Bahá'u'lláh and the Master so thoroughly as to be able to give it to others in its pure form. There are many who have some superficial idea of what the Cause stands for. They, therefore, present it together with all sorts of ideas that are their own. As the Cause is still in its early days we must be most careful lest we fall under this error and injure the Movement we so much adore.

There is no limit to the study of the Cause. The more we read the writings the more truths we can find in them and the more we will see that our previous notions were erroneous."

16.34   Shoghi Effendi trusts, however, that these souls who are attracted by the teachings would be made to live the life and also deepen their knowledge of the Writings of Bahá'u'lláh. For it is only by fully appreciating the spiritual and social import of His Mission that we can be willing to dedicate our life to its service.

By holding study classes where the Word is read and understood and obtaining a thorough knowledge of the spirit that animated the early believers we can make sure that these newcomers are grounded in the teachings and made real and devoted believers. Books such as the Íqán, Some Answered Questions, the Tablets of Bahá'u'lláh, Nabíl's Narrative and Dr. Esslemont's book should be read and read over again by every soul who desires to serve the Movement or considers himself an active member of the group.

FROM THE WRITINGS AND LETTERS WRITTEN BY, OR ON BEHALF OF, THE UNIVERSAL HOUSE OF JUSTICE

16.35 As more and more receptive souls embrace the Cause of God and throw in their lot with those already participating in the global enterprise under way, the development and activity of the individual, the institutions, and the community are sure to receive a mighty thrust forward. May a bewildered humanity see in the relationships being forged among these three protagonists by the followers of Bahá'u'lláh a pattern of collective life that will propel it towards its high destiny. This is our ardent prayer in the Holy Shrines.

16.36 Invariably, opportunities afforded by the personal circumstances of the believers initially involved—or perhaps a single homefront pioneer—to enter into meaningful and distinctive conversation with local residents dictate how the process of growth begins in a cluster. A study circle made up of a few friends or colleagues, a class offered for several neighbourhood children, a group formed for junior youth during after-school hours, a devotional gathering hosted for family and friends—any one of these can serve as a stimulus to growth. What happens next follows no predetermined course. Conditions may justify that one core activity be given precedence, multiplying at a rate faster than the others. It is equally possible that all four would advance at a comparable pace. Visiting teams may be called upon to provide impetus to the fledgling set of activities. But irrespective of the specifics, the outcome must be the same. Within every cluster, the level of cohesion achieved among the core activities must be such that, in their totality, a nascent programme for the sustained expansion and consolidation of the Faith can be perceived. That is to say, in whatever combination and however small in number, devotional gatherings, children's classes and junior youth groups are being maintained by those progressing through the sequence of institute courses and committed to the vision of individual and collective transformation they foster. This initial flow of human resources into the field of systematic action marks the first of several milestones in a process of sustainable growth.

16.37 Let the friends immerse themselves in this ocean, let them organize regular study classes for its constant consideration, and, as reinforcement to their effort, let them remember conscientiously the requirements of daily prayer and reading of the Word of God enjoined upon all Bahá'ís by Bahá'u'lláh.

16.38 Newly enrolled professionals and other experts provide a great resource for the development of Bahá'í scholarship. It is hoped that, as they attain a deeper grasp of the Teachings and their significance, they will be able to assist Bahá'í communities in correlating the beliefs of the Faith with the current thoughts and problems of the world. In some instances Bahá'ís of a particular profession have come together in special conferences or organized themselves into an association for this purpose. This also allows them to support one another as Bahá'ís and to take advantage of their professional status to promote the interests of the Faith. Current examples of professional associations of this type are the Bahá'í Justice Society and the Bahá'í Medical Association, both in the United States. Special encouragement should therefore be given to believers of unusual capacity to consecrate their abilities to the service of the Cause through the unique contribution they can make to this rapidly developing field of Bahá'í endeavour.

16.39 The House of Justice calls upon the members of the community of the Greatest Name, young and old, men and women alike, to strive to develop and offer to humanity a new model of scholarly activity along the lines set out in this compilation, animated by the spirit of inquiry into the limitless meaning of the Divine Teachings. This scholarly endeavour should be characterized by the welcome it offers to all who wish to be involved in it, each in his or her own way, by mutual encouragement and cooperation among its participants, and by the respect accorded to distinguished accomplishment and outstanding achievement. The spirit and approach should be far removed from the arrogance, contention, and exclusiveness which have too often sullied the name of scholarship in the wider society, and which have created barriers to the sound development of this worthy pursuit.

16.40 The House of Justice advises you not to attempt to define too narrowly the form that Bahá'í scholarship should take, or the approach that scholars should adopt. Rather should you strive to develop within your Association respect for a wide range of approaches and endeavours. No doubt there will be some Bahá'ís who will wish to work in isolation, while others will desire consultation and collaboration with those having similar interests. Your aim should be to promote an atmosphere of mutual respect and tolerance within which will be included scholars whose principal interest is in theological issues as well as those scholars whose interests lie in relating the insights provided by the Bahá'í teachings to contemporary thought in the arts and sciences.

OTHER SOURCES

16.41 At the general level, the Bahá'í International Community (BIC) has participated in a number of major international summits and nongovernmental forums. Notable among them have been the United Nations Conference on Environment and Development (the "Earth Summit") in Rio de Janiero in 1992, the World Summit for Social Development in Copenhagen in 1995, and the Fourth World Conference on Women in Beijing that same year, as well as the World Conference Against Racism in 2001 and the World Summit for

Sustainable Development in 2002, both held in South Africa, and the 2005 Annual Meeting of the World Economic Forum in Davos, Switzerland.

Because of the worldview deriving from the Bahá'í system of belief, the community has taken a particularly keen interest in discussions that explore the contribution of religion to questions of development. These have included the World Faiths Development Dialogue Conference, cosponsored by the World Bank and the Archbishop of Canterbury held in Lambeth Palace, London, in 1998, and the Parliament of the World's Religions held in South Africa in 1999. Especially enriching has been the involvement, from 1995 to 2000, in a project sponsored by the International Development Research Centre (IDRC) in Canada, which explored the relationship between science, religion, and development.

The community has found in this series of activities welcome opportunities to give expression to the central conviction animating Bahá'í work in the development field. As early as the Earth Summit, a statement submitted by the BIC to the plenary session, on behalf of all religious nongovernmental organizations, concluded: "The profound and far-reaching changes, the unity and unprecedented cooperation required to reorient the world toward an environmentally sustainable and just future, will only be possible by touching the human spirit, by appealing to those universal values which alone can empower individuals and peoples to act in accordance with the long-term interests of the planet and humanity as a whole." (Bahá'í International Community, *For the Betterment of the World*)

CHAPTER 17:

HEALING OUR WORLD BY HEALING OUR FAMILIES

FROM THE WRITINGS OF BAHÁ'U'LLÁH

17.1 The word of God which the Supreme Pen hath recorded on the eighth leaf of the Most Exalted Paradise is the following: Schools must first train the children in the principles of religion, so that the Promise and the Threat recorded in the Books of God may prevent them from the things forbidden and adorn them with the mantle of the commandments; but this in such a measure that it may not injure the children by resulting in ignorant fanaticism and bigotry.

17.2 Everyone, whether man or woman, should hand over to a trusted person a portion of what he or she earneth through trade, agriculture or other occupation, for the training and education of children, to be spent for this purpose with the knowledge of the Trustees of the House of Justice.

17.3 The Pen of Glory counselleth everyone regarding the instruction and education of children. Behold that which the Will of God hath revealed upon Our arrival in the Prison City and recorded in the Most Holy Book. Unto every father hath been enjoined the instruction of his son and daughter in the art of reading and writing and in all that hath been laid down in the Holy Tablet. He that putteth away that which is commanded unto him, the Trustees are then to take from him that which is required for their instruction, if he be wealthy, and if not the matter devolveth upon the House of Justice. Verily, have We made it a shelter for the poor and needy. He that bringeth up his son or the son of another, it is as though he hath brought up a son of Mine; upon him rest My Glory, My Loving-Kindness, My Mercy, that have compassed the world.

17.4 At the outset of every endeavour, it is incumbent to look to the end of it. Of all the arts and sciences, set the children to studying those which will result in advantage to man, will ensure his progress and elevate his rank. Thus the noisome odours of lawlessness will be dispelled, and thus through the high endeavours of the nation's leaders, all will live cradled, secure and in peace.

The Great Being saith: The learned of the day must direct the people to acquire those branches of knowledge which are of use, that both the learned themselves and the generality of mankind may derive benefits therefrom. Such academic pursuits as begin and end in words alone have never been and will never be of any worth. The majority of Persia's learned doctors devote all their lives to the study of a philosophy the ultimate yield of which is nothing but words.

17.5 O ye that dwell on earth! The religion of God is for love and unity; make it not the cause of enmity or dissension. In the eyes of men of insight and the beholders of the Most Sublime Vision, whatsoever are the effective means for safeguarding and promoting the happiness and welfare of the children of men have already been revealed by the Pen of Glory.

FROM THE WRITINGS AND UTTERANCES OF 'ABDU'L-BAHÁ

17.6 Training in morals and good conduct is far more important than book learning. A child is cleanly, agreeable, of good character, well-behaved—even though he be ignorant—is preferable to a child that is rude, unwashed, ill-natured and yet becoming deeply versed in all the sciences and arts. The reason for this is that the child who conducts himself well, even though he be ignorant, is of benefit to others, while an ill-natured, ill-behaved child is corrupted and harmful to others, even though he be learned. If, however, the child be trained to be both learned and good, the result is light upon light.

17.7 While the children are yet in their infancy feed them from the breast of heavenly grace, foster them in the cradle of all excellence, rear them in the embrace of bounty. Give them the advantage of every useful kind of knowledge. Let them share in every new and rare and wondrous craft and art. Bring them up to work and strive, and accustom them to hardship. Teach them to dedicate their lives to matters of great import, and inspire them to undertake studies that will benefit mankind.

17.8 It followeth that the children's school must be a place of utmost discipline and order, that instruction must be thorough, and provision must be made for the rectification and refinement of character; so that, in his earliest years, within the very essence of the child, the divine foundation will be laid and the structure of holiness raised up.

Know that this matter of instruction, of character rectification and refinement, of heartening and encouraging the child, is of the utmost importance, for such are basic principles of God.

Thus, if God will, out of these spiritual schools illumined children will arise, adorned with all the fairest virtues of humankind, and will shed their light not only across Persia, but around the world.

It is extremely difficult to teach the individual and refine his character once puberty is passed. By then, as experience hath shown, even if every effort be exerted to modify some tendency of his, it all availeth nothing. He may, perhaps, improve somewhat today; but let a few days pass and he forgetteth, and turneth backward to his habitual condition and accustomed ways. Therefore it is in early childhood that a firm foundation must be laid. While the branch is green and tender it can easily be made straight.

Our meaning is that qualities of the spirit are the basic and divine foundation, and adorn the true essence of man; and knowledge is the cause of human progress. The beloved of God must attach great importance to this matter, and carry it forward with enthusiasm and zeal.

17.9 So long as the mother faileth to train her children, and start them on a proper way of life, the training which they receive later on will not take its full effect. It is incumbent upon the Spiritual Assemblies to provide the mothers with a well-planned programme for the education of children, showing how, from infancy, the child must be watched over and taught. These instructions must be given to every mother to serve her as a guide, so that each will train and nurture her children in accordance with the Teachings.

17.10 The education and training of children is among the most meritorious acts of humankind and draweth down the grace and favour of the All-Merciful, for education is the indispensable foundation of all human excellence and alloweth man to work his way to the heights of abiding glory. If a child be trained from his infancy, he will, through the loving care of the Holy Gardener, drink in the crystal waters of the spirit and of knowledge, like a young tree amid the rilling brooks. And certainly he will gather to himself the bright rays of the Sun of Truth, and through its light and heat will grow ever fresh and fair in the garden of life.

Therefore must the mentor be a doctor as well: that is, he must, in instructing the child, remedy its faults; must give him learning, and at the same time rear him to have a spiritual nature. Let the teacher be a doctor to the character of the child, thus will he heal the spiritual ailments of the children of men.

If, in this momentous task, a mighty effort be exerted, the world of humanity will shine out with other adornings, and shed the fairest light. Then will this darksome place grow luminous, and this abode of earth turn into Heaven. The very demons will change to angels then, and wolves to shepherds of the flock, and the wild-dog pack to gazelles that pasture on the plains of oneness, and ravening beasts to peaceful herds, and birds of prey, with talons sharp as knives, to songsters warbling their sweet native notes.

17.11 The Sunday school for the children in which the Tablets and Teachings of Bahá'u'lláh are read, and the Word of God is recited for the children is indeed a blessed thing. Thou must certainly continue this organized activity without cessation, and attach importance to it, so that day by day it may grow and be quickened with the breaths of the Holy Spirit. If this activity is well organized, rest thou assured that it will yield great results. Firmness and steadfastness, however, are necessary, otherwise it will continue for some time, but later be gradually forgotten. Perseverance is an essential condition. In every project firmness and steadfastness will undoubtedly lead to good results; otherwise it will exist for some days, and then be discontinued.

17.12 In a time to come, morals will degenerate to an extreme degree. It is essential that children be reared in the Bahá'í way, that they may find happiness both in this world and the next. If not, they shall be beset by sorrows and troubles, for human happiness is founded upon spiritual behaviour.

17.13 Let the mothers consider that whatever concerneth the education of children is of the first importance. Let them put forth every effort in this regard, for when the bough is green and tender it will grow in whatever way ye train it. Therefore is it incumbent upon the mothers to rear their little ones even as a gardener tendeth his young plants. Let them strive by day and by night to establish within their children faith and certitude, the fear of God, the love of the Beloved of the worlds, and all good qualities and traits. Whensoever a mother seeth that her child hath done well, let her praise and applaud him and cheer his heart; and if the slightest undesirable trait should manifest itself, let her counsel the child and punish him, and use means based on reason, even a slight verbal chastisement should this be necessary. It is not, however, permissible to strike a child, or vilify him, for the child's character will be totally perverted if he be subjected to blows or verbal abuse.

17.14 It is incumbent upon Bahá'í children to surpass other children in the acquisition of sciences and arts, for they have been cradled in the grace of God.

Whatever other children learn in a year, let Bahá'í children learn in a month. The heart of 'Abdu'l-Bahá longeth, in its love, to find that Bahá'í young people, each and all, are known throughout the world for their intellectual attainments. There is no question but that they will exert all their efforts, their energies, their sense of pride, to acquire the sciences and arts.

17.15 O God! Educate these children. These children are the plants of Thine orchard, the flowers of Thy meadow, the roses of Thy garden. Let Thy rain fall upon them; let the Sun of Reality shine upon them with Thy love. Let Thy breeze refresh them in order that they may be trained, grow and develop, and appear in the utmost beauty. Thou art the Giver. Thou art the Compassionate.

17.16   According to the teachings of Bahá'u'lláh the family, being a human unit, must be educated according to the rules of sanctity. All the virtues must be taught the family. The integrity of the family bond must be constantly considered, and the rights of the individual members must not be transgressed. The rights of the son, the father, the mother—none of them must be transgressed, none of them must be arbitrary. Just as the son has certain obligations to his father, the father, likewise, has certain obligations to his son. The mother, the sister and other members of the household have their certain prerogatives. All these rights and prerogatives must be conserved, yet the unity of the family must be sustained. The injury of one shall be considered the injury of all; the comfort of each, the comfort of all; the honor of one, the honor of all.

17.17   The only difference between members of the human family is that of degree. Some are like children who are ignorant, and must be educated until they arrive at maturity. Some are like the sick and must be treated with tenderness and care. None are bad or evil! We must not be repelled by these poor children. We must treat them with great kindness, teaching the ignorant and tenderly nursing the sick.

FROM THE WRITINGS AND LETTERS WRITTEN BY, OR ON BEHALF OF, SHOGHI EFFENDI

17.18   With regard to the statement attributed to 'Abdu'l-Bahá and which you have quoted in your letter regarding a 'problem child'; these statements of the Master, however true in their substance, should never be given a literal interpretation. 'Abdu'l-Bahá could have never meant that a child should be left to himself, entirely free. In fact Bahá'í education, just like any other system of education is based on the assumption that there are certain natural deficiencies in every child, no matter how gifted, which his educators, whether his parents, school masters, or his spiritual guides and preceptors should endeavour to remedy. Discipline of some sort, whether physical, moral or intellectual, is indeed indispensable, and no training can be said to be complete and fruitful if it disregards this element. The child when born is far from being perfect. It is not only helpless, but actually is imperfect, and even is naturally inclined towards evil. He should be trained, his natural inclinations harmonized, adjusted and controlled, and if necessary suppressed or regulated, so as to insure his healthy physical and moral development. Bahá'í parents cannot simply adopt an attitude of non resistance towards their children, particularly those who are unruly and violent by nature. It is not even sufficient that they should pray on their behalf. Rather they should endeavour to inculcate, gently and patiently, into their youthful minds such principles of moral conduct and initiate them into the principles and teachings of the Cause with such tactful and loving care as would enable them to become 'true sons of God' and develop into loyal and intelligent citizens of His Kingdom. This is the high purpose which Bahá'u'lláh Himself has clearly defined as the chief goal of every education.

17.19 He is sorry to hear your little boy is not developing satisfactorily; very few children are really bad. They do, however, sometimes have complicated personalities and need very wise handling to enable them to grow into normal, moral, happy adults. If you feel convinced your son will really benefit from going to....,...'s school you could send him there. But in general we should certainly always avoid sending Bahá'í children to orthodox religious schools, especially Catholic, as the children receive the imprint of religious beliefs we as believers know are out-dated and no longer for this age. He will especially pray for the solution of this problem.

17.20 Regarding your question about children fighting: The statement of the Master, not to strike back, should not be taken so extremely literally that Bahá'í children must accept to be bullied and thrashed. If they can manage to show a better way of setting disputes than by active self-defence, they should naturally do so.

17.21   Regarding children at fifteen a Bahá'í is of age as far as keeping the laws of the Aqdas is concerned—prayer, fasting, etc. But children under fifteen should certainly observe the Bahá'í Holy Days, and not go to school, if this can be arranged on these nine days.

FROM THE WRITINGS AND LETTERS WRITTEN BY, OR ON BEHALF OF, THE UNIVERSAL HOUSE OF JUSTICE

17.22   As to your question about the use of physical punishment in child training, although there is a Tablet of the Master which considers beating as not permissible, this does not necessarily include every form of corporal punishment. In order to have a full grasp of the Master's attitude towards punishment, one has to study all His Tablets in this respect. For the time being no hard and fast rule can be laid down, and parents must use their own wise discretion in these matters until the time is ripe for the principles of Bahá'í education of children to be more clearly elucidated and applied.

17.23   ... If the non-Bahá'í parents of a youth under fifteen permit their child to be a Bahá'í we have no objection whatsoever from the point of view of our Teachings to permitting such a youth to declare as a Bahá'í regardless of age. When he declares is faith in Bahá'u'lláh, he will then be accepted in the community and be treated as other Bahá'í children.

17.24   In letters replying to questions on the registration of children and youth the Universal House of Justice has attempted to avoid laying down rulings that are universally applicable. However, for the assistance of National Spiritual Assemblies it is now providing the following summary of guidelines and elucidations that have been given. We are to emphasize that no hard and fast lines should be drawn, and procedural matters must never be allowed to eclipse the spiritual reality of belief, which is an intensely personal relationship between the soul and its Creator." "Unlike the children of some other religions, Bahá'í children do not automatically inherit the Faith of their parents. However, the parents are responsible for the upbringing and spiritual welfare of their children, Spiritual Assemblies have the duty to assist parents, if necessary, in fulfilling these obligations, so that the children will be reared in the light of the Revelation of Bahá'u'lláh and from their earliest years will learn to love God and His Manifestations and to walk in the way of God's Law. It is natural, therefore, to regard the children of Bahá'ís as Bahá'ís unless there is a reason to conclude the contrary. It is quite wrong to think of Bahá'í children as existing in some sort of spiritual limbo until the age of fifteen at which point they can 'become' Bahá'ís. In the light of this one can conclude the following:

Children born to a Bahá'í couple are regarded as Bahá'ís from the beginning of their lives, and their births should be registered by the Spiritual Assembly.

The birth of a child to a couple, one of whom is a Bahá'í, should also be registered unless the non-Bahá'í parent objects.

A Spiritual Assembly may accept the declaration of faith of a child of non-Bahá'í parents, and register him as Bahá'í child, provided the parents give their consent."

17.25 ... Both children of Bahá'í parents, and children who, with their non-Bahá'í parents' consent, declare their Faith in Bahá'u'lláh before they are fifteen years old, are regarded as Bahá'í and it is within a Spiritual Assembly's discretion to request such children to undertake work of which they are capable in the service of the Faith, such as service on suitable committees. However, upon attaining the age of fifteen a child becomes spiritually mature and is responsible for stating on his own behalf whether or not he wishes to remain a member of the Bahá'í community. If he does not then reaffirm his faith, he must be treated, administratively, as a non-Bahá'í.

17.26 Without minimizing the serious situation facing a world heedless of Bahá'u'lláh's admonitions, it must be remembered that He also refers to the Golden Age of civilization to come. the House of Justice hopes that Bahá'í teachers and parents will do their utmost to encourage the children to study the explanations of the beloved Guardian about the twin processes at work in the world-the steady growth of the Faith, and the devastating forces of disintegration assailing the outworn institutions of present-day society. We are asked to assure you that the House of Justice will remember you and the children of your class at the Holy Threshold.

17.27 ...House of Justice has instructed us to say that children should be trained to understand the spiritual significance of the gatherings of the followers of the Blessed Beauty, and to appreciate the honour and bounty of being able to take part in them, whatever their outward form may be. It is realized that some Bahá'í observances are lengthy and it is difficult for very small children to remain quiet for so long. In such cases one or other of the parents may have to miss part of the meeting in order to care for the child. The Spiritual Assembly can also perhaps help the parents by providing for a children's observance, suited to their capacities, in a separate room during part of the community's observance. Attendance at the whole of the adult celebration thus becomes a sign of growing maturity and a distinction to be earned by good behavior.

In any case, the House of Justice Points out that parents are responsible for their children and should make them behave when they attend Bahá'í meetings. If children persist in creating a disturbance they should be taken out of the meeting. This is not merely necessary to ensure the properly dignified conduct of Bahá'í meeting but is an aspect of the training of children in courtesy, consideration for others, reverence, and obedience to their parents.

CHAPTER 18:

PURIFYING OUR LIVES THROUGH THE BAHÁ'Í FUND

Making a Better World with the Bahá'í Faith: QUOTATIONS

FROM THE WRITINGS OF BAHÁ'U'LLÁH

18.1   To give and to be generous are attributes of Mine; well is it with him that adorneth himself with My virtues.

18.2   Blessed is he that hath set himself towards Thee, and hasted to attain the Day-Spring of the lights of Thy face. Blessed is he who with all his affections hath turned to the Dawning-Place of Thy Revelation and the Fountain-Head of Thine inspiration. Blessed is he that hath expended in Thy path what Thou didst bestow upon him through Thy bounty and favor. Blessed is he who, in his sore longing after Thee, hath cast away all else except Thyself. Blessed is he who hath enjoyed intimate communion with Thee, and rid himself of all attachment to any one save Thee.

18.3   Say: Should your conduct, O people, contradict your professions, how think ye, then, to be able to distinguish yourselves from them who, though professing their faith in the Lord their God, have, as soon as He came unto them in the cloud of holiness, refused to acknowledge Him, and repudiated His truth? Disencumber yourselves of all attachment to this world and the vanities thereof. Beware that ye approach them not, inasmuch as they prompt you to walk after your own lusts and covetous desires, and hinder you from entering the straight and glorious Path.

18.4   Know ye that by "the world" is meant your unawareness of Him Who is your Maker, and your absorption in aught else but Him. The "life to come," on the other hand, signifieth the things that give you a safe approach to God, the All-Glorious, the Incomparable. Whatsoever deterreth you, in this Day, from loving God is nothing but the world. Flee it, that ye may be numbered with the blest. Should a man wish to adorn himself with the ornaments of the earth, to wear its apparels, or partake of the benefits it can bestow, no harm can befall him, if he alloweth nothing whatever to intervene between him and God, for God hath ordained every good thing, whether created in the heavens or in the earth, for such of His servants as truly believe in Him. Eat ye, O people, of the good things which God hath allowed you, and deprive not yourselves from His wondrous bounties. Render thanks and praise unto Him, and be of them that are truly thankful.

18.5 O wayfarer in the path of God! Take thou thy portion of the ocean of His grace, and deprive not thyself of the things that lie hidden in its depths. Be thou of them that have partaken of its treasures. A dewdrop out of this ocean would, if shed upon all that are in the heavens and on the earth, suffice to enrich them with the bounty of God, the Almighty, the All-Knowing, the All-Wise. With the hands of renunciation draw forth from its life-giving waters, and sprinkle therewith all created things, that they may be cleansed from all man-made limitations and may approach the mighty seat of God, this hallowed and resplendent Spot.

18.6 Prove yourselves worthy of his trust and confidence in you, and withhold not from the poor the gifts which the grace of God hath bestowed upon you. He, verily, shall recompense the charitable, and doubly repay them for what they have bestowed.

18.7 Charity is pleasing and praiseworthy in the sight of God and is regarded as a prince among goodly deeds.

18.8 The essence of charity is for the servant to recount the blessings of his Lord, and to render thanks unto Him at all times and under all conditions.

18.9 The beginning of magnanimity is when man expendeth his wealth on himself, on his family and on the poor among his brethren in his Faith.

18.10 O YE THAT PRIDE YOURSELVES ON MORTAL RICHES! Know ye in truth that wealth is a mighty barrier between the seeker and his desire, the lover and his beloved. The rich, but for a few, shall in no wise attain the court of His presence nor enter the city of content and resignation. Well is it then with him, who, being rich, is not hindered by his riches from the eternal kingdom, nor deprived by them of imperishable dominion. By the Most Great Name! The splendor of such a wealthy man shall illuminate the dwellers of heaven even as the sun enlightens the people of the earth!

18.11 Busy not thyself with this world, for with fire We test the gold, and with gold We test Our servants.

18.12 Thou dost wish for gold and I desire thy freedom from it. Thou thinkest thyself rich in its possession, and I recognize thy wealth in thy sanctity therefrom. By My life! This is My knowledge, and that is thy fancy; how can My way accord with thine?

FROM THE WRITINGS AND UTTERANCES OF 'ABDU'L-BAHÁ

18.13 Be ye a refuge to the fearful; bring ye rest and peace to the disturbed; make ye a provision for the destitute; be a treasury of riches for the poor; be a healing medicine for those who suffer pain; be ye doctor and nurse to the ailing; promote ye friendship, and honour, and conciliation, and devotion to God, in this world of non-existence.

18.14 The confirmations of God are the surety for these blessings; the sacred bounty of God bestoweth these great gifts. The friends of God are supported by the Kingdom on high and they win their victories through the massed armies of the most great guidance. Thus for them every difficulty will be made smooth, every problem will most easily be solved.

18.15 Man reacheth perfection through good deeds, voluntarily performed, not through good deeds the doing of which was forced upon him. And sharing is a personally chosen righteous act: that is, the rich should extend assistance to the poor, they should expend their substance for the poor, but of their own free will, and not because the poor have gained this end by force. For the harvest of force is turmoil and the ruin of the social order. On the other hand voluntary sharing, the freely-chosen expending of one's substance, leadeth to society's comfort and peace. It lighteth up the world; it bestoweth honour upon humankind.

18.16 O God, my God! Illumine the brows of Thy true lovers and support them with angelic hosts of certain triumph. Set firm their feet on Thy straight path, and out of Thine ancient bounty open before them the portals of Thy blessings; for they are expending on Thy pathway what Thou hast bestowed upon them, safeguarding Thy Faith, putting their trust in their remembrance of Thee, offering up their hearts for love of Thee, and withholding not what they possess in adoration for Thy Beauty and in their search for ways to please Thee.

O my Lord! Ordain for them a plenteous share, a destined recompense and sure reward.

Verily, Thou art the Sustainer, the Helper, the Generous, the Bountiful, the Ever-Bestowing.

FROM THE WRITINGS AND LETTERS WRITTEN BY, OR ON BEHALF OF, SHOGHI EFFENDI

18.17 We must be like the fountain or spring that is continually emptying itself of all that it has and is continually being refilled from an invisible source. To be continually giving out for the good of our fellows undeterred by fear of poverty and reliant on the unfailing bounty of the Source of all wealth and all good—this is the secret of right living.

18.18 And as the progress and extension of spiritual activities is dependent and conditioned upon material means, it is of absolute necessity that immediately after the establishment of local as well as national Spiritual Assemblies, a Bahá'í Fund be established, to be placed under the exclusive control of the Spiritual Assembly. All donations and contributions should be offered to the Treasurer of the Assembly, for the express purpose of promoting the interests of the Cause, throughout that locality or country. It is the sacred obligation of every conscientious and faithful servant of Bahá'u'lláh, who desires to see His Cause advance, to contribute freely and generously for the increase of that Fund. The members of the Spiritual Assembly will at their own discretion expend it to promote the Teaching Campaign, to help the needy, to establish educational Bahá'í institutions, to extend in every way possible their sphere of service. I cherish the hope that all the friends, realizing the necessity of this measure, will bestir themselves and contribute, however modestly at first, towards the speedy establishment and the increase of that Fund.

18.19 Even though Shoghi Effendi would urge every believer to sacrifice as much as possible for the sake of contributing towards the fund of the National Assembly, yet he would discourage the friends to incur debts for that purpose. We are asked to give what we have, not what we do not possess, especially if such an act causes suffering to others. In such matters we should use judgement and wisdom and take into our confidence other devoted Bahá'ís.

18.20 ... in the first place every believer is free to follow the dictates of his own conscience as regards the manner in which to spend his own money. Secondly, we must always bear in mind that there are so few Bahá'ís in the world, relative to the world's population, and so many people in need, that even if all of us gave all we had, it would not alleviate more than an infinitesimal amount of suffering. This does not mean we must not help the needy, we should; but our contributions to the Faith are the surest way of lifting once and for all time the burden of hunger and misery from mankind, for it is only through the system of Bahá'u'lláh—Divine in origin—that the world can be gotten on its feet and want, fear, hunger, war, etc., be eliminated. Non-Bahá'ís cannot contribute to our work or do it for us; so really our first obligation is to support our own teaching work, as this will lead to the healing of the nations.

FROM THE WRITINGS AND LETTERS WRITTEN BY, OR ON BEHALF OF, THE UNIVERSAL HOUSE OF JUSTICE

18.21   One of the distinguishing features of the Cause of God is its principle of non-acceptance of financial contributions for its own purposes from non-Bahá'ís: support of the Bahá'í fund is a bounty reserved by Bahá'u'lláh to His declared followers. This bounty imposes full responsibility for financial support of the Faith on the believers alone, every one of whom is called upon to do his utmost to ensure that the constant and liberal outpouring of means is maintained and increased to meet the growing needs of the Cause. Many Bahá'í communities are at present dependent on outside help, and for them the aim must be to become self-supporting, confident that the General Lord will, as their efforts increase, eventually enable them to offer for the progress of His Faith material wealth as well as their devotion, their energy and love.

18.22   Giving to the Fund, therefore, is a spiritual privilege, not open to those who have not accepted Bahá'u'lláh, of which no believer should deny himself. It is both a responsibility and a source of bounty. This is an aspect of the Cause which, we feel, is an essential part of the basic teaching and deepening of new believers. The importance of contributing resides in the degree of sacrifice of the giver, the spirit of devotion with which the contribution is made and the unity of the friends in this service; these attract the confirmations of God and enhance the dignity and self-respect of the individuals and the community.

18.23   There is a profound aspect to the relationship between a believer and the Fund, which holds true irrespective of his or her economic condition. When a human soul accepts Bahá'u'lláh as the Manifestation of God for this age and enters into the Divine Covenant, that soul should progressively bring his or her whole life into harmony with the Divine purpose—he becomes a co-worker in to the Cause of God and receives the bounty of being permitted to devote his material possessions, no matter how meagre, to the work of the Faith.

18.24 As regards collection of funds in other countries, the House of Justice does not wish Bahá'í institutions of any country to appeal for funds to the Bahá'ís of another country, unless the National Spiritual Assembly of that country permits it. This does not mean that individuals are not free to contribute to a Bahá'í project in any country that they wish. For example, if a Bahá'í from another country comes to a conference in ... and he wishes to contribute to your school, there would be no objection. However, and organized and indiscriminate appeal for funds to individuals in other countries should not be made without the consent of the National Assembly of that country.

OTHER SOURCES

18.25 Let us take as an example the Bahá'í view of income distribution, which allows for differences but would eliminate both extreme wealth and extreme poverty. The accumulation of excessive fortunes by a small number of individuals, while the masses are in need, is, according to Bahá'í teachings, an iniquity and an injustice. Moderation should, therefore, be established by means of laws and regulations that would hinder the accumulation of excessive fortunes by a few individuals and provide for the essential needs of the masses. (Bahá'í International Community, 1993 Feb 12, *Human Rights and Extreme Poverty*)

SPECIAL SECTION FOR THE HUQUQU'LLÁH

FROM THE WRITINGS OF BAHÁ'U'LLÁH

18.26 Should anyone acquire one hundred mithqals of gold, nineteen mithqals thereof are God's and to be rendered unto Him, the Fashioner of earth and heaven. Take heed, O people, lest ye deprive yourselves of so great a bounty.

18.27 It is clear and evident that the payment of the Right of God is conducive to prosperity, to blessing, and to honour and divine protection. Well is it with them that comprehend and recognize this truth and woe betide them that believe not. And this is on condition that the individual should observe the injunctions prescribed in the Book with the utmost radiance, gladness and willing acquiescence. It behoveth you to counsel the friends to do that which is right and praiseworthy. Whoso hearkeneth to this call, it is to his own behoof, and whoso faileth bringeth loss upon himself. Verily our Lord of Mercy is the All-Sufficing, the All-Praised.

18.28 It is incumbent upon everyone to discharge the obligation of Huquq. The advantages gained from this deed revert to the persons themselves. However, the acceptance of the offerings dependeth on the spirit of joy, fellowship and contentment that the righteous souls who fulfil this injunction will manifest. If such is the attitude acceptance is permissible, and not otherwise. Verily thy Lord is the All-Sufficing, the All-Praised.

18.29 Huququ'lláh is indeed a great law. It is incumbent upon all to make this offering, because it is the source of grace, abundance, and of all good. It is a bounty which shall remain with every soul in every world of the worlds of God, the All-Possessing, the All-Bountiful

18.30 May my Glory rest upon thee! Fix thy gaze upon the glory of the Cause. Speak forth that which will attract the hearts and the minds. To demand the Ḥuqúq is in no wise permissible. This command was revealed in the Book of God for various necessary matters ordained by God to be dependent upon material means. Therefore, if someone, with utmost pleasure and gladness, nay with insistence, wisheth to partake of this blessing, thou mayest accept. Otherwise, acceptance is not permissible.

18.31 According to that which is revealed in the Most Holy Book, Ḥuqúqu'lláh is fixed at the rate of 19 mithqals out of every 100 mithqals worth of gold. This applies to possessions in gold, in silver or other properties.

18.32 The Primal Point hath said that they should pay Ḥuqúqu'lláh on the value of whatsoever they possess, but notwithstanding, We have in this greatest Dispensation exempted the residence and household furnishings; that is, such furnishings as are needful.

18.33 It hath been decreed by God that a property which is not lucrative, that is, yieldeth no profit, is not subject to the payment of Ḥuqúq. Verily He is the Ordainer, the Bountiful.

18.34 The payment of the Right of God is conditional upon one's financial ability. If a person is unable to meet his obligation, God will verily excuse him. He is the All-Forgiving, the All-Generous.

18.35 The Right of God is an obligation upon everyone. This commandment hath been revealed and set down in the Book by the Pen of Glory. However, it is not permissible to solicit or demand it. If one is privileged to pay the Ḥuqúq, and doeth so in a spirit of joy and radiance, such an act is acceptable, and not otherwise. As a reminder to the friends, a general appeal should be made once at the meeting, and that should suffice. They that are assured, steadfast and endowed with insight will act spontaneously and observe what hath been prescribed by God, thereby reaping the benefit of their own deed. Verily, God is independent of all mankind.

18.36 In this day it is incumbent upon everyone to meet the obligation of the Right of God as far as it lieth in his power.

FROM THE WRITINGS AND UTTERANCES OF 'ABDU'L-BAHÁ

18.37 O my heavenly friends! It is certain and evident that the Incomparable One is always praised for His absolute wealth, distinguished for His all-embracing mercy, characterized by His eternal grace, and known for His gifts to the world of existence. Nonetheless, in accordance with His inscrutable wisdom and in order to apply a unique test to distinguish the friend from the stranger, He hath enjoined the Ḥuqúq upon His servants and made it obligatory.

Those who have observed this weighty ordinance have received heavenly blessings and in both worlds their faces have shone radiantly and their nostrils have been perfumed by the sweet savours of God's tender mercy. One of the tokens of His consummate wisdom is that the payment of the Ḥuqúq will enable the donors to become firm and steadfast and will exert a great influence on their hearts and souls. Furthermore the Ḥuqúq will be used for charitable purposes.

18.38 Thou hast enquired about the Ḥuqúq. From one's annual income, all expenses during the year are deductible, and on what is left 19% is payable to the Ḥuqúq. Thus, a person hath earned œ1,000 income out of his business. After deducting his annual expenses of say œ600, he would have a surplus of œ400 on which Ḥuqúq is payable at the rate of 19%. This would amount to œ76 to be offered for charitable purposes to the Ḥuqúq.

The Ḥuqúq is not levied on one's entire possessions each year. A person's wealth may be worth œ100,000. How can he be expected to pay Ḥuqúq on this property every year? For instance, whatever income thou hast earned in a particular year, you should deduct from it your expenses during that year. The Ḥuqúq will then be payable on the remainder. Possessions on which Ḥuqúq was paid the previous year will be exempt from further payment.

18.39 Huquq is applied on everything one possesseth. However, if a person hath paid the Huquq on a certain property, and the income from that property is equal to his needs, no Huquq is payable by that person.

Huquq is not payable on agricultural tools and equipment, and on animals used in ploughing the land, to the extent that these are necessary.

FROM THE WRITINGS AND LETTERS WRITTEN BY, OR ON BEHALF OF, SHOGHI EFFENDI

18.40 Great is the recompense that God has ordained for the true and devoted souls, the pure and detached beings who have spontaneously bequeathed a portion of their earthly possessions to the Cause of God, either during their own lifetimes or through their wills, and have had the privilege and honour of discharging their obligations to Ḥuqúqu'lláh.

Give assurance on my behalf to the donors and to the survivors of those who have ascended unto God, affirming that these efforts and donations are bound to attract divine confirmations, heavenly blessings and incalculable favours, and to promote the manifold interests of the International Bahá'í Community. Well is it with them, inasmuch as God has enabled them to fulfil that which shall elevate their stations in this world and in the world to come.

FROM THE WRITINGS AND LETTERS WRITTEN BY, OR ON BEHALF OF, THE UNIVERSAL HOUSE OF JUSTICE

18.41 The payment of the Ḥuqúqu'lláh is one of the essential spiritual obligations that the wondrous Pen of Bahá'u'lláh has laid down in the Most Holy Book.

18.42 In brief, payment of Ḥuqúqu'lláh is one of the binding spiritual responsibilities of the followers of Bahá'u'lláh and the proceeds thereof revert to the Authority in the Cause to whom all must turn. Moreover, the Ancient Beauty—magnified be His praise—has affirmed that after the establishment of the Universal House of Justice necessary rulings would be enacted in this connection in conformity with that which God has purposed, and that no one, except the Authority to which all must turn, has the right to dispose of this Fund. In other words, whatever portion of one's wealth is due to the Ḥuqúqu'lláh belongs to the World Centre of the Cause of God, not to the individuals concerned.

266 ❓ Making a Better World with the Bahá'í Faith: QUOTATIONS

CHAPTER 19:

EMPOWERING YOUTH TO RENEW OUR COMMUNITIES

268 ❓ Making a Better World with the Bahá'í Faith: QUOTATIONS

FROM THE WRITINGS OF BAHÁ'U'LLÁH

19.1 Blessed is he who in the prime of his youth and the heyday of his life will arise to serve the Cause of the Lord of the beginning and of the end, and adorn his heart with His love. The manifestation of such a grace is greater than the creation of the heavens and of the earth. Blessed are the steadfast and well is it with those who are firm.

19.2 Arise, O people, and, by the power of God's might, resolve to gain the victory over your own selves, that haply the whole earth may be freed and sanctified from its servitude to the gods of its idle fancies...

19.3 Praise be unto Thee, O my God! Thou art He Who by a word of His mouth hath revolutionized the entire creation, and by a stroke of His pen hath divided Thy servants one from another. I bear witness, O my God, that through a word spoken by Thee in this Revelation all created things were made to expire, and through yet another word all such as Thou didst wish were, by Thy grace and bounty, endued with new life.

I render Thee thanks, therefore, and extol Thee, in the name of all them that are dear to Thee, for that Thou hast caused them to be born again, by reason of the living waters which have flowed down out of the mouth of Thy will. Since Thou didst quicken them by Thy bounteousness, O my God, make them steadfastly inclined, through Thy graciousness, towards Thy will; and since Thou didst suffer them to enter into the Tabernacle of Thy Cause, grant by Thy grace that they may not be kept back from Thee.

Unlock, then, to their hearts, O my God, the portals of Thy knowledge, that they may recognize Thee as One Who is far above the reach and ken of the understanding of Thy creatures, and immeasurably exalted above the strivings of Thy people to hint at Thy nature, and may not follow every clamorous impostor that presumeth to speak in Thy name. Enable them, moreover, O my Lord, to cleave so tenaciously to Thy Cause that they may remain unmoved by the perplexing suggestions of them who, prompted by their desires, utter what hath been forbidden unto them in Thy Tablets and Thy Scriptures.

19.4   O SON OF MAN! Ponder and reflect. Is it thy wish to die upon thy bed, or to shed thy life-blood on the dust, a martyr in My path, and so become the manifestation of My command and the revealer of My light in the highest paradise? Judge thou aright, O servant!

FROM THE WRITINGS AND UTTERANCES OF 'ABDU'L-BAHÁ

19.5   O spiritual youth! Praise thou God that thou hast found thy way into the Kingdom of Splendours, and hast rent asunder the veil of vain imaginings, and that the core of the inner mystery hath been made known unto thee.

19.6   Therefore, O ye illumined youth, strive by night and by day to unravel the mysteries of the mind and spirit, and to grasp the secrets of the Day of God. Inform yourselves of the evidences that the Most Great Name hath dawned. Open your lips in praise. Adduce convincing arguments and proofs. Lead those who thirst to the fountain of life; grant ye true health to the ailing. Be ye apprentices of God; be ye physicians directed by God, and heal ye the sick among humankind. Bring those who have been excluded into the circle of intimate friends. Make the despairing to be filled with hope. Waken them that slumber; make the heedless mindful.

Such are the fruits of this earthly life. Such is the station of resplendent glory. Upon you be Baha'u'l-Abha.

19.7   Mortal charm shall fade away, roses shall give way to thorns, and beauty and youth shall live their day and be no more. But that which eternally endureth is the Beauty of the True One, for its splendour perisheth not and its glory lasteth for ever;

its charm is all-powerful and its attraction infinite. Well is it then with that countenance that reflecteth the splendour of the Light of the Beloved One! The Lord be praised, thou hast been illumined with this Light, hast acquired the pearl of true knowledge, and hast spoken the Word of Truth.

19.8 From the beginning to the end of his life man passes through certain periods, or stages, each of which is marked by certain conditions peculiar to itself. For instance, during the period of childhood his conditions and requirements are characteristic of that degree of intelligence and capacity. After a time he enters the period of youth, in which his former conditions and needs are superseded by new requirements applicable to the advance in his degree. His faculties of observation are broadened and deepened; his intelligent capacities are trained and awakened; the limitations and environment of childhood no longer restrict his energies and accomplishments. At last he passes out of the period of youth and enters the stage, or station, of maturity, which necessitates another transformation and corresponding advance in his sphere of life activity. New powers and perceptions clothe him, teaching and training commensurate with his progression occupy his mind, special bounties and bestowals descend in proportion to his increased capacities, and his former period of youth and its conditions will no longer satisfy his matured view and vision.

Similarly, there are periods and stages in the life of the aggregate world of humanity, which at one time was passing through its degree of childhood, at another its time of youth but now has entered its long presaged period of maturity, the evidences of which are everywhere visible and apparent. Therefore, the requirements and conditions of former periods have changed and merged into exigencies which distinctly characterize the present age of the world of mankind. That which was applicable to human needs during the early history of the race could neither meet nor satisfy the demands of this day and period of newness and consummation. Humanity has emerged from its former degrees of limitation and preliminary training. Man must now become imbued with new virtues and powers, new moralities, new capacities. New bounties, bestowals and perfections are awaiting and already descending upon him. The gifts and graces of the period of youth, although timely and sufficient during the adolescence of the world of mankind, are now incapable of meeting the requirements of its maturity. The playthings of childhood and infancy no longer satisfy or interest the adult mind.

19.9 O Lord! Make this youth radiant and confer Thy bounty upon this poor creature. Bestow upon him knowledge, grant him added strength at the break of every morn and guard him within the shelter of Thy protection so that he may be freed from error, may devote himself to the service of Thy Cause, may guide the wayward, lead the hapless, free the captives and awaken the heedless, that all may be blessed with Thy remembrance and praise. Thou art the Mighty and the Powerful.

FROM THE WRITINGS AND LETTERS WRITTEN BY, OR ON BEHALF OF, SHOGHI EFFENDI

19.10 The Bahá'í youth must be taught how to teach the Cause of God. Their knowledge of the fundamentals of the Faith must be deepened and the standard of their education in science and literature enhanced. They must become thoroughly familiar with the language used and the example set by 'Abdu'l-Bahá in His public addresses throughout the West. They must also be acquainted with those essential prerequisites of teaching as recorded in the Holy Books and Tablets.

19.11 I strongly urge you to devote, while you are pursuing your studies, as much time as you possibly can to a thorough study of the history and Teachings of our Beloved Cause. This is the prerequisite of a future successful career of service to the Bahá'í Faith in which I hope and pray you will distinguish yourself in the days to come.

19.12 Even though the Bahá'í Youth should feel with the condition in which they see their non-Bahá'í friends and not indict them for it, they should not let themselves be carried by the wave of world events as they are being carried. Whereas they see before them only a world that is crumbling down we are also seeing a new world being built up. Whereas they experience the destruction of old institutions that commanded their respect, we are beholding the dawn of a new era with its strict commands and new social bonds. Their materialistic outlook shows them the futility of all things while our faith in a regenerated and spiritualized man makes us look to the future and build for it. To make them follow our ways we should sympathize with their plight but should not follow their ways. We should take our stand on a higher plane of moral and spiritual life and, setting for them the true example, urge them up to our level. The young people should read what Bahá'u'lláh and the Master say on such matters and follow them conscientiously. That is if they desire to be true to the teachings and establish them throughout the world.

19.13 The Movement is in need of young people, who have been spiritually awakened, to arise and stem the tide of a material civilization that has brought mankind to the verge of ruin. Should the forces, now playing havoc with society, be let loose, should we neglect our duty to check them and bring them under our control, no man dare imagine what the future will bring.

   It is upon the young people that the greatest suffering will fall. They should, therefore, mobilize their ranks, and, with one accord, arise and consummate their task and establish the Kingdom of God upon the earth.

19.14 Life is not easy for the young people of this generation. They enter life with a heart full of hope, but find before themselves nothing but failures, and see in the future nothing but darkness. What they need is the light manifested by Bahá'u'lláh, for that brightens their soul and stimulates their vigour in facing difficulties.

19.15   The problem with which you are faced is one which concerns and seriously puzzles many of our present-day youth. How to attain spirituality is, indeed, a question to which every young man and woman must sooner or later try to find a satisfactory answer. It is precisely because no such satisfactory reply has been given or found, that modern youth finds itself bewildered, and is being consequently carried away by the materialistic forces that are so powerfully undermining the foundation of man's moral and spiritual life.

Indeed, the chief reason for the evils now rampant in society is a lack of spirituality. The materialistic civilization of our age has so much absorbed the energy and interest of mankind, that people in general no longer feel the necessity of raising themselves above the forces and conditions of their daily material existence. There is not sufficient demand for things that we should call spiritual to differentiate them from the needs and requirements of our physical existence. The universal crisis affecting mankind is, therefore, essentially spiritual its causes. The spirit of the age, taken on the whole, is irreligious. Man's outlook upon life is too crude and materialistic to enable him to elevate himself into the higher realms of the spirit.

It is this condition, so sadly morbid, into which society has fallen, that religion seeks to improve and transform. For the core of religious faith is that mystic feeling that unites man with God. This state of spiritual communion can be brought about and maintained by means of meditation and prayer. And this is the reason why Bahá'u'lláh has so much stressed the importance of worship. It is not sufficient for a believer to merely accept and observe the teachings. He should, in addition, cultivate the sense of spirituality, which he can acquire chiefly by the means of prayer. The Bahá'í Faith, like all other Divine religions, is thus fundamentally mystic in character. Its chief goal is the development of the individual and society, through the acquisition of spiritual virtues and powers. It is the soul of man that has first to be fed. And this spiritual nourishment prayer can best provide. Laws and institutions, as viewed by Bahá'u'lláh, can become really effective only when our inner spiritual life has been perfected and transformed. Otherwise religion will degenerate into a mere organization, and become a dead thing.

The believers, particularly the young ones, should therefore fully realize the necessity of praying. For prayer is absolutely indispensable to their inner spiritual development, and this, already stated, is the very foundation and purpose of the Religion of God.

19.16 The responsibility of young believers is very great, as they must not only fit themselves to inherit the work of the older Bahá'ís and carry on the affairs of the Cause in general, but the world which lies ahead of them—as promised by Bahá'u'lláh—will be a world chastened by its sufferings, ready to listen to His Divine Message at last, and consequently a very high character will be expected of the exponents of such a religion. To deepen their knowledge, to perfect themselves in the Bahá'í standards of virtue and upright conduct, should be the paramount duty of every young Bahá'í.

19.17 If the younger Bahá'í generation, in whom Shoghi Effendi has great hopes, take the pain of studying the Cause deeply and thoroughly, read its history, find its underlying principles and become both well informed and energetic, they surely can achieve a great deal. It is upon their shoulders that the Master has laid the tremendous work of teaching. They are the ones to raise the call of the Kingdom and arouse the people from slumber. If they fail the Cause is doomed to stagnation....

19.18 His hope, as well as that of the friends, is that you should increase both in number and spirituality. The future of this Cause, which is so dear to us all, depends upon the energy and devotion of the rising generation. It is you who before long will be called to shoulder its responsibilities and undertake its spread. To do that, however, you ought to be well equipped. You ought to have your intellectual as well as spiritual side equally developed....

19.19 ... the Guardian fully realizes the difficulties that stand in the way of co-operation between the young and old believers. This is a problem that confronts the Cause almost everywhere, specially in those communities where the number of young and old Bahá'ís is nearly the same. The solution, as in all such cases, is to be found through intelligent and mutual compromise. The old believers have to give up something of their old conceptions and ways of working in order to better adapt themselves to the changing social conditions and circumstances. The young too must learn to act with wisdom, tact and moderation, and to take advantage and benefit from the age-long experience of their older fellow-believers. The old and the young have each something specific to contribute to the progress and welfare of the Bahá'í community The energy of youth should be tempered and guided by the wisdom of old age.'

19.20 If ever it could be said that a religion belonged to the youth, then surely the Bahá'í Faith today is that religion. The whole world is suffering, it is sunk in misery, crushed beneath its heavy problems. The task of healing its ills and building up its future devolves mainly upon the youth. They are the generation who, after the war, will have to solve the terrible difficulties created by the war and all that brought it about. And they will not be able to upbuild the future except by the laws and principles laid down by Bahá'u'lláh. So their task is very great and their responsibility very grave.

19.21 Being a Bahá'í you are certainly aware of the fact that Bahá'u'lláh considered education as one of the most fundamental factors of a true civilization. This education, however, in order to be adequate and fruitful, should be comprehensive in nature and should take into consideration not only the physical and the intellectual side of man but also his spiritual and ethical aspects. This should be the programme of the Bahá'í youth all over the world.

And no doubt the best means through which this educational development can be attained is by joining the different associations and gatherings which intend to promote the ideals of this new international civilization. Although the Guardian prefers that Bahá'ís should join those associations which are within the orbit of Bahá'í activities, he nevertheless approves and even encourages any person who would like to join any non-Bahá'í movements, provided that these movements will not promote any ideal or principle which will harm and check the advance of the Cause.

19.22 It is on young and active Bahá'ís, like you, that the Guardian centers all his hopes for the future progress and expansion of the Cause, and it is on their shoulders that he lays the responsibility for the upkeep of the spirit of selfless service among their fellow-believers. Without that spirit no work can be successfully achieved. With it triumph, though hardly won, is but inevitable. You should therefore, try all your best to carry aflame within you the torch of faith, for through it you will surely find guidance, strength and eventual success.

...every one of them is able, in his own measure, to deliver the Message ... Everyone is a potential teacher. He has only to use what God has given him and thus prove that he is faithful to his trust.

19.23 The youth should be encouraged to train themselves in public speaking while they are still pursuing their studies in schools or colleges.

19.24 He urges you to make up your minds to do great, great deeds for the Faith; the condition of the world is steadily growing worse, and your generation must provide the saints, heroes, martyrs and administrators of future years. With dedication and will power you can rise to great heights.

FROM THE WRITINGS AND LETTERS WRITTEN BY, OR ON BEHALF OF, THE UNIVERSAL HOUSE OF JUSTICE

19.25 Indeed, let them welcome with confidence the challenges awaiting them. Imbued with this excellence and a corresponding humility, with tenacity and a loving servitude, today's youth must move towards the front ranks of the professions, trades, arts and crafts which are necessary to the further progress of humankind—this to ensure that the spirit of the Cause will cast its illumination on all these important areas of human endeavor. Moreover, while aiming at mastering the unifying concepts and swiftly advancing technologies of this era of communications, they can, indeed they must also guarantee the transmittal to the future of those skills which will preserve the marvelous, indispensable achievements of the past. The transformation which is to occur in the functioning of society will certainly depend to a great extent on the effectiveness of the preparations the youth make for the world they will inherit.

19.26 For any person, whether Bahá'í or not, his youthful years are those in which he will make many decisions which will set the course of his life. In these years he is most likely to choose his life's work, complete his education, begin to earn his own living, marry, and start to raise his own family. Most important of all, it is during this period that the mind is most questing and that the spiritual values that will guide the person's future behaviour are adopted. These factors present Bahá'í youth with their greatest opportunities, their greatest challenge, and their greatest tests—opportunities to truly apprehend the Teachings of their Faith and to give them to their contemporaries, challenges to overcome the pressures of the world and to provide leadership for their and succeeding generations, and tests enabling them to exemplify in their lives the high moral standards set forth in the Bahá'í Writings. Indeed the Guardian wrote of the Bahá'í youth that it is they who can contribute so decisively to the virility, the purity, and the driving force of the life of the Bahá'í community, and upon whom must depend the future orientation of its destiny, and the complete unfoldment of the potentialities with which God has endowed it'. "When studying at school or university Bahá'í youth will often find themselves in the unusual and slightly embarrassing position of having a more profound insight into a subject than their instructors. The Teachings of Bahá'u'lláh throw light on so many aspects of human life and knowledge that a Bahá'í must learn, earlier than most, to weigh the information that is given to him rather than to accept it blindly. A Bahá'í has the advantage of the Divine Revelation for this Age, which shines like a searchlight on so many problems that baffle modern thinkers; he must therefore develop the ability to learn everything from those around him, showing proper humility before his teachers, but always relating what he hears to the Bahá'í teachings, for they will enable him to sort out the gold from the dross of human error.

19.27 We sincerely hope that the forefront of the volunteers, the Bahá'í youth will arise for the sake of God and, through their driving force, their ability to endure inhospitable and arduous conditions, and their contentment with the bare necessities of life, they will offer an inspiring example to the peoples and communities they set out to serve, will exert an abiding influence on their personal lives, and will promote with distinction the vital interest of God's Cause at this crucial stage in the fortunes of the Plan.

19.28 Three great fields of service lie open before young Bahá'ís, in which they will simultaneously be remaking the character of human society and preparing themselves for the work they can undertake later in their lives.

First, the foundation of all their accomplishments, is their study of the teachings, the spiritualization of their lives, and the forming of their characters in accordance with the standards of Bahá'u'lláh. As the moral standards of the people around us collapse and decay, whether of the centuries-old civilizations of the East, the more recent cultures of Christendom and Islam, or of the rapidly changing tribal societies of the world, the Bahá'ís must increasingly stand out as pillars of righteousness and forbearance. The life of a Bahá'í will be characterized by truthfulness and decency; he will walk uprightly among his fellowmen, dependent upon none save God, yet linked by bonds of love and brotherhood with mankind; he will be entirely detached from the loose standards, the decadent theories, the frenetic experimentation, the desperation of present-day society, will look upon his neighbors with a bright and friendly face, and be a beacon light and haven for all those who would emulate his strength of character and assurance of soul.

The second field of service, which is linked intimately with the first, is teaching the Faith, particularly to their fellow youth, among whom are some of the most open and seeking minds in the world. Not yet having acquired all the responsibilities of a family or a long-established home and job, youth can the more easily choose where they will live and study or work. In the world at large young people travel hither and thither seeking amusement, education, and experiences. Bahá'í youth, bearing the incomparable treasure of the Word of God for this Day, can harness this mobility into service for mankind and can choose their places of residence, their areas of travel, and their types of work with the goal in mind of how they can best serve the Faith.

The third field of service is the preparation by youth for their later years. It is the obligation of a Bahá'í to educate his children; likewise it is the duty of the children to acquire knowledge of the arts and sciences and to learn a trade or a profession whereby they, in turn, can earn their living and support their families. This, for a Bahá'í youth, is in itself a service to God, a service, moreover, which can be combined with teaching the Faith and often with pioneering. The Bahá'í community will need men and women of many skills and qualifications; for, as it grows in size the sphere of its activities in the life of society will increase and diversify. Let Bahá'í youth, therefore, consider the best ways in which they can use and develop their native abilities for the service of mankind and the Cause of God, whether this be as farmers, teachers, doctors, artisans, musicians, or any one of the multitude of livelihoods that are open to them.

CHAPTER 20:

ENSURING UNITY OF OUR COMMUNITY WITHIN THE COVENANT

FROM THE WRITINGS OF BAHÁ'U'LLÁH

20.1 The first duty prescribed by God for His servants is the recognition of Him Who is the Day Spring of His Revelation and the Fountain of His laws, Who representeth the Godhead in both the Kingdom of His Cause and the world of creation. Whoso achieveth this duty hath attained unto all good; and whoso is deprived thereof, hath gone astray, though he be the author of every righteous deed. It behoveth every one who reacheth this most sublime station, this summit of transcendent glory, to observe every ordinance of Him Who is the Desire of the world. These twin duties are inseparable. Neither is acceptable without the other. Thus hath it been decreed by Him Who is the Source of Divine inspiration.

They whom God hath endued with insight will readily recognize that the precepts laid down by God constitute the highest means for the maintenance of order in the world and the security of its peoples. He that turneth away from them, is accounted among the abject and foolish. We, verily, have commanded you to refuse the dictates of your evil passions and corrupt desires, and not to transgress the bounds which the Pen of the Most High hath fixed, for these are the breath of life unto all created things. The seas of Divine wisdom and divine utterance have risen under the breath of the breeze of the All-Merciful. Hasten to drink your fill, O men of understanding! They that have violated the Covenant of God by breaking His commandments, and have turned back on their heels, these have erred grievously in the sight of God, the All-Possessing, the Most High.

20.2 Follow not, therefore, your earthly desires, and violate not the Covenant of God, nor break your pledge to Him. With firm determination, with the whole affection of your heart, and with the full force of your words, turn ye unto Him, and walk not in the ways of the foolish.... Break not the bond that uniteth you with your Creator, and be not of those that have erred and strayed from His ways....

20.3   The days of your life are far spent, O people, and your end is fast approaching. Put away, therefore, the things ye have devised and to which ye cleave, and take firm hold on the precepts of God, that haply ye may attain that which He hath purposed for you, and be of them that pursue a right course. Delight not yourselves in the things of the world and its vain ornaments, neither set your hopes on them. Let your reliance be on the remembrance of God, the Most Exalted, the Most Great. He will, erelong, bring to naught all the things ye possess. Let Him be your fear, and forget not His covenant with you, and be not of them that are shut out as by a veil from Him.

20.4   Whoso layeth claim to a Revelation direct from God, ere the expiration of a full thousand years, such a man is assuredly a lying imposter.... Should a man appear, ere the lapse of a full thousand years—each year consisting of twelve months according to the Qur'án, and of nineteen months of nineteen days each, according to the Bayan—and if such a man reveal to your eyes all the signs of God, unhesitatingly reject him!

FROM THE WRITINGS AND UTTERANCES OF 'ABDU'L-BAHÁ

20.5   The sacred and youthful branch, the guardian of the Cause of God as well as the Universal House of Justice, to be universally elected and established, are both under the care and protection of the Abha Beauty, under the shelter and unerring guidance of His Holiness, the Exalted One (may my life be offered up for them both). Whatsoever they decide is of God. Whoso obeyeth him not, neither obeyeth them, hath not obeyed God; whoso rebelleth against him and against them hath rebelled against God; whoso opposeth him hath opposed God; whoso contendeth with them hath contended with God; whoso disputeth with him hath disputed with God; whoso denieth him hath denied God; whoso disbelieveth in him hath disbelieved in God; whoso deviateth, separateth himself and turneth aside from him hath in truth deviated, separated himself and turned aside from God.

20.6 Inasmuch as great differences and divergences of denominational belief had arisen throughout the past, every man with a new idea attributing it to God, Bahá'u'lláh desired that there should not be any ground or reason for disagreement among the Bahá'ís. Therefore, with His own pen He wrote the Book of His Covenant, addressing His relations and all people of the world, saying, "Verily, I have appointed One Who is the Center of My Covenant. All must obey Him; all must turn to Him; He is the Expounder of My Book, and He is informed of My purpose. All must turn to Him. Whatsoever He says is correct, for, verily, He knoweth the texts of My Book. Other than He, no one doth know My Book." The purpose of this statement is that there should never be discord and divergence among the Bahá'ís but that they should always be unified and agreed…. Therefore, whosoever obeys the Center of the Covenant appointed by Bahá'u'lláh has obeyed Bahá'u'lláh, and whosoever disobeys Him has disobeyed Bahá'u'lláh….

Beware! Beware! lest anyone should speak from the authority of his own thoughts or create a new thing out of himself. Beware! Beware! According to the explicit Covenant of Bahá'u'lláh you should care nothing at all for such a person. Bahá'u'lláh shuns such souls.

20.7 As to the most great characteristic of the revelation of Bahá'u'lláh, a specific teaching not given by any of the Prophets of the past: It is the ordination and appointment of the Center of the Covenant. By this appointment and provision He has safeguarded and protected the religion of God against differences and schisms, making it impossible for anyone to create a new sect or faction of belief.

20.8 … Bahá'u'lláh covenanted, not that I ('Abdu'l-Bahá) am the Promised One, but that 'Abdu'l-Bahá is the Expounder of the Book and the Centre of His Covenant, and that the Promised One of Bahá'u'lláh will appear after one thousand or thousands of years. This is the Covenant which Bahá'u'lláh made. If a person shall deviate, he is not acceptable at the Threshold of Bahá'u'lláh. In case of differences, 'Abdu'l-Bahá must be consulted. They must revolve around his good pleasure. After 'Abdu'l-Bahá, whenever the Universal House of Justice is organized it will ward off differences.

20.9 And it is a basic principle of the Law of God that in every Prophetic Mission, He entereth into a Covenant with all believers—a Covenant that endureth until the end of that Mission, until the promised day when the Personage stipulated at the outset of the Mission is made manifest. Consider Moses, He Who conversed with God. Verily, upon Mount Sinai, Moses entered into a Covenant regarding the Messiah, with all those souls who would live in the day of the Messiah. And those souls, although they appeared many centuries after Moses, were nevertheless—so far as the Covenant, which is outside time, was concerned—present there with Moses. The Jews, however, were heedless of this and remembered it not, and thus they suffered a great and clear loss.

20.10 Centuries, nay, countless ages, must pass away ere the Day-Star of Truth shineth again in its mid-summer splendor, or appeareth once more in the radiance of its vernal glory... Concerning the Manifestations that will come down in the future "in the shadows of the clouds," know, verily, that in so far as their relation to the Source of their inspiration is concerned, they are under the shadow of the Ancient Beauty. In their relation, however, to the age in which they appear, each and every one of them "doeth whatsoever He willeth."

20.11 Abraham, on Him be peace, made a covenant concerning Moses and gave the glad-tidings of His coming. Moses made a covenant concerning the promised Christ, and announced the good news of His advent to the world. Christ made a covenant concerning the Paraclete and gave the tidings of His coming. The Prophet Muhammad made a covenant concerning the Báb, and the Báb was the One promised by Muhammad, for Muhammad gave the tidings of His coming. The Báb made a Covenant concerning the Blessed Beauty, Bahá'u'lláh, and gave the glad-tidings of His coming for the Blessed Beauty was the One promised by the Báb. Bahá'u'lláh made a covenant concerning a Promised One Who will become manifest after one thousand or thousands of years. That Manifestation is Bahá'u'lláh's Promised One, and will appear after a thousand or thousands of years. He, moreover, with His Supreme

Pen, entered into a great Covenant and Testament with all the Bahá'ís whereby they were all commanded to follow the Centre of the Covenant after His ascension, and depart, not even to a hair's breadth, from obeying Him.

20.12 In the Book of the Covenant Bahá'u'lláh declares that by these two verses this Personage is meant. In all His Books and Tablets He has praised those who are firm in the Covenant and rebuked those who are not. He said, "Verily, shun those who are shaken in the Covenant. Verily, God is the Confirmer of the firm ones." In His prayers He has said, "O God! Render those who are firm in the Covenant blessed, and degrade those who are not. O God! Be the Protector of him who protecteth Him, and confirm him who confirms the Center of the Covenant." Many utterances are directed against the violators of the Covenant, the purpose being that no dissension should arise in the blessed Cause; that no one should say, "My opinion is this"; and that all may know Who is the authoritative expounder and whatsoever He says is correct. Bahá'u'lláh has not left any possible room for dissension. Naturally, there are some who are antagonistic, some who are followers of self-desire, others who hold to their own ideas and still others who wish to create dissension in the Cause. For example, Judas Iscariot was one of the disciples, yet he betrayed Christ. Such a thing has happened in the past, but in this day the Blessed Perfection has declared, "This person is the expounder of My Book and all must turn to Him." The purpose is to ward off dissension and differences among His followers. Notwithstanding this safeguard and provision against disagreement, there are certain souls here in America and a few in 'Akká who have violated this explicit command. For twenty years these violators have accomplished nothing. Have they accomplished anything in Chicago? The friends here must be like the friends in San Francisco. Whenever they sense the least violation from anyone, they should say, "Begone! You shall not associate with us."

FROM THE WRITINGS AND LETTERS WRITTEN BY, OR ON BEHALF OF, SHOGHI EFFENDI

20.13 To direct and canalize these forces let loose by this Heaven-sent process, and to insure their harmonious and continuous operation after His ascension, an instrument divinely ordained, invested with indisputable authority, organically linked with the Author of the Revelation Himself, was clearly indispensable. That instrument Bahá'u'lláh had expressly provided through the institution of the Covenant, an institution which he had firmly established prior to His ascension. This same Covenant He had anticipated in His Kitáb-i-Aqdas, had alluded to it as He bade His last farewell to the members of His family, who had been summoned to His bed-side, in the days immediately preceding His ascension, and had incorporated it in a special document which He designated as "the Book of My Covenant," and which He entrusted, during His last illness, to His eldest son 'Abdu'l-Bahá.

  Written entirely in His own hand ... this unique and epoch-making Document, designated by Bahá'u'lláh as His "Most Great Tablet," and alluded to by Him as the "Crimson Book" in His "Epistle to the Son of the Wolf," can find no parallel in the Scriptures of any previous Dispensation, not excluding that of the Báb Himself. For nowhere in the books pertaining to any of the world's religious systems, not even among the writings of the Author of the Bábí Revelation, do we find any single document establishing a Covenant endowed with an authority comparable to the Covenant which Bahá'u'lláh had Himself instituted.

20.14 ... it is made indubitably clear and evident that the Guardian of the Faith has been made the Interpreter of the Word and that the Universal House of Justice has been invested with the function of legislating on matters not expressly revealed in the teachings. The interpretation of the Guardian, functioning within his own sphere, is as authoritative and binding as the enactments of the International House of Justice, whose exclusive right and prerogative is to pronounce upon and deliver the final judgment on such laws and ordinances as Bahá'u'lláh has not expressly revealed. Neither can, nor will ever, infringe upon the sacred and prescribed domain of the other. Neither will seek to curtail the specific and undoubted authority with which both have been divinely invested.

20.15 People who have withdrawn from the Cause because they no longer feel that they can support its Teachings and Institutions sincerely, are not Covenant-breakers—they are non-Bahá'ís and should just be treated as such. Only those who ally themselves actively with known enemies of the Faith who are Covenant-breakers, and who attack the Faith in the same spirit as these people, can be considered, themselves, to be Covenant-breakers. As you know, up to the present time, no one has been permitted to pronounce anybody a Covenant-breaker but the Guardian[1] himself.
[1 Now the Universal House of Justice]

20.16 ... Covenant Breaking is truly a Spiritual disease, and the whole view-point and attitude of a Covenant Breaker is so poisonous that the Master likened it to leprosy, and warned the friends to breathe the same air was dangerous. This should not be taken literally; He meant when you are close enough to breathe the same air you are close enough to contact their corrupting influence. Your sister should never imagine she, loyal and devoted, has become a 'carrier'.

20.17 Regarding Mr. ... question about the Covenant-breakers, Bahá'u'lláh and the Master in many places and very emphatically have told us to shun entirely all Covenant-breakers as they are afflicted with what we might try and define as a contagious spiritual disease; they have also told us, however, to pray for them. These souls are not lost forever. In the Aqdas, Bahá'u'lláh says that God will forgive Mirza Yahya if he repents. It follows, therefore, that God will forgive any soul if he repents. Most of them don't want to repent, unfortunately. If the leaders can be forgiven it goes without saying that their followers can also be forgiven. "Also, it has nothing to do with unity in the Cause; if a man cuts a cancer out of his body to preserve his health and very life, no one would suggest that for the sake of unity it should be reintroduced into the otherwise healthy organism. On the contrary, what was once a part of him has so radically changed as to have become a poison.

20.18 Ex-communication is a spiritual thing ... Only actual enemies of the Cause are ex-communicated. On the other hand, those who conspicuously disgrace the Faith or refuse to abide by its laws can be deprived, as a punishment, of their voting rights; this in itself is a severe action, and he therefore always urges all National Assemblies (who can take such action) to first warn and repeatedly warn the evil-doer before taking the step of depriving him of his voting rights. He feels your Assembly must act with the greatest wisdom in such matters, and only impose this sanction if a believer is seriously injuring the Faith in the eyes of the public through his conduct or flagrantly breaking the laws of God. If such a sanction were lightly used the friends would come to attach no importance to it, or to feel the N.S.A. used it every time they got angry with some individual's disobedience to them. We must always remember that, sad and often childish as it seems, some of those who make the worst nuisances of themselves to their National Bodies are often very loyal believers, who think they are protecting the true interests of their Faith by attacking N.S.A. decisions!

20.19 With regard to avoiding association with declared Covenant-breakers. Shoghi Effendi says that this does not mean that if one or more of these attends a non-Bahá'í meeting any Bahá'ís present should feel compelled to leave the meeting or to refuse to take part in the meeting, especially if that part has been prearranged. Also if in the course of some business it should become necessary to negotiate with one of these people, in order to clear up the business, that is permissible, provided the association is confined to the matter of the business in hand. It is different if one of these people should come to Bahá'í meetings. Then it would become necessary to ask him in a most tactful and dignified way to leave the meeting as Bahá'ís are forbidden to associate with him.

20.20 ... we believe that God's Mercy exceeds His Justice, and that through the repentance of a soul, the prayers and supplications of other souls, and the goodness of God, even a person who has passed away in great spiritual darkness can be forgiven, educated spiritually in the next world and progress.

20.21 Probably no group of people in the world have softer tongues, or proclaim more loudly their innocence, then those who in their heart of hearts, and by their every act, are enemies of the Center of the Covenant. The Master well knew this, and that is why He said we must shun their company, but pray for them. If you put a leper in a room with healthy people, he cannot catch their health; on the contrary they are very likely to catch his horrible ailment.

20.22 ... the believers need to be deepened in their knowledge and appreciation of the Covenants of both Bahá'u'lláh and 'Abdu'l-Bahá. This is the stronghold of the faith of every Bahá'í, and that which enables him to withstand every test and the attacks of the enemies outside the Faith, and the far more dangerous, insidious, lukewarm people inside the Faith who have no real attachment to the Covenant, and consequently uphold the intellectual aspect of the teachings while at the same time undermining the spiritual foundation upon which the whole Cause of God rests.

 He feels you and your dear family should do all you can do to teach the believers the Will and Testament and to strengthen their understanding of its important provisions; for all the authority of the administrative bodies, as well as of the Guardian himself, is mainly derived from this tremendous document.

FROM THE WRITINGS AND LETTERS WRITTEN BY, OR ON BEHALF OF, THE UNIVERSAL HOUSE OF JUSTICE

20.23 A Covenant in the religious sense is a binding agreement between God and man, whereby God requires of man certain behaviour in return for which He guarantees certain blessings, or whereby He gives man certain bounties in return for which He takes from those who accept them an undertaking to behave in a certain way. There is, for example, the Greater Covenant which every Manifestation of God makes with His followers, promising that in the fulness of time a new Manifestation will be sent, and taking from them the undertaking to accept Him when this occurs. There is also the Lesser Covenant that a Manifestation of God makes with His followers that they will accept His appointed successor after Him. If they do so, the Faith can remain united and pure. If not, the Faith becomes divided and its force spent. It is a Covenant of this kind that Bahá'u'lláh made with His followers regarding 'Abdu'l-Bahá and that 'Abdu'l-Bahá perpetuated through the Administrative Order...

20.24 ...There is, though, a great difference between this and previous Dispensations, for Bahá'u'lláh has written that this is "the Day which shall not be followed by night." ("God Passes By", p. 245). He has given us His Covenant which provides for a continuing centre of divine guidance in the world. The Bahá'í Faith has not lacked for ambitious men who would seize the reins of authority and distort the Faith for their own ends, but in every case they have broken themselves and dashed their hopes on the rock of the Covenant.

20.25 To read the writings of Covenant-breakers is not forbidden to the believers and does not constitute in itself an act of Covenant-breaking. Indeed, some of the Bahá'ís have the unpleasant duty to read such literature as part of their responsibilities for protecting the Cause of Bahá'u'lláh. However, the friends are warned in the strongest terms against reading such literature because Covenant- breaking is a spiritual poison and the calumnies and distortions of the truth which the Covenant-breakers give out are such that they can undermine the faith of the believer and plant the seeds of doubt unless he is fore-armed with an unshakable belief in Bahá'u'lláh and His Covenant and a knowledge of the true facts. "Personal relations with Covenant-breakers, however, such as personal contact or entering into correspondence with one is strictly forbidden. In this connection, however, it is important to remember two qualifications: "First, the civil rights of Covenant-breakers must be scrupulously upheld. For example, if a Bahá'í owes a debt to a person who breaks the Covenant he must be sure that it is repaid and that his obligations are met. "Secondly, although the believers are required to avoid, if possible, all contact with Covenant-breakers it sometimes happens that contact on business matters cannot be avoided. For example, in one city the head of the rate collection department was a Covenant-breaker. In such situations the believers should restrict their contact with the Covenant-breaker to a purely formal business level and to an absolute minimum.

20.26 At the time of our beloved Shoghi Effendi's death it was evident, from the circumstances and from the explicit requirements of the Holy Texts[1], that it had been impossible for him to appoint a successor in accordance with the provisions of the Will and Testament of 'Abdu'l-Bahá....

[1 Shoghi Effendi had no children and all the surviving Aghsan had broken the Covenant.]

20.27 ... under the Covenant of God, Shoghi Effendi was, during his ministry as Guardian of the Cause, the point of authority in the Faith to which all were to turn... The same thing applies to the position occupied by the Universal House of Justice in its relationship to the friends.

20.28 The Universal House of Justice, which the Guardian said would be regarded by posterity as "the last refuge of a tottering civilization," is now, in the absence of the Guardian, the sole infallibly guided institution in the world to which all must turn, and on it rests the responsibility for ensuring the unity and progress of the Cause of God in accordance with the revealed Word.

20.29 The Covenant of Bahá'u'lláh is unbroken, its all-encompassing power inviolate. The two unique features which distinguish it from all religious covenants of the past are unchanged and operative. The revealed Word, in its original purity, amplified by the divinely guided interpretations of 'Abdu'l-Bahá and Shoghi Effendi, remains immutable, unadulterated by any man-made creeds or dogmas, unwarrantable inferences, or unauthorized interpretations. The channel of Divine guidance, providing flexibility in all the affairs of mankind, remains open through that institution which was founded by Bahá'u'lláh and endowed by Him with supreme authority and unfailing guidance, and of which the Master wrote: "Unto this body all things must be referred." How clearly we can see the truth of Bahá'u'lláh's assertion: "The Hand of Omnipotence hath established His Revelation upon an enduring foundation. Storms of human strife are powerless to undermine its basis, nor will men's fanciful theories succeed in damaging its structure."

CHAPTER 21:

EXPLORING THE WORLD IN SERVICE TO HUMANITY

FROM THE WRITINGS OF BAHÁ'U'LLÁH

21.1 They that have forsaken their country for the purpose of teaching Our Cause—these shall the Faithful Spirit strengthen through its power. A company of Our chosen angels shall go forth with them, as bidden by Him Who is the Almighty, the All-Wise. How great the blessedness that awaiteth him that hath attained the honor of serving the Almighty! By My life! No act, however great, can compare with it, except such deeds as have been ordained by God, the All-Powerful, the Most Mighty. Such a service is, indeed, the prince of all goodly deeds, and the ornament of every goodly act. Thus hath it been ordained by Him Who is the Sovereign Revealer, the Ancient of Days.

21.2 Whoso ariseth to teach Our Cause must needs detach himself from all earthly things, and regard, at all times, the triumph of Our Faith as his supreme objective. This hath, verily, been decreed in the Guarded Tablet. And when he determineth to leave his home, for the sake of the Cause of his Lord, let him put his whole trust in God, as the best provision for his journey, and array himself with the robe of virtue. Thus hath it been decreed by God, the Almighty, the All-Praised.

If he be kindled with the fire of His love, if he forgoeth all created things, the words he uttereth shall set on fire them that hear him. Verily, thy Lord is the Omniscient, the All-Informed. Happy is the man that hath heard Our voice, and answered Our call. He, in truth, is of them that shall be brought nigh unto Us.

21.3 Center your energies in the propagation of the Faith of God. Whoso is worthy of so high a calling, let him arise and promote it. Whoso is unable, it is his duty to appoint him who will, in his stead, proclaim this Revelation, whose power hath caused the foundations of the mightiest structures to quake, every mountain to be crushed into dust, and every soul to be dumbfounded. Should the greatness of this Day be revealed in its fullness, every man would forsake a myriad lives in his longing to partake, though it be for one moment, of its great glory—how much more this world and its corruptible treasures!

21.4 ... whosoever ariseth to aid our Cause God will render him victorious over ten times ten thousand souls, and, should he wax in his love for Me, him will We cause to triumph over all that is in heaven and all that is on earth.

21.5 Whensoever ye be invited to a banquet or festive occasion, respond with joy and gladness, and whoever fulfilleth his promise will be safe from reproof.

21.6 Be unrestrained as the wind, while carrying the Message of Him Who hath caused the Dawn of Divine Guidance to break. Consider, how the wind, faithful to that which God hath ordained, bloweth upon all the regions of the earth, be they inhabited or desolate. Neither the sight of desolation, nor the evidences of prosperity, can either pain or please it. It bloweth in every direction, as bidden by its Creator. So should be every one that claimeth to be a lover of the one true God. It behoveth him to fix his gaze upon the fundamentals of His Faith, and to labor diligently for its propagation. Wholly for the sake of God he should proclaim His Message, and with that same spirit accept whatever response his words may evoke in his hearer. He who shall accept and believe, shall receive his reward; and he who shall turn away, shall receive none other than his own punishment.

FROM THE WRITINGS AND UTTERANCES OF 'ABDU'L-BAHÁ

21.7 O ye lovers of God! Make firm your steps; fulfil your pledge to one another; go forth in harmony to scatter abroad the sweet savours of God's love, and to establish His Teachings, until ye breathe a soul into the dead body of this world, and bring true healing in the physical and spiritual realms to everyone who aileth.

21.8 O ye homeless and wanderers in the Path of God! Prosperity, contentment, and freedom, however much desired and conducive to the gladness of the human heart, can in no wise compare with the trials of homelessness and adversity in the pathway of God for such exile and banishment are blessed by the divine favour, and are surely followed by the mercy of Providence. The joy of tranquillity in one's home, and the sweetness of freedom from all cares shall pass away, whilst the blessings of homelessness shall endure forever, and its far-reaching results shall be made manifest.

Abraham's migration from His native land caused bountiful gifts of the All-Glorious to be made manifest, and the setting of canaan's brightest star unfolded to the eyes the radiance of Joseph. The flight of Moses, the Prophet of Sinai, revealed the Flame of the Lord's burning Fire, and the rise of Jesus breathed the breaths of the Holy Spirit into to the world. The departure of Muhammad, the Beloved of God, from the city of His birth was the cause of the exaltation of God's Holy Word, and the banishment of the Sacred Beauty led to the diffusion of the light of His divine Revelation throughout all regions. "Take ye good heed, O people of insight!"

21.9 Should one of them turn his face toward some direction and summon the people to the Kingdom of God, all the ideal forces and lordly confirmations will rush to his support and reinforcement.

21.10 Either travel yourselves, personally, throughout those states or choose others and send them, so that they may teach the souls.

21.11 Thou hast the desire to travel that thou mayest spread the fragrances of God. This is highly suitable. Assuredly divine confirmations will assist thee and the power of the Covenant and Testament will secure for thee triumph and victory.

21.12 O phoenix of that immortal flame kindled in the sacred Tree! Bahá'u'lláh—may my life, my soul, my spirit be offered up as a sacrifice unto His lowly servants—hath, during His last days on earth, given the most emphatic promise that, through the outpourings of the grace of God and the aid and assistance vouchsafed from His Kingdom on high, souls will arise and holy beings appear who, as stars, would adorn the firmament of divine guidance; illumine the dayspring of loving-kindness and bounty; manifest the signs of the unity of God; shine with the light of sanctity and purity; receive their full measure of divine inspiration; raise high the sacred torch of faith; stand firm as the rock and immoveable as the mountain; and grow to become luminaries in the heavens of His Revelation, mighty channels of His grace, means for the bestowal of God's bountiful care, heralds calling forth the name of the One true God, and establishers of the world's supreme foundation.

These shall labour ceaselessly, by day and by night, shall heed neither trials nor woe, shall suffer no respite in their efforts, shall seek no repose, shall disregard all ease and comfort, and, detached and unsullied, shall consecrate every fleeting moment of their lives to the diffusion of the divine fragrance and the exaltation of God's holy Word. Their faces will radiate heavenly gladness, and their hearts be filled with joy. Their souls will be inspired, and their foundation stand secure. They shall scatter in the world, and travel throughout all regions. They shall raise their voices in every assembly, and adorn and revive every gathering. They shall speak in every tongue, and interpret every hidden meaning. They shall reveal the mysteries of the Kingdom, and manifest unto everyone the signs of God. They shall burn brightly even as a candle in the heart of every assembly, and beam forth as a star upon every horizon. The gentle breezes wafted from the garden of their hearts shall perfume and revive the souls of men, and the revelations of their minds, even as showers, will reinvigorate the peoples and nations of the world.

I am waiting, eagerly waiting for these holy ones to appear; and yet, how long will they delay their coming? My prayer and ardent supplication, at eventide and at dawn, is that these shining stars may soon shed their radiance upon the world, that their sacred countenances may be unveiled to mortal eyes, that the hosts of divine assistance may achieve their victory, and the billows of grace, rising from His oceans above, may flow upon all mankind. Pray ye also and supplicate unto Him that through the bountiful aid of the Ancient Beauty these souls may be unveiled to the eyes of the world.

21.13 O that I could travel, even though on foot and in the utmost poverty, to these regions, and, raising the call of "Ya Baha'u'l-Abha" in cities, villages, mountains, deserts and oceans, promote the divine teachings! This, alas, I cannot do. How intensely I deplore it! Please God, ye may achieve it.

FROM THE WRITINGS AND LETTERS WRITTEN BY, OR ON BEHALF OF, SHOGHI EFFENDI

21.14 Nor should any of the pioneers, at this early stage in the upbuilding of Bahá'í national communities, overlook the fundamental prerequisite for any successful teaching enterprise, which is to adapt the presentation of the fundamental backgrounds, the ideologies, and the temperament of the divers races and nations whom they are called upon to enlighten and attract. The susceptibilities of these races and nations, from both the northern and southern climes, springing from either the Germanic or Latin stock, belonging to either the Catholic or Protestant communion, some democratic, others totalitarian in outlook, some socialistic, others capitalistic in their tendencies, differing widely in their customs and standards of living, should at all times be carefully considered, and under no circumstances neglected.

These pioneers, in their contact with the members of divers creeds, races and nations, covering a range which offers no parallel in either the north or south continents, must neither antagonize them nor compromise with their own essential principles. They must be neither provocative nor supine, neither fanatical nor excessively liberal, in their exposition of the fundamental and distinguishing features of their Faith. They must be either wary or bold, they must act swiftly or mark time, they must use the direct or indirect method, they must be challenging or conciliatory, in strict accordance with the spiritual receptivity of the soul with whom they come in contact, whether he be a nobleman or a commoner, a northerner or a southerner, a layman or a priest, a capitalist or a socialist, a statesman or a prince, an artisan or a beggar. In their presentation of the Message of Bahá'u'lláh they must neither hesitate nor falter. They must be neither contemptuous of the poor nor timid before the great. In their exposition of its verities they must neither overstress nor whittle down the truth which they champion, whether they hearer belong to royalty, or be a prince of the church, or a politician, or a tradesman, or a man of the street. To all alike, high or low, rich or poor, they must proffer, with open hands, with a radiant heart, with an eloquent tongue, with infinite patience, with uncompromising loyalty, with great wisdom, with unshakable courage, the Cup of Salvation at so critical an hour, to the confused, the hungry, the distraught and fear-stricken multitudes, in the north, in the west, in the south and in the heart, of that sorely tried continent.

21.15 I am moved, at this juncture, as I am reminded of the share which, ever since the inception of the Faith in the West, the handmaidens of Bahá'u'lláh, as distinguished from the men, have had in opening up, single-handed, so many, such diversified, and widely-scattered countries over the whole surface of the globe, not only to pay a tribute to such apostolic fervor as is truly reminiscent of those heroic men who were responsible for the birth of the Faith of Bahá'u'lláh, but also to stress the significance of such a preponderating share which the women of the West have had and are having in the establishment of His Faith throughout the whole world. 'Among the miracles,' 'Abdu'l-Bahá Himself has testified, 'which distinguish this sacred Dispensation is this, that women have evinced a greater boldness than men when enlisted in the ranks of the Faith.' So great and splendid a testimony applies in particular to the West, and though it has received thus far abundant and convincing confirmation must, as the years roll away, be further reinforced, as the American believers usher in the most glorious phase of their teaching activities under the Seven Year Plan. The 'boldness' which, in the words of 'Abdu'l-Bahá, has characterized their accomplishments in the past must suffer no eclipse as they stand on the threshold of still greater and nobler accomplishments. Nay rather, it must, in the course of time and throughout the length and breadth of the vast and virgin territories of Latin America, be more convincingly demonstrated, and win for the beloved Cause victories more stirring than any it has as yet achieved.

21.16 For over thirty years, with an enlarged heart, and many other ailments, she remained at her post in Bulgaria. Never well-to-do, she often suffered actual poverty and want; want of heat, want of clothing, want of food, when her money failed to reach her because Bulgaria had come under the Soviet zone of influence. She was bombed, lost her possessions, she was evacuated, she lived in drafty, cold dormitories for many, many months in the country, she returned valiant to the capital of Bulgaria after the war, and continued, on foot, to carry out her teaching work.

The Guardian himself urged her strongly, when the war first began to threaten to cut her off in Bulgaria, to go to Switzerland. She was a Canadian subject, and ran great risks by remaining, not to mention the danger and the privations of war. However, she begged the Guardian not to insist, and assured him her one desire was to remain with her spiritual children. This she did, up to the last breath of her glorious life. Her tomb will become a national shrine, immensely loved and revered, as the Faith rises in stature in that country.

He thinks that every Bahá'í, and most particularly those who have left their homes and gone to serve in foreign fields, should know of, and turn their gaze to, Marion Jack.

21.17 Whenever you feel at all discouraged you should remember how many years it took for the administration to get as well established as it is at present in North America. Problems repeat themselves, and in the earlier stages in the U.S.A. the body of the believers was very loosely knit together, many of the friends were, as they now are in Latin America, affiliated with various more or less progressive cults (from) which they had come to the Faith and from which they could not be suddenly cut off; they had to be weaned and educated; the same thing you must now do. He urges you therefore to be very patient with the believers and, through loving consultation and education, gradually insist that the old allegiances must give way to the great and all-satisfying bond they have now found with Bahá'u'lláh and His Faith.

21.18 Let them dedicate thyselves—young and old, men and women alike—and go forth and settle in new districts, travel, and teach in spite of lack of experience, and be assured that Bahá'u'lláh has promised to aid all those who arise in His Name. His strength will sustain them; their own weakness is unimportant.

21.19 The Bahá'í teacher must be all confidence. Therein lies his strength and the secret of his success. Though single-handed, and no matter how great the apathy of the people around you may be, you should have faith that the hosts of the Kingdom are on your side, and that through their help you are bound to overcome the forces of darkness that are facing the Cause of God. Persevere, be happy and confident, therefore.

21.20 He feels the Persians can render the utmost assistance to the teaching work, wherever they settle; but they must go on the basis of pioneers, and take up residence where they can render the best service to the Cause of God. It does little good for the Faith to have large groups of Persians settled in a city, and thus constitute an Assembly. When they move the Assembly falls. What we need in all areas is native believers. The pioneers should be in the minority, and aid the natives to shoulder the responsibilities of the Faith.

Thus he feels you should encourage the friends leaving Persia, to settle in outlying areas, in smaller cities, where there are no Bahá'ís, or few, and teach there.

21.21 The Guardian feels that the Persians should not congregate in a few chosen places, but rather that they should ... spread out in the various cities of these countries where there are no Bahá'ís. If this is done, it will greatly facilitate the teaching work in those countries, and at the same time will overcome the problem of establishing Persian colonies ...

One of the problems ... is that so many of the Persian pioneers congregate in certain cities, and this creates actually a Persian colony, and little or nothing seems to be done about teaching the natives. If the Persian pioneers dispersed to various cities, then of course they would automatically begin to teach the natives, because they would not be burdened with the necessity of Assembly functioning and association with other Persian Bahá'ís.

The same situation exists with regard to American pioneers in these countries. They all want to congregate in one place, and thus little or nothing is done for the country itself.

21.22 Concerning the abolition of the institution of paid national teachers, the Guardian wishes to re-affirm his former statements on this matter, and to stress once more that great care be taken to avoid the difficulties and the misunderstandings which in former days had caused so much trouble among the friends. The main point to be emphasized in this connection is that of making the teaching of the Cause not the work of a limited group but the chief duty and responsibility of every Bahá'í. This is why no salaried teachers should any longer exist. But occasionally to defray the expenses of a teaching trip of a certain Bahá'í, particularly when it is done spontaneously, can do no harm to the Cause. Such an action, provided it is done with care and only when circumstances make it necessary, constitutes no violation of the principles already referred to. The danger in all activities of this nature is to give the impression that the teaching of the Cause is an institution, depending on the support of paid teachers. Those who willingly and with utmost detachment arise to promote the Cause should, undoubtedly, be helped in every way. But they have no claim whatever on the financial help which some friends may freely choose to extend to them.

FROM THE WRITINGS AND LETTERS WRITTEN BY, OR ON BEHALF OF, THE UNIVERSAL HOUSE OF JUSTICE

21.23 The duties of teaching and pioneering are enjoined upon all believers. There are no special categories of believers for these functions. Any Bahá'í who spreads the Message of Bahá'u'lláh is a teacher, any Bahá'í who moves to another area to spread the Faith is a pioneer.

21.24 No special training is required for a pioneer. A believer who leaves his home spontaneously and goes to teach the Faith elsewhere without consulting anybody is as much a pioneer as one who goes after consultation with the committee responsible. This is a matter of principle, no matter how desirable it may be that all prospective pioneers first consult to ensure the best use of their services.

21.25 A pioneer has no special administrative status except in the case where he goes to a new area where there are no Bahá'ís. He then usually remains the channel of communication between the new Bahá'í group, as it is formed, and the National Committee in charge, until such time as a Local Spiritual Assembly is formed. At that point his special status ceases altogether. Any services he may perform in advising or teaching the new believers spring from the fact that he is an older believer, and not from his being a pioneer. Many pioneers who go to places where Bahá'ís of long standing already live often receive the counsel and spiritual support of the older native believers rather than vice-versa. Similarly there is no special significance in the dwelling of a pioneer- it frequently happens that the homes of some of the new believers, being less cramped than the quarters of the pioneer, are the places used for meetings of the community."

PART III: CHANNELING SPIRITUAL FORCES

CHAPTER 22:

SHARING A SPIRIT OF FAITH

310 ❓ Making a Better World with the Bahá'í Faith: QUOTATIONS

FROM THE WRITINGS OF BAHÁ'U'LLÁH

22.1   Now is the time to cheer and refresh the down-cast through the invigorating breeze of love and fellowship, and the living waters of friendliness and charity.

22.2   Guidance hath ever been given by words, and now it is given by deeds. Every one must show forth deeds that are pure and holy, for words are the property of all alike, whereas such deeds as these belong only to Our loved ones. Strive then with heart and soul to distinguish yourselves by your deeds. In this wise We counsel you in this holy and resplendent tablet.

22.3   The summons and the message which We gave were never intended to reach or to benefit one land or one people only. Mankind in its entirety must firmly adhere to whatsoever hath been revealed and vouchsafed unto it. Then and only then will it attain unto true liberty.

22.4   Every word is endowed with a spirit, therefore the speaker or expounder should carefully deliver his words at the appropriate time and place, for the impression which each word maketh is clearly evident and perceptible. The Great Being saith: One word may be likened unto fire, another unto light, and the influence which both exert is manifest in the world. Therefore an enlightened man of wisdom should primarily speak with words as mild as milk, that the children of men may be nurtured and edified thereby and may attain the ultimate goal of human existence which is the station of true understanding and nobility. And likewise He saith: One word is like unto springtime causing the tender saplings of the rose-garden of knowledge to become verdant and flourishing, while another word is even as a deadly poison. It behoveth a prudent man of wisdom to speak with utmost leniency and forbearance so that the sweetness of his words may induce everyone to attain that which befitteth man's station.

22.5   It behoveth the people of God to be forbearing. They should impart the Word of God according to the hearer's particular measure of understanding and capacity, that perchance the children of men may be roused from heedlessness and set their faces towards this Horizon which is immeasurably exalted above every horizon.

22.6   ... If he be kindled with the fire of His love, if he forgoeth all created things, the words he uttereth shall set on fire them that hear him.

22.7   Moderation is indeed highly desirable. Every person who in some degree turneth towards the truth can himself later comprehend most of what he seeketh. However, if at the outset a word is uttered beyond his capacity, he will refuse to hear it and will arise in opposition.

FROM THE WRITINGS AND UTTERANCES OF 'ABDU'L-BAHÁ

22.8   ... Never lose thy trust in God. Be thou ever hopeful, for the bounties of God never cease to flow upon man. If viewed from one perspective they seem to decrease, but from another they are full and complete. Man is under all conditions immersed in a sea of God's blessings. Therefore, be thou not hopeless under any circumstances, but rather be firm in thy hope.

22.9   It is my hope that the breaths of the Holy Spirit will so be breathed into your hearts that your tongues will disclose the mysteries, and set forth and expound the inner meanings of the Holy Books; that the friends will become physicians, and will, through the potent medicine of the heavenly Teachings, heal the long-standing diseases that afflict the body of this world; that they will make the blind to see, the deaf to hear, the dead to come alive; that they will awaken those who are sound asleep.

Rest ye assured that the confirmations of the Holy Spirit will descend upon you, and that the armies of the Abha Kingdom will grant you the victory.

22.10 With hearts overflowing with the love of God, with tongues commemorating the mention of God, with eyes turned to the Kingdom of God, they must deliver the Glad Tidings of the manifestation of the Lord of Hosts to all the people. Know ye of a certainty that in whatever meeting ye may enter, in the apex of that meeting the Holy Spirit shall be waving and the heavenly confirmations of the Blessed Perfection shall encompass all."

22.11 O ye believers of God! Do ye not look upon the smallness of your number and the multitudes of the nations. Five grains of wheat will be endued with heavenly blessing, whereas a thousand tons of tares will yield no results or effect. One fruitful tree will be conducive to the life of society, whereas a thousand forests of wild trees offer no fruits. The plain is covered with pebbles, but precious stones are rare. One pearl is better than a thousand wildernesses of sand, especially this pearl of great price, which is endowed with divine blessing. Ere long thousands of other pearls will be born from it. When that pearl associates and becomes the intimate of the pebbles, they also all change into pearls.

... rest ye not, seek ye no composure, attach not yourselves to the luxuries of this ephemeral world, free yourselves from every attachment, and strive with heart and soul to become fully established in the Kingdom of God. Gain ye the heavenly treasures. Day by day become ye more illumined. Draw ye nearer and nearer unto the threshold of oneness. Become ye the manifestors of spiritual favors and the dawning-places of infinite lights!...

As regards the teachers, they must completely divest themselves from the old garments and be invested with a new garment. According to the statement of Christ, they must attain to the station of rebirth:—that is, whereas in the first instance they were born from the womb of the mother, this time they must be born from the womb of the world of nature. Just as they are now totally unaware of the experiences of the foetal world, they must also forget entirely the defects of the world of nature. They must be baptized with the water of life, the fire of the love of God and the breaths of the Holy Spirit;

be satisfied with little food, but take a large portion from the heavenly table. They must disengage themselves from temptation and covetousness, and be filled with the spirit. Through the effect of their pure breath, they must change the stone into the brilliant ruby and the shell into pearl. Like unto the cloud of vernal shower, they must transform the black soil into the rose garden and orchard. They must make the blind seeing, the deaf hearing, the extinguished one enkindled and set aglow, and the dead quickened.

22.12 The aim is this: The intention of the teacher must be pure, his heart independent, his spirit attracted, his thought at peace, his resolution firm, his magnanimity exalted and in the love of God a shining torch. Should he become as such, his sanctified breath will even affect the rock; otherwise there will be no result whatsoever. As long as a soul is not perfected, how can he efface the defects of others. Unless he is detached from aught else save God, how can he teach severance to others!

22.13 The contribution thou hast made for teaching is highly acceptable and it shall be eternally mentioned in the divine Kingdom for it is the cause of the diffusion of fragrances and the exaltation of the Word of God.

22.14 Although the reality of Divinity is sanctified and boundless, the aims and needs of the creatures are restricted. God's grace is like the rain that cometh down from heaven: the water is not bounded by the limitations of form, yet on whatever place it poureth down, it taketh on limitations—dimensions, appearance, shape—according to the characteristics of that place. In a square pool, the water, previously unconfined, becometh a square; in a six-sided pool it becometh a hexagon, in an eight-sided pool an octagon, and so forth. The rain itself hath no geometry, no limits, no form, but it taketh on one form or another, according to the restrictions of its vessel. In the same way, the Holy Essence of the Lord God is boundless, immeasurable, but His graces and splendours become finite in the creatures, because of their limitations, wherefore the prayers of given persons will receive favourable answers in certain cases.

22.15 Follow thou the way of thy Lord, and say not that which the ears cannot bear to hear, for such speech is like luscious food given to small children. However palatable, rare and rich the food may be, it cannot be assimilated by the digestive organs of a suckling child. Therefore unto everyone who hath a right, let his settled measure be given.

'Not everything that a man knoweth can be disclosed, nor can everything that he can disclose be regarded as timely, nor can every timely utterance be considered as suited to the capacity of those who hear it.' Such is the consummate wisdom to be observed in thy pursuits. Be not oblivious thereof, if thou wishest to be a man of action under all conditions. First diagnose the disease and identify the malady, then prescribe the remedy, for such is the perfect method of a skillful physician.

22.16 In accordance with the divine teachings in this glorious Dispensation we should not belittle anyone and call him ignorant, saying: 'You know not but I know.' Rather, we should look upon others with respect, and when attempting to explain and demonstrate, we should speak as if we are investigating the truth, saying: 'Here these things are before us. Let us investigate to determine where and in what form the truth can be found.'

The teacher should not consider himself as learned and others ignorant. Such a thought breeds pride, and pride is unconducive to influence. The teacher should not see in himself any superiority; he should speak with the utmost kindliness, lowliness and humility, for such speech exerts influence and educates the souls.

22.17 The powers of earth cannot withstand the privileges and bestowals which God has ordained for this great and glorious century. It is a need and exigency of the time. Man can withstand anything except that which is divinely intended and indicated for the age and its requirements. Now, Praise be to God! in all countries of the world, lovers of peace are to be found and these principles are being spread among mankind, especially in this country. Praise be to God! this thought is prevailing and souls are continually arising as defenders of the oneness of humanity, endeavoring to assist and establish international peace. There is no doubt that this wonderful democracy will be able to realize it and the banner of international agreement will be unfurled here to spread onward and outward among all the nations of the world. I give thanks to God that I find you imbued with such susceptibilities and lofty aspirations and I hope that you will be the means of spreading this light to all men. Thus may the Sun of Reality shine upon the East and West. The enveloping clouds shall pass away and the heat of the divine rays will dispel the mist. The reality of man shall develop and come forth as the image of God his creator. The thoughts of man shall take such upward flight that former accomplishments shall appear as the play of children;—for the ideas and beliefs of the past and the prejudices regarding race and religion have ever been lowering and destructive to human evolution. I am most hopeful that in this century these lofty thoughts shall be conducive to human welfare. Let this century be the sun of previous centuries the effulgences of which shall last forever, so that in times to come they shall glorify the twentieth century, saying the twentieth century was the century of lights, the twentieth century was the century of life, the twentieth century was the century of international peace, the twentieth century was the century of divine bestowals and the twentieth century has left traces which shall last forever.

22.18 Let us then trust in the bounty and bestowal of God. Let us be exhilarated with the divine breath, illumined and exalted by the heavenly glad-tidings. God has ever dealt with man in mercy and kindness. He who conferred the divine spirit in former times is abundantly able and capable at all times and periods to grant the same bestowals. Therefore let us be hopeful. The God who gave to the world formerly will do so now and in the future. God who breathed the breath of the Holy Spirit upon His servants will breathe it upon them now and hereafter. There is no cessation to His bounty. The divine spirit is penetrating from eternity to eternity for it is the bounty of God and the bounty of God is eternal. Can you conceive of limitation of the divine power in atomic verities or cessation of the divine bounty in existing organisms? Could you conceive the power now manifest in this glass in cohesion of its atoms, becoming non-existent? The energy by which the water of the sea is constituted, failing to exert itself and the sea disappearing? A shower of rain today and no more showers afterward? The effulgence of the sun terminated and no more light or heat?

22.19 You have assembled here this afternoon in the utmost love, engaged in the commemoration of God. It is my hope that this gathering may increase in number day by day; that you may become more and more attracted, more spiritual, more illumined, acquire knowledge of the teachings of Bahá'u'lláh from each other and be able to spread the message of truth. May your hearts become so attracted that the instant a question is asked, you will be able to give the right answer and that the truth of the Holy Spirit may speak through your tongues. Be ye helpful through the providence and favor of the Blessed Perfection, for His favors change a drop into an ocean, cause a seed to become a tree and make an atom as glorious as the sun. His graces are boundless. The treasure houses of God are filled with bounties. God, Who hath shown favors unto others, will certainly bestow favors upon you. I offer supplication to the Kingdom of Abha and seek extraordinary blessings and confirmations in your behalf in order that your tongues may become fluent, your hearts like clear mirrors flooded with the rays of the Sun of Truth, your thoughts expanded, your comprehension more vivid and that you may progress in the plane of human perfections.

22.20 O friends of God! Praise be unto God that the invisible bounties of the Sun of Truth are encompassing you from all directions, and the doors of mercy are opened from all parts. Now is the time to be benefited and filled therewith. Seize the opportunity, and lose not the chance. Keep yourselves entirely clear of the world's conditions of gloom, and show forth the characters and qualities of divine souls, that ye may consider to what an extent the radiance of the Divine Sun is shining and brilliant, and how the signs of favor are showing forth from the invisible World of Unity.

FROM THE WRITINGS AND LETTERS WRITTEN BY, OR ON BEHALF OF, SHOGHI EFFENDI

22.21 The opportunities which the turmoil of the present age presents, with all the sorrows which it evokes, the fears which it excites, the disillusionment which it produces, the perplexities which it creates, the indignation which it arouses, the revolt which it provokes, the grievances it engenders, the spirit of restless search which it awakens, must, in like manner, be exploited for the purpose of spreading far and wide the knowledge of the redemptive power of the Faith of Bahá'u'lláh, and for enlisting fresh recruits in the ever-swelling army of His followers.

22.22 ... Having ... obtained a clear understanding of the true character of our mission, the methods to adopt, the course to pursue, and having attained sufficiently the individual regeneration—the essential requisite of teaching—let us arise to teach His Cause with righteousness, conviction, understanding and vigor. Let this be the paramount and most urgent duty of every Bahá'í. Let us make it the dominating passion of our life. Let us scatter to the uttermost corners of the earth, sacrifice our personal interests, comforts, tastes and pleasures; mingle with the divers kindreds and peoples of the world; familiarize ourselves with their manners, traditions, thoughts and customs; arouse, stimulate and maintain universal interest in the Movement, and at the same time endeavor by all the means in our power, by concentrated and persistent attention, to enlist the unreserved allegiance and the active support of the more hopeful and receptive among our hearers. Let us too bear in mind the example which our beloved Master has clearly set before us. Wise and tactful in His approach, wakeful and attentive in His early intercourse, broad and liberal in all His public utterances, cautious and gradual in the unfolding of the essential verities of the Cause, passionate in His appeal yet sober in argument, confident in tone, unswerving in conviction, dignified in His manners—such were the distinguishing features of our Beloved's noble presentation of the Cause of Bahá'u'lláh.

22.23 Having on his own initiative, and undaunted by any hindrances with which either friend or foe may, unwittingly or deliberately, obstruct his path, resolved to arise and respond to the call of teaching, let him carefully consider every avenue of approach which he might utilize in his personal attempts to capture the attention, maintain the interest, and deepen the faith, of those whom he seeks to bring into the fold of his Faith. Let him survey the possibilities which the particular circumstances in which he lives offer him, evaluate their advantages, and proceed intelligently and systematically to utilize them for the achievement of the object he has in mind. Let him also attempt to devise such methods as association with clubs, exhibitions, and societies, lectures on subjects akin to the teachings and ideals of his Cause such as temperance, morality, social welfare, religious and racial tolerance, economic cooperation, Islam, and Comparative Religion, or participation in social, cultural, humanitarian, charitable, and educational organizations and enterprises which, while safeguarding the integrity of his Faith, will open up to him a multitude of ways and means whereby he can enlist successively the sympathy, the support, and ultimately the allegiance of those with whom he comes in contact. Let him, while such contacts are being made, bear in mind the claims which his Faith is constantly making upon him to preserve its dignity, and station, to safeguard the integrity of its laws and principles, to demonstrate its comprehensiveness and universality, and to defend fearlessly its manifold and vital interests. Let him consider the degree of his hearer's receptivity, and decide for himself the suitability of either the direct or indirect method of teaching, whereby he can impress upon the seeker the vital importance of the Divine Message, and persuade him to throw in his lot with those who have already embraced it. Let him remember the example set by 'Abdu'l-Bahá, and His constant admonition to shower such kindness upon the seeker, and exemplify to such a degree the spirit of the teachings he hopes to instill into him, that the recipient will be spontaneously impelled to identify himself with the Cause embodying such teachings. Let him refrain, at the outset, from insisting on such laws and observances as might impose too severe a strain on the seeker's newly-awakened faith, and endeavor to nurse him, patiently, tactfully, and yet determinedly, into full maturity, and aid him to proclaim his unqualified acceptance of whatever has been ordained by Bahá'u'lláh. Let him, as soon as that stage has been attained, introduce him to the body of his fellow-believers, and seek, through constant fellowship and active participation in the local activities of his community, to enable him to contribute his share to the enrichment of its life, the furtherance of its tasks, the consolidations of its interests, and the coordination of its activities with those of its sister communities. Let him not be content until he has infused into his spiritual child so deep a longing as to impel him to arise independently, in his turn, and devote his energies to the quickening of other souls, and the upholding of the laws and principles laid down by his newly-adopted Faith.

22.24 The individual alone must assess its [the individual's duty] character, consult his conscience, prayerfully consider all its aspects, manfully struggle against the natural inertia that weighs him down in his effort to arise, shed, heroically and irrevocably, the trivial and superfluous attachments which hold him back, empty himself of every thought that may tend to obstruct his path, mix, in obedience to the counsels of the Author of His Faith, and in imitation of the One Who is its true Exemplar, with men and women, in all walks of life, seek to touch their hearts, through the distinction which characterizes his thoughts, his words and acts, and win them over tactfully, lovingly, prayerfully and persistently, to the Faith he himself has espoused.

22.25 The Cause of God has room for all. It would, indeed, not be the Cause of God if it did not take in and welcome everyone—poor and rich, educated and ignorant, the unknown and the prominent—God surely wants them all, as He created them all."

22.26 These people [the indigenous people], finding the Bahá'ís / sincerely/ lacking in either prejudice—or that even worse attitude, condescension—might not only take interest in our Teachings, but also help us to reach their people in the proper way.

It is a great mistake to believe that because people are illiterate or live primitive lives, they are lacking in either intelligence or sensibility. On the contrary, they may well look on us, with the evils of our civilization, with its moral corruption, its ruinous wars, its hypocrisy and conceit, as people who merit watching with both suspicion and contempt. We should meet them as equals, well-wishers, people who admire and respect their ancient descent and who feel that they will be interested, as we are, in a /living religion/—and not in the dead forms of present-day churches.

22.27 ... the upper classes ... need the right type of people to approach them, and a method that can suit their mentality. Our teaching methods should allow a certain degree of elasticity in establishing contacts with various types of individual seekers. Every inquirer has to be approached from his own angle. Those who are essentially of the mystic type should first be given those teachings of the Cause which emphasize the nature and value of spiritual realities; while those who are practically minded and of a positive type are naturally more ready and inclined to accept the social aspect of the Teachings. But of course, gradually the /entire/ Message, in all its aspects and with the full implications it entails, should be explained to the newcomer. For to be a believer means to accept the Cause in its wholeness, and not to adhere to some of its teachings. However, as already stated, this ought to be done gradually and tactfully. For conversion is after all a slow process.

22.28 ... Do not feel discouraged if your labors do not always yield an abundant fruitage. For a quick and rapidly-won success is not always the best and most lasting. The harder you strive to attain your goal, the greater will be the confirmations of Bahá'u'lláh, and the more certain you can feel to attain success. Be cheerful, therefore, and exert yourself with full faith and confidence. For Bahá'u'lláh has promised His Divine assistance to everyone who arises with a pure and detached heart to spread His holy Word, even though he may be bereft of every human knowledge and capacity, and notwithstanding the forces of darkness and of opposition which may be arrayed against him. The goal is clear, the path safe and certain, and the assurances of Bahá'u'lláh as to the eventual success of our efforts quite emphatic. Let us keep firm, and wholeheartedly carry on the great work which He has entrusted into our hands.

22.29 The believers ought to give the Message even to those who do not seem to be ready for it, because they can never judge the real extent to which the Word of God can influence the hearts and minds of the people, even those who appear to lack any power of receptivity to the Teachings.

22.30 ... Unless and until the believers really come to realize they are one spiritual family, knit together by a bond more lasting than mere physical ties can ever be, they will not be able to create that warm community atmosphere which alone can attract the hearts of humanity, frozen for lack of real love and feeling.

22.31 Not all of us are capable of serving in the same way, but the one way every Bahá'í can spread the Faith is by example. This moves the hearts of people far more deeply than words ever can.

    The love we show others, the hospitality and understanding, the willingness to help them, these are the very best advertisements of the Faith.

22.32 All the Bahá'ís, new and old alike, should devote themselves as much as possible to teaching the Faith; they should also realize that the atmosphere of true love and unity which they manifest within the Bahá'í Community will directly affect the public, and be the greatest magnet for attracting people to the Faith and confirming them.

22.33 ... If the Bahá'ís want to be really effective in teaching the Cause they need to be much better informed and able to discuss intelligently, intellectually, the present condition of the world and its problems... .

    We Bahá'ís should, in other words, arm our minds with knowledge in order to better demonstrate to, especially, the educated classes, the truths enshrined in our Faith.

22.34 We must be careful not to teach in a fanatical way. We should teach as the Master taught. He was the perfect Exemplar of the Teachings. He proclaimed the universal truths, and, through love and wise demonstration of the universal verities of the Faith, attracted the hearts and the minds.

22.35 Teaching is the source of Divine Confirmation. It is not sufficient to pray diligently for guidance, but this prayer must be followed by meditation as to the best methods of action and then action itself. Even if the action should not immediately produce results, or perhaps not be entirely correct, that does not make so much difference, because prayers can only be answered through action and if someone's action is wrong, God can use that method of showing the pathway which is right.

FROM THE WRITINGS AND LETTERS WRITTEN BY, OR ON BEHALF OF, THE UNIVERSAL HOUSE OF JUSTICE

22.36 If Bahá'ís are to fulfil Bahá'u'lláh's mandate, however, it is obviously vital that they come to appreciate that the parallel efforts of promoting the betterment of society and of teaching the Bahá'í Faith are not activities competing for attention. Rather, are they reciprocal features of one coherent global programme. Differences of approach are determined chiefly by the differing needs and differing stages of inquiry that the friends encounter. Because free will is an inherent endowment of the soul, each person who is drawn to explore Bahá'u'lláh's teachings will need to find his own place in the never-ending continuum of spiritual search. He will need to determine, in the privacy of his own conscience and without pressure, the spiritual responsibility this discovery entails. In order to exercise this autonomy intelligently, however, he must gain both a perspective on the processes of change in which he, like the rest of the earth's population, is caught up and a clear understanding of the implications for his own life. The obligation of the Bahá'í community is to do everything in its power to assist all stages of humanity's universal movement towards reunion with God. The Divine Plan bequeathed it by the Master is the means by which this work is carried out.

CHAPTER 23:

INSPIRING AN UPLIFTING SPIRIT OF MORALITY IN SOCIETY

326 ❓ Making a Better World with the Bahá'í Faith: QUOTATIONS

FROM THE WRITINGS OF BAHÁ'U'LLÁH

23.1 Be pure, O people of God, be pure; be righteous, be righteous…. Say: O people of God! That which can ensure the victory of Him Who is the Eternal Truth, His hosts and helpers on earth, have been set down in the sacred Books and Scriptures, and are as clear and manifest as the sun. These hosts are such righteous deeds, such conduct and character, as are acceptable in His sight. Whoso ariseth, in this Day, to aid Our Cause, and summoneth to his assistance the hosts of a praiseworthy character and upright conduct, the influence flowing from such an action will, most certainly, be diffused throughout the whole world.

23.2 Say: He is not to be numbered with the people of Baha who followeth his mundane desires, or fixeth his heart on things of the earth. He is My true follower who, if he come to a valley of pure gold, will pass straight through it aloof as a cloud, and will neither turn back, nor pause. Such a man is, assuredly, of Me. From his garment the Concourse on high can inhale the fragrance of sanctity…. And if he met the fairest and most comely of women, he would not feel his heart seduced by the least shadow of desire for her beauty. Such an one, indeed, is the creation of spotless chastity. Thus instructeth you the Pen of the Ancient of Days, as bidden by your Lord, the Almighty, the All-Bountiful.

23.3 … The Almighty beareth Me witness: To act like the beasts of the field is unworthy of man. Those virtues that befit his dignity are forbearance, mercy, compassion and loving-kindness towards all the peoples and kindreds of the earth. Say: O friends! Drink your fill from this crystal stream that floweth through the heavenly grace of Him Who is the Lord of Names. Let others partake of its waters in My name, that the leaders of men in every land may fully recognize the purpose for which the Eternal Truth hath been revealed, and the reason for which they themselves have been created.

23.4 O FRIEND! In the garden of thy heart plant naught but the rose of love, and from the nightingale of affection and desire loosen not thy hold. Treasure the companionship of the righteous and eschew all fellowship with the ungodly.

23.5 The winds of despair are, alas, blowing from every direction, and the strife that divideth and afflicteth the human race is daily increasing. The signs of impending convulsions and chaos can now be discerned, inasmuch as the prevailing order appeareth to be lamentably defective. I beseech God, exalted be His glory, that He may graciously awaken the peoples of the earth, may grant that the end of their conduct may be profitable unto them, and aid them to accomplish that which beseemeth their station.

23.6 The world is in travail, and its agitation waxeth day by day. Its face is turned towards waywardness and unbelief. Such shall be its plight, that to disclose it now would not be meet and seemly. Its perversity will long continue. And when the appointed hour is come, there shall suddenly appear that which shall cause the limbs of mankind to quake. Then, and only then, will the Divine Standard be unfurled, and the Nightingale of Paradise warble its melody.

23.7 The company of the ungodly increaseth sorrow, whilst fellowship with the righteous cleanseth the rust from off the heart. He that seeketh to commune with God, let him betake himself to the companionship of His loved ones; and he that desireth to hearken unto the word of God, let him give ear to the words of His chosen ones.

23.8 O SON OF SPIRIT! The bird seeketh its nest; the nightingale the charm of the rose; whilst those birds, the hearts of men, content with transient dust, have strayed far from their eternal nest, and with eyes turned towards the slough of heedlessness are bereft of the glory of the divine presence. Alas! How strange and pitiful; for a mere cupful, they have turned away from the billowing seas of the Most High, and remained far from the most effulgent horizon.

FROM THE WRITINGS AND UTTERANCES OF 'ABDU'L-BAHÁ

23.9 O thou son of the Kingdom! All things are beneficial if joined with the love of God; and without His love all things are harmful, and act as a veil between man and the Lord of the Kingdom. When His love is there, every bitterness turneth sweet, and every bounty rendereth a wholesome pleasure. For example, a melody, sweet to the ear, bringeth the very spirit of life to a heart in love with God, yet staineth with lust a soul engrossed in sensual desires. And every branch of learning, conjoined with the love of God, is approved and worthy of praise; but bereft of His love, learning is barren—indeed, it bringeth on madness. Every kind of knowledge, every science, is as a tree: if the fruit of it be the love of God, then is it a blessed tree, but if not, that tree is but dried-up wood, and shall only feed the fire.

23.10 Then divine policy shall govern the world, for the divine policy is the oneness of humanity. God is just and kind to all. He considers all as His servants. He excludes none, and His judgments are correct and true. No matter how complete human policy and foresight may appear, they are imperfect. If we do not seek the counsel of God or if we refuse to follow His dictates, it is presumptive evidence that we are knowing and wise, whereas God is ignorant; that we are sagacious and God is not. God forbid! We seek shelter in His mercy for this suggestion! No matter how far the human intelligence may advance, it is still but a drop, while divine omniscience is the ocean. Shall we say that a drop is imbued or endowed with qualities of which the ocean is devoid? Shall we believe that the policy and plan of this atom of a human soul are superior to the wisdom of the Omniscient? There is no greater ignorance than this. Briefly, some are mere children; with the utmost love we must educate them to make them wise. Others are sick and ailing; we must tenderly treat them until they recover. Some have unworthy morals; we must train them toward the standard of true morality. Other than this we are all the servants of one God and under the providence and protection of one Father.

23.11 Consider history. What has brought unity to nations, morality to peoples and benefits to mankind? If we reflect upon it, we will find that establishing the divine religions has been the greatest means toward accomplishing the oneness of humanity. The foundation of divine reality in religion has done this, not imitations of ancestral religious forms. Imitations are opposed to each other and have ever been the cause of strife, enmity, jealousy and war. The divine religions are collective centers in which diverse standpoints may meet, agree and unify. They accomplish oneness of native lands, races and policies. For instance, Christ united various nations, brought peace to warring peoples and established the oneness of humankind. The conquering Greeks and Romans, the prejudiced Egyptians and Assyrians were all in a condition of strife, enmity and war, but Christ gathered these varied peoples together and removed the foundations of discord—not through racial, patriotic or political power, but through divine power, the power of the Holy Spirit. This was not otherwise possible. All other efforts of men and nations remain as mere mention in history, without accomplishment.

23.12 The religions of God have the same foundation, but the dogmas appearing later have differed. Each of the divine religions has two aspects. The first is essential. It concerns morality and development of the virtues of the human world. This aspect is common to all. It is fundamental; it is one; there is no difference, no variation in it. As regards the inculcation of morality and the development of human virtues, there is no difference whatsoever between the teachings of Zoroaster, Jesus and Bahá'u'lláh. In this they agree; they are one. The second aspect of the divine religions is nonessential. It concerns human needs and undergoes change in every cycle according to the exigency of the time. For example, in the time of Moses divorce was conformable to the needs and conditions; Moses, therefore, established it. But in the time of Christ, divorces were numerous and the cause of corruption; as they were not suitable for the time, he made divorce unlawful and likewise changed other laws. These are needs and conditions which have to do with the conduct of society; therefore, they undergo change according to the exigency of the time. Moses dwelt in the desert. As there were no penitentiaries, no means of restitution in the desert and wilderness, the laws of God were an eye for an eye, a tooth for a tooth. Could this be carried out now? If a man destroys another man's eye, are you willing to destroy the eye of the offender? If a man's teeth are broken or his ear cut off, will you demand a corresponding mutilation of his assailant? This would not be conformable to conditions of humanity at the present time. If a man steals, shall his hand be cut off? This punishment was just and right in the law of Moses, but it was applicable to the desert, where there were no prisons and reformatory institutions of later and higher forms of government. Today you have government and organization, a police system, a judge and trial by jury. The punishment and penalty is now different. Therefore, the nonessentials which deal with details of community are changed according to the exigency of the time and conditions. But the essential foundation of the teachings of Moses, Zoroaster, Jesus and Bahá'u'lláh is identical, is one; there is no difference whatsoever.

23.13 The real bond of integrity is religious in character, for religion indicates the oneness of the world of humanity. Religion serves the world of morality. Religion purifies the hearts. Religion impels men to achieve praiseworthy deeds. Religion becomes the cause of love in human hearts, for religion is a divine foundation, the foundation ever conducive to life. The teachings of God are the source of illumination to the people of the world. Religion is ever constructive, not destructive.

The foundation of all the divine religions is one. All are based upon reality. Reality does not admit plurality, yet amongst mankind there have arisen differences concerning the Manifestations of God. Some have been Zoroastrians, some are Buddhists, some Jews, Christians, Muslims and so on. This has become a source of divergence, whereas the teachings of the holy Souls Who founded the divine religions are one in essence and reality. All these have served the world of humanity. All have summoned souls to peace and accord. All have proclaimed the virtues of humanity. All have guided souls to the attainment of perfections, but among the nations certain imitations of ancestral forms of worship have arisen. These imitations are not the foundation and essence of the divine religions. Inasmuch as they differ from the reality and the essential teachings of the Manifestations of God, dissensions have arisen, and prejudice has developed. Religious prejudice thus becomes the cause of warfare and battle.

23.14 Until man acquires perfections himself, he will not be able to teach perfections to others. Unless man attains life himself, he cannot convey life to others. Unless he finds light, he cannot reflect light. We must, therefore, endeavor ourselves to attain to the perfections of the world of humanity, lay hold of everlasting life and seek the divine spirit in order that we may thereby be enabled to confer life upon others, be enabled to breathe life into others.

23.15 When man allows the spirit, through his soul, to enlighten his understanding, then does he contain all Creation; because man, being the culmination of all that went before and thus superior to all previous evolutions, contains all the lower world within himself. Illumined by the spirit through the instrumentality of the soul, man's radiant intelligence makes him the crowning-point of Creation.

But on the other hand, when man does not open his mind and heart to the blessing of the spirit, but turns his soul towards the material side, towards the bodily part of his nature, then is he fallen from his high place and he becomes inferior to the inhabitants of the lower animal kingdom. In this case the man is in a sorry plight! For if the spiritual qualities of the soul, open to the breath of the Divine Spirit, are never used, they become atrophied, enfeebled, and at last incapable; whilst the soul's material qualities alone being exercised, they become terribly powerful—and the unhappy, misguided man, becomes more savage, more unjust, more vile, more cruel, more malevolent than the lower animals themselves. All his aspirations and desires being strengthened by the lower side of the soul's nature, he becomes more and more brutal, until his whole being is in no way superior to that of the beasts that perish. Men such as this, plan to work evil, to hurt and to destroy; they are entirely without the spirit of Divine compassion, for the celestial quality of the soul has been dominated by that of the material. If, on the contrary, the spiritual nature of the soul has been so strengthened that it holds the material side in subjection, then does the man approach the Divine; his humanity becomes so glorified that the virtues of the Celestial Assembly are manifested in him; he radiates the Mercy of God, he stimulates the spiritual progress of mankind, for he becomes a lamp to show light on their path.

FROM THE WRITINGS AND LETTERS WRITTEN BY, OR ON BEHALF OF, SHOGHI EFFENDI

23.16 Not only must irreligion and its monstrous offspring, the triple curse that oppresses the soul of mankind in this day, be held responsible for the ills which are so tragically besetting it, but other evils and vices, which are, for the most part, the direct consequences of the "weakening of the pillars of religion," must also be regarded as contributory factors to the manifold guilt of which individuals and nations stand convicted. The signs of moral downfall, consequent to the dethronement of religion and the enthronement of these usurping idols, are too numerous and too patent for even a superficial observer of the state of present-day society to fail to notice. The spread of lawlessness, of drunkenness, of gambling, and of crime; the inordinate love of pleasure, of riches, and other earthly vanities; the laxity in morals, revealing itself in the irresponsible attitude towards marriage, in the weakening of parental control, in the rising tide of divorce, in the deterioration in the standard of literature and of the press, and in the advocacy of theories that are the very negation of purity, of morality and chastity—these evidences of moral decadence, invading both the East and the West, permeating every stratum of society, and instilling their poison in its members of both sexes, young and old alike, blacken still further the scroll upon which are inscribed the manifold transgressions of an unrepentant humanity.

Small wonder that Bahá'u'lláh, the Divine Physician, should have declared: "In this day the tastes of men have changed, and their power of perception hath altered. The contrary winds of the world, and its colors, have provoked a cold, and deprived men's nostrils of the sweet savors of Revelation."

Brimful and bitter indeed is the cup of humanity that has failed to respond to the summons of God as voiced by His Supreme Messenger, that has dimmed the lamp of its faith in its Creator, that has transferred, in so great a measure, the allegiance owed Him to the gods of its own invention, and polluted itself with the evils and vices which such a transference must necessarily engender.

23.17 The steady and alarming deterioration in the standard of morality as exemplified by the appalling increase of crime, by political corruption in ever widening and ever higher circles, by the loosening of the sacred ties of marriage, by the inordinate craving for pleasure and diversion, and by the marked and progressive slackening of parental control, is no doubt the most arresting and distressing aspect of the decline that has set in, and can be clearly perceived, in the fortunes of the entire nation.

Parallel with this, and pervading all departments of life—an evil which the nation, and indeed all those within the capitalist system, though to a lesser degree, share with that state and its satellites regarded as the sworn enemies of that system—is the crass materialism, which lays excessive and ever-increasing emphasis on material well-being, forgetful of those things of the spirit on which alone a sure and stable foundation can be laid for human society. It is this same cancerous materialism, born originally in Europe, carried to excess in the North American continent, contaminating the Asiatic peoples and nations, spreading its ominous tentacles to the borders of Africa, and now invading its very heart, which Bahá'u'lláh in unequivocal and emphatic language denounced in His Writings, comparing it to a devouring flame and regarding it as the chief factor in precipitating the dire ordeals and world-shaking crises that must necessarily involve the burning of cities and the spread of terror and consternation in the hearts of men.

23.18 Having on his own initiative, and undaunted by any hindrances with which either friend or foe may, unwittingly or deliberately, obstruct his path, resolved to arise and respond to the call of teaching, let him carefully consider every avenue of approach which he might utilize in his personal attempts to capture the attention, maintain the interest, and deepen the faith, of those whom he seeks to bring into the fold of his Faith. Let him survey the possibilities which the particular circumstances in which he lives offer him, evaluate their advantages, and proceed intelligently and systematically to utilize them for the achievement of the object he has in mind. Let him also attempt to devise such methods as association with clubs, exhibitions, and societies, lectures on subjects akin to the teachings and ideals of his Cause such as temperance, morality, social welfare, religious and racial tolerance, economic cooperation, Islam, and Comparative Religion, or participation in social, cultural, humanitarian, charitable, and educational organizations and enterprises which, while safeguarding the integrity of his Faith, will open up to him a multitude of ways and means whereby he can enlist successively the sympathy, the support, and ultimately the allegiance of those with whom he comes in contact. Let him, while such contacts are being made, bear in mind the claims which his Faith is constantly making upon him to preserve its dignity, and station, to safeguard the integrity of its laws and principles, to demonstrate its comprehensiveness and universality, and to defend fearlessly its manifold and vital interests. Let him consider the degree of his hearer's receptivity, and decide for himself the suitability either the direct or indirect method of teaching, whereby he can impress upon the seeker the vital importance of the Divine Message, and persuade him to throw in his lot with those who have already embraced it. Let him remember the example set by 'Abdu'l-Bahá, and His constant admonition to shower such kindness upon the seeker, and exemplify to such a degree the spirit of the teachings he hopes to instill into him, that the recipient will be spontaneously impelled to identify himself with the Cause embodying such teachings. Let him refrain, at the outset, from insisting on such laws and observances as might impose too severe a strain on the seeker's newly awakened faith, and endeavor to nurse him, patiently, tactfully, and yet determinedly, into full maturity, and aid him to proclaim his unqualified acceptance of whatever has been ordained by Bahá'u'lláh. Let him, as soon as that stage has been attained, introduce him to the body of his fellow-believers, and seek, through constant fellowship and active participation in the local activities of his community, to enable him to contribute his share to the enrichment of its life, the furtherance of its tasks, the consolidations of its interests, and the coordination of its activities with those of its sister communities. Let him not be content until he has infused into his spiritual child so deep a longing as to impel him to arise independently, in his turn, and devote his energies to the quickening of other souls, and the upholding of the laws and principles laid down by his newly adopted Faith.

23.19 Such a chaste and holy life, with its implications of modesty, purity, temperance, decency, and clean-mindedness, involves no less than the exercise of moderation in all that pertains to dress, language, amusements, and all artistic and literary avocations. It demands daily vigilance in the control of one's carnal desires and corrupt inclinations. It calls for the abandonment of a frivolous conduct, with its excessive attachment to trivial and often misdirected pleasures. It requires total abstinence from all alcoholic drinks, from opium, and from similar habit-forming drugs. It condemns the prostitution of art and of literature, the practices of nudism and of companionate marriage, infidelity in marital relationships, and all manner of promiscuity, of easy familiarity, and of sexual vices. It can tolerate no compromise with the theories, the standards, the habits, and the excesses of a decadent age. Nay rather it seeks to demonstrate, through the dynamic force of its example, the pernicious character of such theories, the falsity of such standards, the hollowness of such claims, the perversity of such habits, and the sacrilegious character of such excesses.

23.20 In the passage 'eschew all fellowship with the ungodly,' Bahá'u'lláh means that we should shun the company of those who disbelieve in God and are wayward. The word 'ungodly' is a reference to such perverse people. The words 'Be thou as a flame of fire to My enemies and a river of life eternal to My loved ones', should flee from the enemies of God and instead seek the fellowship of His lovers.

23.21 He heartily agrees with you that unless we practice the Teachings we cannot possibly expect the Faith to grow, because the fundamental purpose of all religions—including our own—is to bring man nearer to God, and to change his character, which is of the utmost importance. Too much emphasis is often laid on the social and economic aspects of the Teachings; but the moral aspect cannot be over-emphasized.

23.22 We cannot segregate the human heart from the environment outside us and say that once one of these is reformed everything will be improved. Man is organic with the world. His inner life moulds the environment and is itself also deeply affected by it. The one acts upon the other and every abiding change in the life of man is the result of these mutual reactions.

No movement in the world directs its attention upon both these aspects of human life and has full measures for their improvement, save the teachings of Bahá'u'lláh. And this is its distinctive feature. If we desire therefore the good of the world we should strive to spread those teachings and also practise them in our own life. Through them will the human heart be changed, and also our social environment provides the atmosphere in which we can grow spiritually and reflect in full the light of God shining through the revelation of Bahá'u'lláh.

23.23 In the teaching there is nothing against dancing, but the friends should remember that the standard of Bahá'u'lláh is modesty and chastity. The atmosphere of modern dance halls, where so much smoking and drinking and promiscuity goes on, is very bad, but decent dances are not harmful in themselves. There is certainly no harm in classical dancing or learning dancing in school. There is also no harm in taking part in dramas. Likewise in cinema acting. The harmful thing, nowadays, is not the art itself the unfortunate corruption which often surrounds these arts. As Bahá'ís we need to avoid none of the arts, but acts and the atmosphere that sometimes go with these professions we should avoid.

23.24 Also, you raise the question of what will be the source of inspiration to Bahá'í musicians and composers; the music of the past or the Word? We cannot possibly foresee, standing as we do on the threshold of Bahá'í culture, what forms and characteristics the arts of the future, inspired by this Mighty New Revelation, will have. All we can be sure of is that they will be wonderful; as every Faith has given rise to a culture which flowered in different forms, so too our beloved Faith may be expected to do the same thing. It is premature to try and grasp what they will be at present.

FROM THE WRITINGS AND LETTERS WRITTEN BY, OR ON BEHALF OF, THE UNIVERSAL HOUSE OF JUSTICE

23.25   As you readily understand, Bahá'ís are exhorted to lead a chaste and holy life, and, according to Bahá'í Law, sexual intercourse is permissible only between a man and the woman who is his wife. In sexual morality, as in other realms of behaviour, people often stumble and fall short of the ideal. It is the task of Spiritual Assemblies to ensure that the friends are deepened in their understanding of the teachings, and are exhorted to apply them in their lives. In caring for its community, a Spiritual Assembly should act as a loving father rather than as a stern judge in such matters. Nevertheless, if a believer's behaviour is blatantly and flagrantly immoral and, therefore, is harmful to the good name of the Faith, the Assembly must counsel him (or her), urge him to reform his conduct, warn him of the consequences if he does not mend his ways and, ultimately, if the believer persists in misbehaviour, the Assembly must deprive him of his administrative rights. This deprivation remains in force until such time that he has rectified his behaviour.

23.26   Bahá'í teachings on sexual morality center on marriage and the family as the bedrock of the whole structure of human society and are designed to protect and strengthen that divine institution. Thus Bahá'í Law restricts permissible sexual intercourse to that between a man and the woman to whom he is married.

Thus, it should not be so much a matter of whether a practicing homosexual can be a Bahá'í as whether, having become a Bahá'í, the homosexual can overcome his problem through knowledge of the teachings and reliance on Bahá'u'lláh.

23.27 ...Bahá'ís in their deep love for Bahá'u'lláh, should be eager to apply every spiritual precept in their own lives while at the same time exercising patience, forbearance and forgiveness in respect to the shortcomings of others. It is for the Institutions of the Faith to adopt such programmes as will deepen the believers in their understanding of the teachings so that they will unhesitatingly and eagerly follow him.

There is no doubt that the standard of spotless chastity inculcated by Bahá'u'lláh in His teachings can be attained by the friends only when they stand forth firmly and courageously as uncompromising adherents of the Bahá'í way of life fully conscious that they represent teachings which are the very antithesis of the corrosive forces which are so tragically destroying the fabric of man's moral values. The present trend in modern society and its conflict with our challenging principles of moral conduct, far from influencing the believers to compromise their resolve to adhere undeviatingly to the standards of purity and chastity set forth for them by their Faith, must stimulate them to discharge their sacred obligations with determination and thus combat the evil forces undermining the foundations of individual morality.

340 ❓ Making a Better World with the Bahá'í Faith: QUOTATIONS

CHAPTER 24:

INFUSING A SPIRIT OF SERVICE INTO ALL MANKIND

342 Making a Better World with the Bahá'í Faith: QUOTATIONS

FROM THE WRITINGS OF BAHÁ'U'LLÁH

24.1 That one indeed is a man who, today, dedicateth himself to the service of the entire human race. The Great Being saith: Blessed and happy is he that ariseth to promote the best interests of the peoples and kindreds of the earth.

24.2 Be of them whom the tumult of the world, however much it may agitate them in the path of their Creator, can never sadden, whose purpose the blame of the blamer will never defeat.

24.3 Wherefore, be thankful to God, for having strengthened thee to aid His Cause, for having made the flowers of knowledge and understanding to spring forth in the garden of thine heart. Thus hath His grace encompassed thee, and encompassed the whole of creation. Beware, lest thou allow anything whatsoever to grieve thee. Rid thyself of all attachment to the vain allusions of men, and cast behind thy back the idle and subtle disputations of them that are veiled from God. Proclaim, then, that which the Most Great Spirit will inspire thee to utter in the service of the Cause of thy Lord, that thou mayest stir up the souls of all men and incline their hearts unto this most blessed and all-glorious Court....

24.4 O Thou Whose nearness is my wish, Whose presence is my hope, Whose remembrance is my desire, Whose court of glory is my goal, Whose abode is my aim, Whose name is my healing, Whose love is the radiance of my heart, Whose service is my highest aspiration!

24.5 Thy might beareth me witness! Were it not to celebrate Thy praise, my tongue would be of no use to me, and were it not for the sake of rendering service to Thee, my existence would avail me not. But for the pleasure of beholding the splendours of Thy realm of glory, why should I cherish sight? And but for the joy of giving ear to Thy most sweet voice, of what use is hearing?

24.6 Let each morn be better than its eve and each morrow richer than its yesterday.

24.7 The Great Being saith: The man of consummate learning and the sage endowed with penetrating wisdom are the two eyes to the body of mankind. God willing, the earth shall never be deprived of these two greatest gifts. That which hath been set forth and will be revealed in the future is but a token of this Servant's ardent desire to dedicate Himself to the service of all the kindreds of the earth.

24.8 Make thou every effort to render service unto God, that from thee may appear that which will immortalize thy memory in His glorious and exalted heaven.

24.9 How vast is the tabernacle of the Cause of God! It hath overshadowed all the peoples and kindreds of the earth, and will, erelong, gather together the whole of mankind beneath its shelter. Thy day of service is now come. Countless Tablets bear the testimony of the bounties vouchsafed unto thee. Arise for the triumph of My Cause, and, through the power of thine utterance, subdue the hearts of men. Thou must show forth that which will ensure the peace and the well-being of the miserable and the down-trodden. Gird up the loins of thine endeavor, that perchance thou mayest release the captive from his chains, and enable him to attain unto true liberty.

FROM THE WRITINGS AND UTTERANCES OF 'ABDU'L-BAHÁ

24.10 Soon will your swiftly-passing days be over, and the fame and riches, the comforts, the joys provided by this rubbish-heap, the world, will be gone without a trace. Summon ye, then, the people to God, and invite humanity to follow the example of the Company on high. Be ye loving fathers to the orphan, and a refuge to the helpless, and a treasury for the poor, and a cure for the ailing. Be ye the helpers of every victim of oppression, the patrons of the disadvantaged. Think ye at all times of rendering some service to every member of the human race. Pay ye no heed to aversion and rejection, to disdain, hostility, injustice: act ye in the opposite way. Be ye sincerely kind, not in appearance only. Let each one of God's loved ones centre his attention on this: to be the Lord's mercy to man; to be the Lord's grace. Let him do some good to every person whose path he crosseth, and be of some benefit to him. Let him improve the character of each and all, and reorient the minds of men. In this way, the light of divine guidance will shine forth, and the blessings of God will cradle all mankind: for love is light, no matter in what abode it dwelleth; and hate is darkness, no matter where it may make its nest. O friends of God! That the hidden Mystery may stand revealed, and the secret essence of all things may be disclosed, strive ye to banish that darkness for ever and ever.

24.11 What bounty greater than this that science should be considered as an act of worship and art as service to the Kingdom of God.

24.12 Service to the friends is service to the Kingdom of God, and consideration shown to the poor is one of the greatest teachings of God.

24.13 Soon will our handful of days, our vanishing life, be gone, and we shall pass, empty-handed, into the hollow that is dug for those who speak no more; wherefore must we bind our hearts to the manifest Beauty, and cling to the lifeline that faileth never. We must gird ourselves for service, kindle love's flame, and burn away in its heat. We must loose our tongues till we set the wide world's heart afire, and with bright rays of guidance blot out the armies of the night, and then, for His sake, on the field of sacrifice, fling down our lives.

Thus let us scatter over every people the treasured gems of the recognition of God, and with the decisive blade of the tongue, and the sure arrows of knowledge, let us defeat the hosts of self and passion, and hasten onward to the site of martyrdom, to the place where we die for the Lord. And then, with flying flags, and to the beat of drums, let us pass into the realm of the All-Glorious, and join the Company on high.

Well is it with the doers of great deeds.

24.14 Wherefore, rest ye neither day nor night and seek no ease. Tell ye the secrets of servitude, follow the pathway of service, till ye attain the promised succour that cometh from the realms of God.

24.15 O my spiritual loved ones! Praise be to God, ye have thrust the veils aside and recognized the compassionate Beloved, and have hastened away from this abode to the placeless realm. Ye have pitched your tents in the world of God, and to glorify Him, the Self-Subsistent, ye have raised sweet voices and sung songs that pierced the heart. Well done! A thousand times well done! For ye have beheld the Light made manifest, and in your reborn beings ye have raised the cry, 'Blessed be the Lord, the best of all creators!' Ye were but babes in the womb, then were ye sucklings, and from a precious breast ye drew the milk of knowledge, then came ye to your full growth, and won salvation. Now is the time for service, and for servitude unto the Lord. Release yourselves from all distracting thoughts, deliver the Message with an eloquent tongue, adorn your assemblages with praise of the Beloved, till bounty shall descend in overwhelming floods and dress the world in fresh greenery and blossoms. This streaming bounty is even the counsels, admonitions, instructions, and injunctions of Almighty God.

24.16 For service in love for mankind is unity with God. He who serves has already entered the Kingdom and is seated at the right hand of his Lord.

24.17 In man there are two natures; his spiritual or higher nature and his material or lower nature. In one he approaches God, in the other he lives for the world alone. Signs of both these natures are to be found in men. In his material aspect he expresses untruth, cruelty and injustice; all these are the outcome of his lower nature. The attributes of his Divine nature are shown forth in love, mercy, kindness, truth and justice, one and all being expressions of his higher nature. Every good habit, every noble quality belongs to man's spiritual nature, whereas all his imperfections and sinful actions are born of his material nature. If a man's Divine nature dominates his human nature, we have a saint.

FROM THE WRITINGS AND LETTERS WRITTEN BY, OR ON BEHALF OF, SHOGHI EFFENDI

24.18　There are so many movements in the world at present akin to various Bahá'í principles; indeed we can almost say that the principles of Bahá'u'lláh have been adopted by thinking people all over this planet. But what they do not realize, and what the Bahá'ís must therefore teach them, is that these principles, however perfect, will never be able to create a new society unless and until they are animated by the spirit which alone changes the hearts of and characters of men and that spirit is recognition of their Divine origin in a teacher sent from God in other words, Bahá'u'lláh. When they recognize this, their hearts will change and a change of heart is what people need, not merely a change of intellectual outlook.

24.19　It is the duty of those who are in charge of the organization of society to give every individual the opportunity of acquiring the necessary talent in some kind of profession, and also the means of utilizing such a talent, both for its own sake and for the sake of earning the means of his livelihood. Every individual, no matter how handicapped and limited he may be, is under the obligation of engaging in some work or profession, for work, specially when performed in the spirit of service, is according to Bahá'u'lláh a form of worship. It has not only a utilitarian purpose, but has a value in itself, because it draws us nearer to God, and enables us to better grasp His purpose for us in this world. It is obvious, therefore, that the inheritance of wealth cannot make anyone immune from daily work.

FROM THE WRITINGS AND LETTERS WRITTEN BY, OR ON BEHALF OF, THE UNIVERSAL HOUSE OF JUSTICE

24.20　May you all persevere in your individual efforts to teach the Faith, but with added zest, to study the Writings, but with greater earnestness. May you pursue your education and training for future service to mankind, offering as much (your free time as possible to activities on behalf of the Cause. May those of you already bent on your life's work and who may have already founded families strive toward becoming the living embodiments of Bahá'í ideals, both in the spiritual nurturing of your families and in your active involvement in the effort on the home front or abroad in the pioneering field. May all respond to the current demands upon the Faith by displaying a fresh measure of dedication to the tasks at hand.

CHAPTER 25:

CULTIVATING A SPIRIT OF TRUST

350 ❓ Making a Better World with the Bahá'í Faith: QUOTATIONS

FROM THE WRITINGS OF BAHÁ'U'LLÁH

25.1 We will now mention unto thee Trustworthiness and the station thereof in the estimation of God, thy Lord, the Lord of the Mighty Throne. One day of days We repaired unto Our Green Island. Upon Our arrival, We beheld its streams flowing, and its trees luxuriant, and the sunlight playing in their midst. Turning Our face to the right, We beheld what the pen is powerless to describe; nor can it set forth that which the eye of the Lord of Mankind witnessed in that most sanctified, that most sublime, that blest, and most exalted Spot. Turning, then, to the left We gazed on one of the Beauties of the Most Sublime Paradise, standing on a pillar of light, and calling aloud saying: "O inmates of earth and heaven! Behold ye My beauty, and My radiance, and My revelation, and My effulgence. By God, the True One! I am Trustworthiness and the revelation thereof, and the beauty thereof. I will recompense whosoever will cleave unto Me, and recognize My rank and station, and hold fast unto My hem. I am the most great ornament of the people of Baha, and the vesture of glory unto all who are in the kingdom of creation. I am the supreme instrument for the prosperity of the world, and the horizon of assurance unto all beings." Thus have We sent down for thee that which will draw men nigh unto the Lord of creation.

25.2 O people of Baha! Trustworthiness is in truth the best of vestures for your temples and the most glorious crown for your heads. Take ye fast hold of it at the behest of Him Who is the Ordainer, the All-Informed.

25.3 Adorn your heads with the garlands of trustworthiness and fidelity, your hearts with the attire of the fear of God, your tongues with absolute truthfulness, your bodies with the vesture of courtesy. These are in truth seemly adornings unto the temple of man, if ye be of them that reflect.

25.4 They who are the people of God have no ambition except to revive the world, to ennoble its life, and regenerate its peoples. Truthfulness and good-will have, at all times, marked their relations with all men. Their outward conduct is but a reflection of their inward life, and their inward life a mirror of their outward conduct. No veil hideth or obscureth the verities on which their Faith is established. Before the eyes of all men these verities have been laid bare, and can be unmistakably recognized. Their very acts attest the truth of these words

25.5 Beautify your tongues, O people, with truthfulness, and adorn your souls with the ornament of honesty. Beware, O people, that ye deal not treacherously with any one. Be ye the trustees of God amongst His creatures, and the emblems of His generosity amidst His people. They that follow their lusts and corrupt inclinations, have erred and dissipated their efforts. They, indeed, are of the lost. Strive, O people, that your eyes may be directed towards the mercy of God, that your hearts may be attuned to His wondrous remembrance, that your souls may rest confidently upon His grace and bounty, that your feet may tread the path of His good-pleasure. Such are the counsels which I bequeath unto you. Would that ye might follow My counsels!

25.6 O OPPRESSORS ON EARTH! Withdraw your hands from tyranny, for I have pledged Myself not to forgive any man's injustice. This is My covenant which I have irrevocably decreed in the preserved tablet and sealed with My seal.

25.7 Say: Let truthfulness and courtesy be your adorning. Suffer not yourselves to be deprived of the robe of forbearance and justice, that the sweet savors of holiness may be wafted from your hearts upon all created things. Say: Beware, O people of Baha, lest ye walk in the ways of them whose words differ from their deeds. Strive that ye may be enabled to manifest to the peoples of the earth the signs of God, and to mirror forth His commandments. Let your acts be a guide unto all mankind, for the professions of most men, be they high or low, differ from their conduct. It is through your deeds that ye can distinguish yourselves from others. Through them the brightness of your light can be shed upon the whole earth. Happy is the man that heedeth My counsel, and keepeth the precepts prescribed by Him Who is the All-Knowing, the All-Wise.

25.8 The fruits that best befit the tree of human life are trustworthiness and godliness, truthfulness and sincerity; but greater than all, after recognition of the unity of God, praised and glorified be He, is regard for the rights that are due to one's parents. This teaching hath been mentioned in all the Books of God, and reaffirmed by the Most Exalted Pen.

25.9 By My beauty! All your doings hath My pen graven with open characters upon tablets of chrysolite.

25.10 Lay not aside the fear of God, O ye the learned of the world, and judge fairly the Cause of this unlettered One to Whom all the Books of God, the Protector, the Self-Subsisting, have testified. …Will not the dread of Divine displeasure, the fear of Him Who hath no peer or equal, arouse you?

25.11 "The companions of God," Bahá'u'lláh Himself has declared, "are, in this day, the lump that must leaven the peoples of the world. They must show forth such trustworthiness, such truthfulness and perseverance, such deeds and character that all mankind may profit by their example." "I swear by Him Who is the Most Great Ocean!" He again affirms, "Within the very breath of such souls as are pure and sanctified far-reaching potentialities are hidden. So great are these potentialities that they exercise their influence upon all created things." "He is the true servant of God," He, in another passage has written, "who, in this day, were he to pass through cities of silver and gold, would not deign to look upon them, and whose heart would remain pure and undefiled from whatever things can be seen in this world, be they its goods or its treasures. I swear by the Sun of Truth! The breath of such a man is endowed with potency, and his words with attraction." "By Him Who shineth above the Dayspring of sanctity!" He, still more emphatically, has revealed, "If the whole earth were to be converted into silver and gold, no man who can be said to have truly ascended into the heaven of faith and certitude would deign to regard it, much less to seize and keep it…. They who dwell within the Tabernacle of God, and are established upon the seats of everlasting glory, will refuse, though they be dying of hunger, to stretch their hands, and seize unlawfully the property of their neighbor, however vile and worthless he may be. The purpose of the one true God in manifesting Himself is to summon all mankind to truthfulness and sincerity, to piety and trustworthiness, to resignation and submissiveness to the will of God, to forbearance and kindliness, to uprightness and wisdom. His object is to array every man with the mantle of a saintly character, and to adorn him with the ornament of holy and goodly deeds." "We have admonished all the loved ones of God," He insists, "to take heed lest the hem of Our sacred vesture be smirched with the mire of unlawful deeds, or be stained with the dust of reprehensible conduct." "Cleave unto righteousness, O people of Baha," He thus exhorts them, "This, verily, is the commandment which this wronged One hath given unto you, and the first choice of His unrestrained will for every one of you." "A good character," He explains, "is, verily, the best mantle for men from God. With it He adorneth the temples of His loved ones. By My life! The light of a good character surpasseth the light of the sun and the radiance thereof."

FROM THE WRITINGS AND UTTERANCES OF 'ABDU'L-BAHÁ

25.12 O ye my loved ones! The world is wrapped in the thick darkness of open revolt and swept by a whirlwind of hate. It is the fires of malevolence that have cast up their flames to the clouds of heaven, it is a blood-drenched flood that rolleth across the plains and down the hills, and no one on the face of the earth can find any peace. Therefore must the friends of God engender that tenderness which cometh from Heaven, and bestow love in the spirit upon all humankind. With every soul must they deal according to the Divine counsellings and admonitions; to all must they show forth kindness and good faith; to all must they wish well. They must sacrifice themselves for their friends, and wish good fortune to their foes. They must comfort the ill-natured, and treat their oppressors with loving-kindness. They must be as refreshing water to the thirsty, and to the sick, a swift remedy, a healing balm to those

Chapter 25: Cultivating a Spirit of Trust 355

in pain and a solace to every burdened heart. They must be a guiding light to those who have gone astray, a sure leader for the lost. They must be seeing eyes to the blind, hearing ears to the deaf, and to the dead eternal life, and to the despondent joy forever.

25.13 We should at all times manifest our truthfulness and sincerity, nay rather, we must be constant in our faithfulness and trustworthiness, and occupy ourselves in offering prayers for the good of all.

25.14 For the attributes of the people of faith are justice and fair-mindedness; forbearance and compassion and generosity; consideration for others; candor, trustworthiness, and loyalty; love and loving-kindness; devotion and determination and humanity.

25.15 Wherefore, O my loving friends! Consort with all the peoples, kindreds and religions of the world with the utmost truthfulness, uprightness, faithfulness, kindliness, good-will and friendliness, that all the world of being may be filled with the holy ecstasy of the grace of Baha, that ignorance, enmity, hate and rancor may vanish from the world and the darkness of estrangement amidst the peoples and kindreds of the world may give way to the Light of Unity. Should other peoples and nations be unfaithful to you show your fidelity unto them, should they be unjust toward you show justice towards them, should they keep aloof from you attract them to yourselves, should they show their enmity be friendly towards them, should they poison your lives, sweeten their souls, should they inflict a wound upon you, be a salve to their sores. Such are the attributes of the sincere! Such are the attributes of the truthful.

25.16 O ye beloved of the Lord! It is incumbent upon you to be submissive to all monarchs that are just and to show your fidelity to every righteous king. Serve ye the sovereigns of the world with utmost truthfulness and loyalty. Show obedience unto them and be their well-wishers. Without their leave and permission do not meddle with political affairs, for disloyalty to the just sovereign is disloyalty to God Himself.

25.17 "O army of God!" writes 'Abdu'l-Bahá, "Through the protection and help vouchsafed by the Blessed Beauty—may my life be a sacrifice to His loved ones—ye must conduct yourselves in such a manner that ye may stand out distinguished and brilliant as the sun among other souls. Should any one of you enter a city, he should become a center of attraction by reason of his sincerity, his faithfulness and love, his honesty and fidelity, his truthfulness and loving-kindness towards all the peoples of the world, so that the people of that city may cry out and say: 'This man is unquestionably a Bahá'í, for his manners, his behavior, his conduct, his morals, his nature, and disposition reflect the attributes of the Bahá'ís.' Not until ye attain this station can ye be said to have been faithful to the Covenant and Testament of God." "The most vital duty, in this day," He, moreover, has written, "is to purify your characters, to correct your manners, and improve your conduct. The beloved of the Merciful must show forth such character and conduct among His creatures, that the fragrance of their holiness may be shed upon the whole world, and may quicken the dead, inasmuch as the purpose of the Manifestation of God and the dawning of the limitless lights of the Invisible is to educate the souls of men, and refine the character of every living man...." "Truthfulness," He asserts, "is the foundation of all human virtues. Without truthfulness progress and success, in all the worlds of God, are impossible for any soul. When this holy attribute is established in man, all the divine qualities will also be acquired."

FROM THE WRITINGS AND LETTERS WRITTEN BY, OR ON BEHALF OF, SHOGHI EFFENDI

25.18 These are the days for rendering the divine Cause victorious and effective aid! The victory of God's Faith is dependent upon teaching; and teaching is conditional upon righteous actions and goodly deeds and conduct. The foundation-stone of a life lived in the way of God is the pursuit of moral excellence and the acquisition of a character endowed with qualities that are well-pleasing in His sight. The Bahá'ís should adorn themselves with this holy raiment; with this mighty sword they should conquer the citadels of men's hearts. People have grown weary and impatient of rhetoric and discourse, of preaching and sermonizing. In this day, the one thing that can deliver the world from its travail and attract the hearts of its peoples is deeds, not words; example, not precept; saintly virtues, not statements and charters issued by governments and nations on socio-political affairs. In all matters, great or small, word must be the complement of deed, and deed the companion of word: each must supplement, support and reinforce the other. It is in this respect that the Bahá'ís must seek distinction over other peoples and nations, whom the Pen of the Most High has epitomized in the following words: "Their words are the pride of the world, and their deeds are the shame of the nations."

25.19 Nothing but the abundance of our actions, nothing but the purity of our lives and the integrity of our character, can in the last resort establish our claim that the Bahá'í spirit is in this day the sole agency that can translate a long-cherished ideal into an enduring achievement.

25.20 This is the day for excellence of character and conduct. We should all adorn ourselves with these ornaments of the Kingdom while still in this world of being, so that we may render fit service to the Threshold of the Most Merciful.

25.21 The people of Baha, under the jurisdiction of whatsoever state or government they may be residing, should conduct themselves with honesty and sincerity, trustworthiness and rectitude. They should concern themselves with men's hearts, and hold themselves aloof from the fluctuations and limitations of the contingent world. They are neither thirsty for prominence, nor acquisitive of power; they are neither adepts at dissimulation and hypocrisy, nor are they seekers after wealth and influence; they neither crave for the pomp and circumstance of high office, nor do they lust after the glory of titles and ranks. They are averse to affectation and ostentation, and shrink from the use of coercive force; they have closed their eyes to all but God, and set their hearts on the firm and incontrovertible promises of their Lord; they have severed the bonds of earthly expectations and attachments, and connected their lives to the One Peerless Beloved. Oblivious to themselves, they have occupied their energies in working towards the good of society; and, steadfastly adhering to the sound and wholesome principles of God's Faith, they have turned their backs on the morbid imaginings, the incoherent theories, and pernicious ideas of the victims of caprice and folly. While vigilantly refusing to accept political posts, they should whole-heartedly welcome the chance to assume administrative positions; for the primary purpose of the people of Baha is to advance the interests and promote the welfare of the nation, not to further the devious ends and designs of the profligate and shameless. Such is the method of the Bahá'ís; such is the conduct of all spiritually illumined souls; and aught else is manifest error.

25.22 The permanence and stability achieved by any association, group or nation is a result of—and dependent upon—the soundness and worth of the principles upon which it bases the running of its affairs and the direction of its activities. The guiding principles of the Bahá'ís are: honesty, love, charity and trustworthiness; the setting of the common good above private interest; and the practice of godliness, virtue and moderation. Ultimately, then, their preservation and happiness are assured. Whatever misfortunes they may encounter, wrought by the wiles of the schemer and ill-wisher, shall all pass away like waves, and hardship shall be succeeded by joy. The friends are under the protection of the resistless power and inscrutable providence of God. There is no doubt that every blessed soul who brings his life into harmony with this all-swaying power shall give lustre to his works and win an ample recompense. The actions of those who choose to set themselves against it should provoke not antipathy on our part, but prayers for their guidance. Such was the way of the Bahá'ís in days gone by, and so must it be, now and for always.

25.23 You brought up the question of showing forth honesty and trustworthiness when engaged in the service of the state. These are qualities that must distinguish all the activities of the friends, and the acquisition of which is a religious duty incumbent on every believer. That some of the leaders whom they serve may be unappreciative of their efforts, or fail correctly to value their services, should give no cause for surprise. The reason for such conduct is the remoteness of such men from the True Source of justice, equity and fair-mindedness. We should keep our vision centred on God, not on the doings of His creatures. Every spotless action, every sincere intent of ours will win the commendation of the True One, will be exalted and magnified by Him, and requited with a bounteous recompense.

25.24 The Guardian feels that your attitude towards the corrupt practice of accepting commissions from fellow physicians and pharmacists is most admirable. The more upright and noble the Bahá'ís are in their conduct, the more they will impress the public with the spiritual vitality of the Faith they believe in.

FROM THE WRITINGS AND LETTERS WRITTEN BY, OR ON BEHALF OF, THE UNIVERSAL HOUSE OF JUSTICE

25.25 First, the foundation of all their other accomplishments is their study of the teachings, the spiritualization of their lives and the forming of their characters in accordance with the standards of Bahá'u'lláh. As the moral standards of the people around us collapse and decay, whether of the centuries-old civilizations of the East, the more recent cultures of Christendom and Islam; or of the rapidly changing tribal societies of the world, the Bahá'ís must increasingly stand out as pillars of righteousness and forbearance. The life of a Bahá'í will be characterized by truthfulness and decency; he will walk uprightly among his fellowmen, dependent upon none save God, yet linked by bonds of love and brotherhood with all mankind; he will be entirely detached from the loose standards, the decadent theories, the frenetic experimentation, the desperation of present-day society, will look upon his neighbours with a bright and friendly face and be a beacon light and a haven for all those who would emulate his strength of character and assurance of soul.

OTHER SOURCES

25.26 The task of creating a global development strategy that will accelerate humanity's coming-of-age constitutes a challenge to reshape fundamentally all the institutions of society. The protagonists to whom the challenge addresses itself are all of the inhabitants of the planet: the generality of humankind, members of governing institutions at all levels, persons serving in agencies of international coordination, scientists and social thinkers, all those endowed with artistic talents or with access to the media of communication, and leaders of non-governmental organizations. The response called for must base itself on an unconditioned recognition of the oneness of humankind, a commitment to the establishment of justice as the organizing principle of society, and a determination to exploit to their utmost the possibilities that a systematic dialogue between the scientific and religious genius of the race can bring to the building of human capacity. The enterprise requires a radical rethinking of most of the concepts and assumptions currently governing social and economic life. It must be wedded, as well, to a conviction that, however long the process and whatever setbacks may be encountered, the governance of human affairs can be conducted along lines that serve humanity's real needs. (Baha'i International Community, 1995 Mar 03, *The Prosperity of Humankind*).

CONCLUSION

CHAPTER 26:

DECIDING HOW YOU WILL MAKE A DIFFERENCE

364 ❓ Making a Better World with the Bahá'í Faith: QUOTATIONS

FROM THE WRITINGS OF BAHÁ'U'LLÁH

26.1 The Word of God hath set the heart of the world afire; how regrettable if ye fail to be enkindled with its flame! Please God, ye will regard this blessed night as the night of unity, will knit your souls together, and resolve to adorn yourselves with the ornament of a goodly and praiseworthy character. Let your principal concern be to rescue the fallen from the slough of impending extinction, and to help him embrace the ancient Faith of God. Your behavior towards your neighbor should be such as to manifest clearly the signs of the one true God, for ye are the first among men to be re-created by His Spirit, the first to adore and bow the knee before Him, the first to circle round His throne of glory. I swear by Him Who hath caused Me to reveal whatever hath pleased Him! Ye are better known to the inmates of the Kingdom on high than ye are known to your own selves. Think ye these words to be vain and empty? Would that ye had the power to perceive the things your Lord, the All-Merciful, doth see—things that attest the excellence of your rank, that bear witness to the greatness of your worth, that proclaim the sublimity of your station! God grant that your desires and unmortified passions may not hinder you from that which hath been ordained for you.

26.2 The Book of God is wide open, and His Word is summoning mankind unto Him. No more than a mere handful, however, hath been found willing to cleave to His Cause, or to become the instruments for its promotion. These few have been endued with the Divine Elixir that can, alone, transmute into purest gold the dross of the world, and have been empowered to administer the infallible remedy for all the ills that afflict the children of men. No man can obtain everlasting life, unless he embraceth the truth of this inestimable, this wondrous, and sublime Revelation.

26.3 Praised be Thou, O my God, inasmuch as Thou hast aided us to recognize and love Him. I, therefore, beseech Thee by Him and by Them Who are the Day-Springs of Thy Divinity, and the Manifestations of Thy Lordship, and the Treasuries of Thy Revelation, and the Depositories of Thine inspiration, to enable us to serve and obey Him, and to empower us to become the helpers of His Cause and the dispersers of His adversaries. Powerful art Thou to do all that pleaseth Thee. No God is there beside Thee, the Almighty, the All-Glorious, the One Whose help is sought by all men!

26.4 Thus have We inspired thee, and infused into thy heart that which will make thee independent of the allusions of mankind.

26.5 The purpose underlying the revelation of every heavenly Book, nay, of every divinely-revealed verse, is to endue all men with righteousness and understanding, so that peace and tranquillity may be firmly established amongst them. Whatsoever instilleth assurance into the hearts of men, whatsoever exalteth their station or promoteth their contentment, is acceptable in the sight of God. How lofty is the station which man, if he but choose to fulfill his high destiny, can attain!

26.6 This is My counsel unto thee and unto the beloved of God. Whosoever wisheth, let him turn thereunto; whosoever wisheth, let him turn away. God, verily, is independent of him and of that which he may see and witness.

FROM THE WRITINGS AND UTTERANCES OF 'ABDU'L-BAHÁ

26.7 Know thou of a certainty that Love is the secret of God's holy Dispensation, the manifestation of the All-Merciful, the fountain of spiritual outpourings. Love is heaven's kindly light, the Holy Spirit's eternal breath that vivifieth the human soul. Love is the cause of God's revelation unto man, the vital bond inherent, in accordance with the divine creation, in the realities of things. Love is the one means that ensureth true felicity both in this world and the next. Love is the light that guideth in darkness, the living link that uniteth God with man, that assureth the progress of every illumined soul. Love is the most great law that ruleth this mighty and heavenly cycle, the unique power that bindeth together the divers elements of this material world, the supreme magnetic force that directeth the movements of the spheres in the celestial realms. Love revealeth with unfailing and limitless power the mysteries latent in the universe. Love is the spirit of life unto the adorned body of mankind, the establisher of true civilization in this mortal world, and the shedder of imperishable glory upon every high-aiming race and nation.

Whatsoever people is graciously favoured therewith by God, its name shall surely be magnified and extolled by the Concourse from on high, by the company of angels, and the denizens of the Abhá Kingdom. And whatsoever people turneth its heart away from this Divine Love—the revelation of the Merciful—shall err grievously, shall fall into despair, and be utterly destroyed. That people shall be denied all refuge, shall become even as the vilest creatures of the earth, victims of degradation and shame.

O ye beloved of the Lord! Strive to become the manifestations of the love of God, the lamps of divine guidance shining amongst the kindreds of the earth with the light of love and concord.

All hail to the revealers of this glorious light!

26.8 O ye loving friends! Strive ye with heart and soul to make this world the mirror-image of the Kingdom, that this nether world may teem with the blessings of the world of God, that the voices of the Company on high may be raised in acclamation, and signs and tokens of the bounties and bestowals of Bahá'u'lláh may encompass all the earth.

26.9 O Thou, my God, Who guidest the seeker to the pathway that leadeth aright, Who deliverest the lost and blinded soul out of the wastes of perdition, Thou Who bestowest upon the sincere great bounties and favours, Who guardest the frightened within Thine impregnable refuge, Who answerest, from Thine all-highest horizon, the cry of those who cry out unto Thee. Praised be Thou, O my Lord! Thou hast guided the distracted out of the death of unbelief, and hast brought those who draw nigh unto Thee to the journey's goal, and hast rejoiced the assured among Thy servants by granting them their most cherished desires, and hast, from Thy Kingdom of beauty, opened before the faces of those who yearn after Thee the gates of reunion, and hast rescued them from the fires of deprivation and loss—so that they hastened unto Thee and gained Thy presence, and arrived at Thy welcoming door, and received of gifts an abundant share.

O my Lord, they thirsted, Thou didst lift to their parched lips the waters of reunion. O Tender One, Bestowing One, Thou didst calm their pain with the balm of Thy bounty and grace, and didst heal their ailments with the sovereign medicine of Thy compassion. O Lord, make firm their feet on Thy straight path, make wide for them the needle's eye, and cause them, dressed in royal robes, to walk in glory for ever and ever.

Verily art Thou the Generous, the Ever-Giving, the Precious, the Most Bountiful. There is none other God but Thee, the Mighty, the Powerful, the Exalted, the Victorious.

O my spiritual loved ones! Praise be to God, ye have thrust the veils aside and recognized the compassionate Beloved, and have hastened away from this abode to the placeless realm. Ye have pitched your tents in the world of God, and to glorify Him, the Self-Subsistent, ye have raised sweet voices and sung songs that pierced the heart. Well done! A thousand times well done! For ye have beheld the Light made manifest, and in your reborn beings ye have raised the cry, 'Blessed be the Lord, the best of all creators!' Ye were but babes in the womb, then were ye sucklings, and from a precious breast ye drew the milk of knowledge, then came ye to your full growth, and won salvation. Now is the time for service, and for servitude unto the Lord. Release yourselves from all distracting thoughts, deliver the Message with an eloquent tongue, adorn your assemblages with praise of the Beloved, till bounty shall descend in overwhelming floods and dress the world in fresh greenery and blossoms. This streaming bounty is even the counsels, admonitions, instructions, and injunctions of Almighty God.

O ye my loved ones! The world is wrapped in the thick darkness of open revolt and swept by a whirlwind of hate. It is the fires of malevolence that have cast up their flames to the clouds of heaven, it is a blood-drenched flood that rolleth across the plains and down the hills, and no one on the face of the earth can find any peace. Therefore must the friends of God engender that tenderness which cometh from Heaven, and bestow love in the spirit upon all humankind. With every soul must they deal according to the Divine counsellings and admonitions; to all must they show forth kindness and good faith; to all must they wish well. They must sacrifice themselves for their friends, and wish good fortune to their foes. They must comfort the ill-natured, and treat their oppressors with loving-kindness. They must be as refreshing water to the thirsty, and to the sick, a swift remedy, a healing balm to those in pain and a solace to every burdened heart. They must be a guiding light to those who have gone astray, a sure leader for the lost. They must be seeing eyes to the blind, hearing ears to the deaf, and to the dead eternal life, and to the despondent joy forever.

26.10 From amongst all mankind hath He chosen you, and your eyes have been opened to the light of guidance and your ears attuned to the music of the Company above; and blessed by abounding grace, your hearts and souls have been born into new life. Thank ye and praise ye God that the hand of infinite bestowals hath set upon your heads this gem-studded crown, this crown whose lustrous jewels will forever flash and sparkle down all the reaches of time.

26.11 Raise ye a clamour like unto a roaring sea; like a prodigal cloud, rain down the grace of heaven. Lift up your voices and sing out the songs of the Abha Realm. Quench ye the fires of war, lift high the banners of peace, work for the oneness of humankind and remember that religion is the channel of love unto all peoples. Be ye aware that the children of men are sheep of God and He their loving Shepherd, that He careth tenderly for all His sheep and maketh them to feed in His own green pastures of grace and giveth them to drink from the wellspring of life. Such is the way of the Lord. Such are His bestowals. Such, from among His teachings, is His precept of the oneness of mankind.

The portals of His blessings are opened wide and His signs are published abroad and the glory of truth is blazing forth; inexhaustible are the blessings. Know ye the value of this time. Strive ye with all your hearts, raise up your voices and shout, until this dark world be filled with light, and this narrow place of shadows be widened out, and this dust heap of a fleeting moment be changed into a mirror for the eternal gardens of heaven, and this globe of earth receive its portion of celestial grace.

26.12 Act in accordance with the counsels of the Lord: that is, rise up in such wise, and with such qualities, as to endow the body of this world with a living soul, and to bring this young child, humanity, to the stage of adulthood. So far as ye are able, ignite a candle of love in every meeting, and with tenderness rejoice and cheer ye every heart. Care for the stranger as for one of your own; show to alien souls the same loving kindness ye bestow upon your faithful friends. Should any come to blows with you, seek to be friends with him; should any stab you to the heart, be ye a healing salve unto his sores; should any taunt and mock at you, meet him with love. Should any heap his blame upon you, praise ye him; should he offer you a deadly poison, give him the choicest honey in exchange; and should he threaten your life, grant him a remedy that will heal him evermore. Should he be pain itself, be ye his medicine; should he be thorns, be ye his roses and sweet herbs. Perchance such ways and words from you will make this darksome world turn bright at last; will make this dusty earth turn heavenly, this devilish prison place become a royal palace of the Lord—so that war and strife will pass and be no more, and love and trust will pitch their tents on the summits of the world. Such is the essence of God's admonitions; such in sum are the teachings for the Dispensation of Baha.

26.13 I am greatly pleased with you all and rejoice that you have shown me the utmost kindness and affection. It is my desire that Bahá'u'lláh shall be pleased with you, that you may follow His precepts and become worthy of His confirmations. The requirements are that your minds must be illumined, your souls must be rejoiced with the glad tidings of God, you must become imbued with spiritual moralities, your daily life must evidence faith and assurance, your hearts must be sanctified and pure, reflecting a high degree of love and attraction toward the Kingdom of Abha. You must become the lamps of Bahá'u'lláh so that you may shine with eternal light and be the proofs and evidences of His truth. Then will such signs of purity and chastity be witnessed in your deeds and actions that men will behold the heavenly radiance of your lives and say, "Verily, ye are the proofs of Bahá'u'lláh. Verily, Bahá'u'lláh is the True One, for He has trained such souls as these, each one of which is a proof in himself." They will say to others, "Come and witness the conduct of these souls; come and listen to their words, behold the illumination of their hearts, see the evidences of the love of God in them, consider their praiseworthy morals, and discover the foundations of the oneness of humanity firmly implanted within them. What greater proof can there be than these people that the message of Bahá'u'lláh is truth and reality?" It is my hope that each one of you shall be a herald of God, proclaiming the evidences of His appearance, in words, deeds and thoughts. Let your actions and utterances be a witness that you are of the Kingdom of Bahá'u'lláh. These are the duties enjoined upon you by Bahá'u'lláh.

26.14 It is my wish that you shall arise to live according to these teachings and exhortations; that all of us may be divinely strengthened, enter the paradise of the spiritual Kingdom, diffuse the lights of the Sun of Truth, cause the waves of this Most Great Ocean to reach all human souls so that this world of earth may be transformed into the world of heaven and this devastated ground be changed into the paradise of Abha.

FROM THE WRITINGS AND LETTERS WRITTEN BY, OR ON BEHALF OF, THE UNIVERSAL HOUSE OF JUSTICE

26.15 ...There are mighty agencies in this world, governments, foundations, institutions of many kinds with tremendous financial resources which are working to improve the material lot of human beings. Anything we Bahá'ís could add to such resources in the way of special funds or contributions would be a negligible drop in the ocean. However, alone among men we have the Divinely-given remedy for the real ills of mankind; no one else is doing or can do this most important work, and if we divert our energy and our funds into fields in which others are already doing more than we can hope to do, we shall be delaying the diffusion of the Divine Message which is the most important task of all.

Because of such an attitude, as also because of our refusal to become involved in politics, Bahá'ís are often accused of holding aloof from the 'real problems' of their fellow-men. But when we hear this accusation let us not forget that those who make it are usually idealistic materialists to whom material good is the only 'real' good, whereas we know that the working of the material world is merely a reflection of spiritual conditions and until the spiritual conditions can be changed there can be no lasting change for the better in material affairs.

We should also remember that most people have no clear concept of the sort of world they wish to build, nor how to go about building it. Even those who are concerned to improve conditions are therefore reduced to combatting every apparent evil that takes their attention. Willingness to fight against evils, whether in the form of conditions or embodied in evil men, has thus become for most people the touchstone by which they judge a person's moral worth. Bahá'ís, on the other hand, know the goal they are working towards and know what they must do, step by step, to attain it. Their whole energy is directed towards the building of the good, a good which has such a positive strength that in the face of it the multitude of evils—which are in essence negative—will fade away and be no more. To enter into the quixotic tournament of demolishing one by one the evils in the world is, to a Bahá'í a vain waste of time and effort. His whole life is directed towards proclaiming the Message of Bahá'u'lláh, reviving the spiritual life of his fellow-men, uniting them in a Divinely-created World Order, and then, as that Order grows in strength and influence, he will see the power of that Message transforming the whole of human society and progressively solving the problems and removing the injustice which have so long bedeviled the world.

APPENDIX:
SOURCES AND BIBLIOGRAPHY

374 ❓ Making a Better World with the Bahá'í Faith: QUOTATIONS

SOURCES FOR MAKING A BETTER WORLD WITH THE BAHÁ'Í FAITH

Chapter 1
1.1　　Bahá'u'lláh, Gleanings from the Writings of Bahá'u'lláh, p. 214
1.2　　Bahá'u'lláh, Gleanings from the Writings of Bahá'u'lláh, p. 13
1.3　　Bahá'u'lláh, Gleanings from the Writings of Bahá'u'lláh, p. 7
1.4　　Bahá'u'lláh, Epistle to the Son of the Wolf, p. 37
1.5　　Bahá'u'lláh, Gleanings from the Writings of Bahá'u'lláh, p. 286
1.6　　'Abdu'l-Bahá, Selections from the Writings of 'Abdu'l-Bahá, p. 60
1.7　　'Abdu'l-Bahá, Selections from the Writings of 'Abdu'l-Bahá, p. 128
1.8　　'Abdu'l-Bahá, Selections from the Writings of 'Abdu'l-Bahá, p. 26
1.9　　'Abdu'l-Bahá, Selections from the Writings of 'Abdu'l-Bahá, p. 282
1.10　 'Abdu'l-Bahá, The Promulgation of Universal Peace, p. 322
1.11　 'Abdu'l-Bahá, The Promulgation of Universal Peace, p. 214
1.12　 'Abdu'l-Bahá, The Promulgation of Universal Peace, p. 336
1.13　 'Abdu'l-Bahá, The Promulgation of Universal Peace, p. 153
1.14　 'Abdu'l-Bahá, Foundations of World Unity, p. 103
1.15　 Shoghi Effendi, The World Order of Bahá'u'lláh, p. 42
1.16　 The Universal House of Justice, A Wider Horizon, Selected Letters 1983-1992, p. 5
1.17　 The Universal House of Justice, 1985 Oct, The Promise of World Peace, p. 3
1.18　 From a letter written on behalf of the Universal House of Justice to the National Spiritual Assembly of Italy, November 19, 1974. Lights of Guidance, p. 122
1.19　 Commissioned by The Universal House of Justice, One Common Faith

Chapter 2
2.1　　Bahá'u'lláh, Gleanings from the Writings of Bahá'u'lláh, p. 10
2.2　　Bahá'u'lláh, The Proclamation of Bahá'u'lláh
2.3　　Baha'u'llah, Epistle to the Son of the Wolf, p. 24
2.4　　Baha'u'llah, The Kitab-i-Aqdas, p. 73
2.5　　Baha'u'llah, Epistle to the Son of the Wolf, p. 11
2.6　　Baha'u'llah, The Summons of the Lord of Hosts, p. 4
2.7　　'Abdu'l-Bahá, Selections from the Writings of 'Abdu'l-Bahá, p. 100
2.8　　'Abdu'l-Bahá, Selections from the Writings of 'Abdu'l-Bahá, p. 252
2.9　　'Abdu'l-Bahá, The Promulgation of Universal Peace, p. 105
2.10　 'Abdu'l-Bahá, The Promulgation of Universal Peace, p. 313
2.11　 'Abdu'l-Bahá, The Promulgation of Universal Peace, p. 28
2.12　 Shoghi Effendi, Summary Statement - 1947, Special UN Committee on Palestine
2.13　 Shoghi Effendi, God Passes By, p. 281
2.14　 The Universal House of Justice, 1985 Oct, The Promise of World Peace, p. 1
2.15　 The Universal House of Justice, 1985 Oct, The Promise of World Peace, p. 1

Chapter 3
3.1　　Baha'u'llah, Gleanings from the Writings of Baha'u'llah, p. 243
3.2　　Baha'u'llah, Tablets of Baha'u'llah, p. 23
3.3　　Bahá'u'lláh, The Hidden Words, Arabic #64
3.4　　Bahá'u'lláh, Bahá'í Prayers, p. 3
3.5　　Baha'u'llah, Gleanings from the Writings of Baha'u'llah, p. 340
3.6　　'Abdu'l-Bahá, Selections from the Writings of 'Abdu'l-Bahá, p. 30
3.7　　'Abdu'l-Bahá, Selections from the Writings of 'Abdu'l-Bahá, p. 31
3.8　　'Abdu'l-Bahá, Selections from the Writings of 'Abdu'l-Bahá, p. 23
3.9　　'Abdu'l-Bahá, The Promulgation of Universal Peace, p. 11
3.10　 'Abdu'l-Bahá, The Promulgation of Universal Peace, p. 180
3.11　 'Abdu'l-Bahá, The Promulgation of Universal Peace, p. 171
3.12　 'Abdu'l-Bahá, The Promulgation of Universal Peace, p. 56
3.13　 'Abdu'l-Bahá, The Promulgation of Universal Peace, p. 191

3.14 'Abdu'l-Bahá, The Promulgation of Universal Peace, p. 320
3.15 'Abdu'l-Bahá, The Promulgation of Universal Peace, p. 92
3.16 From a letter written on behalf of the Guardian to the National Spiritual Assembly of the United States, July 19, 1956. Lights of Guidance, p. 131
3.17 From a letter of the Universal House of Justice to the Bahá'ís of the East and West, December 18, 1963. Lights of Guidance, p. 135
3.18 From a letter to an individual on behalf of the Universal House of Justice, 1996 July 02
3.19 Baha'i International Community, 1992 May 29, Statement on Baha'u'llah, p. 15

Chapter 4
4.1 Baha'u'llah, Tablets of Baha'u'llah, p. 165
4.2 Bahá'u'lláh, Tablets of Bahá'u'lláh, p. 127
4.3 Baha'u'llah, Tablets of Baha'u'llah, p. 22
4.4 Baha'u'llah, The Kitab-i-Aqdas, p. 88
4.5 Baha'u'llah, Tablets of Baha'u'llah, p. 89
4.6 Bahá'u'lláh, Tablets of Bahá'u'lláh, p. 138
4.7 Baha'u'llah, Gleanings from the Writings of Baha'u'llah, p. 7
4.8 'Abdu'l-Bahá, Selections from the Writings of 'Abdu'l-Bahá, p. 279
4.9 'Abdu'l-Bahá, Selections from the Writings of 'Abdu'l-Bahá, p. 33
4.10 'Abdu'l-Bahá, Selections from the Writings of 'Abdu'l-Bahá, p. 301
4.11 'Abdu'l-Bahá, The Secret of Divine Civilization, p. 4
4.12 'Abdu'l-Bahá, The Promulgation of Universal Peace, p. 300
4.13 'Abdu'l-Bahá, The Promulgation of Universal Peace, p. 182
4.14 'Abdu'l-Bahá, The Promulgation of Universal Peace, p. 170
4.15 'Abdu'l-Bahá, Paris Talks, p. 15
4.16 Shoghi Effendi, The World Order of Bahá'u'lláh, p. 41
4.17 Shoghi Effendi, The World Order of Bahá'u'lláh, p. 163
4.18 From a letter written on behalf of Shoghi Effendi to an individual believer, December 23, 1942. Lights of Guidance, p. 412
4.19 Shoghi Effendi through his Secretary, Principles of Bahai Administration, p. 27
4.20 The Universal House of Justice, 1985 Oct, The Promise of World Peace, p. 3
4.21 The Universal House of Justice, 2001 Apr 19, Unity of Nations and the Lesser Peace, p. 7
4.22 The Universal House of Justice, 2001 May 24, To Believers Gathered for Terrace Events, p. 2
4.23 Bahá'í International Community, 1993 Aug 03, Ending Religious Intolerance
4.24 Baha'i International Community, 1995 Oct, Turning Point For All Nations
4.25 Baha'i International Community, 1992 May 29, Statement on Baha'u'llah, p. 13

Chapter 5
5.1 Bahá'u'lláh, Gleanings from the Writings of Bahá'u'lláh, p. 6
5.2 Bahá'u'lláh, Gleanings from the Writings of Bahá'u'lláh, p. 249
5.3 Bahá'u'lláh, The Proclamation of Bahá'u'lláh, p. 120
5.4 Bahá'u'lláh, The Kitáb-i-Aqdas, p. 45
5.5 Bahá'u'lláh, Gleanings from the Writings of Bahá'u'lláh, p. 303
5.6 Bahá'u'lláh, Gleanings from the Writings of Bahá'u'lláh, p. 296
5.7 Bahá'u'lláh, Gleanings from the Writings of Bahá'u'lláh, p. 250
5.8 Bahá'u'lláh, Gleanings from the Writings of Bahá'u'lláh, p. 216
5.9 Bahá'u'lláh, Gleanings from the Writings of Bahá'u'lláh, p. 253
5.10 'Abdu'l-Bahá, Selections from the Writings of 'Abdu'l-Bahá, p. 300
5.11 'Abdu'l-Bahá, The Secret of Divine Civilization, p. 64
5.12 'Abdu'l-Bahá, The Secret of Divine Civilization, p. 66
5.13 'Abdu'l-Bahá, The Promulgation of Universal Peace, p. 180
5.14 'Abdu'l-Bahá, The Promulgation of Universal Peace, p. 300
5.15 'Abdu'l-Bahá, The Promulgation of Universal Peace, p. 175
5.16 Shoghi Effendi, The Unfolding Destiny of the British Baha'i Community, p. 128
5.17 The Universal House of Justice, 1985 Oct, The Promise of World Peace
5.18 The Universal House of Justice, 1985 Oct, The Promise of World Peace
5.19 The Universal House of Justice, Messages 1963 to 1986, p. 681
5.20 The Universal House of Justice, Messages 1963 to 1986, p. 681

Appendix: Sources and Bibliography ❷ 377

5.21 The Universal House of Justice, Messages 1963 to 1986, p. 683
5.22 The Universal House of Justice, Messages 1963 to 1986, p. 690
5.23 The Universal House of Justice, Messages 1963 to 1986, p. 694
5.24 The Universal House of Justice, 1985 Oct, The Promise of World Peace, p. 3
5.25 The Universal House of Justice, 1985 Oct, The Promise of World Peace, p. 4
5.26 The Universal House of Justice, 1985 Oct, The Promise of World Peace, p. 4
5.27 The Universal House of Justice, 1985 Oct, The Promise of World Peace, p. 5
5.28 Baha'i International Community, 1999 Mar 20, Peace Among the Nations

Chapter 6
6.1 Bahá'u'lláh, Tablets of Bahá'u'lláh, p. 161
6.2 Bahá'u'lláh, The Kitáb-i-Aqdas, p. 91
6.3 Bahá'u'lláh, Tablets of Bahá'u'lláh, p. 170
6.4 Bahá'u'lláh, Tablets of Bahá'u'lláh, p. 171
6.5 Bahá'u'lláh, Gleanings from the Writings of Bahá'u'lláh, p. 270
6.6 Bahá'u'lláh, Gleanings from the Writings of Bahá'u'lláh, p. 333
6.7 Bahá'u'lláh, Gleanings from the Writings of Bahá'u'lláh, p. 156
6.8 Bahá'u'lláh, Gleanings from the Writings of Bahá'u'lláh, p. 199
6.9 Bahá'u'lláh, Gleanings from the Writings of Bahá'u'lláh, p. 189
6.10 Bahá'u'lláh, The Compilation of Compilations vol. I, p. 246
6.11 Bahá'u'lláh, The Compilation of Compilations vol. I, p. 247
6.12 Bahá'u'lláh, The Compilation of Compilations vol. I, p. 247
6.13 Bahá'u'lláh , The Compilation of Compilations vol. I, p. 247
6.14 Bahá'u'lláh, Gleanings from the Writings of Bahá'u'lláh, p. 177
6.15 'Abdu'l-Bahá, Selections from the Writings of 'Abdu'l-Bahá, p. 125
6.16 'Abdu'l-Bahá, Selections from the Writings of 'Abdu'l-Bahá, p. 126
6.17 'Abdu'l-Bahá, Some Answered Questions, p. 213
6.18 'Abdu'l-Bahá, The Compilation of Compilations vol. I, p. 252
6.19 'Abdu'l-Bahá, The Promulgation of Universal Peace, p. 309
6.20 'Abdu'l-Bahá, The Promulgation of Universal Peace, p. 84
6.21 'Abdu'l-Bahá, The Promulgation of Universal Peace, p. 181
6.22 'Abdu'l-Bahá, The Promulgation of Universal Peace, p. 300
6.23 'Abdu'l-Bahá: Promulgation of Universal Peace, p. 311
6.24 From a letter dated June 1933 written by Shoghi Effendi to the High Commissioner for Palestine
6.25 From a letter dated January 1929 written by Shoghi Effendi to the believers of the East- translated from the Persian, The Compilation of Compilations vol. I, p. 297
6.26 From a letter dated 9 July 1931 written on behalf of Shoghi Effendi to an individual believer, The Compilation of Compilations vol. I, p. 298
6.27 From a letter dated 26 July 1946 written on behalf of Shoghi Effendi to an individual believer, The Compilation of Compilations vol. I, p. 306
6.28 The Universal House of Justice, 1985 Oct, The Promise of World Peace, p. 3
6.29 Bahá'í International Community, 1989 Jan 02, Position Statement on Education
6.30 Bahá'í International Community, 1989 Jan 02, Position Statement on Education
6.31 Bahá'í International Community, 1989 Jan 02, Position Statement on Education
6.32 Bahá'í International Community, 1989 Jan 02, Position Statement on Education
6.33 Bahá'í International Community, 1990 Mar 09, New Delivery Systems for Basic Education
6.34 For the Betterment of the World, The Bahá'í International Community

Chapter 7
7.1 Bahá'u'lláh, Compilation on Women, Compiled by the Research Department of the Universal House of Justice
7.2 Bahá'u'lláh, Compilation on Women, Compiled by the Research Department of the Universal House of Justice
7.3 Bahá'u'lláh, Compilation on Women, Compiled by the Research Department of the Universal House of Justice
7.4 Baha'u'llah, Prayers and Meditations by Baha'u'llah, p. 313
7.5 Baha'u'llah, Prayers and Meditations by Baha'u'llah, p. 147

7.6 Baha'u'llah, The Kitab-i-Aqdas, p. 37
7.7 Baha'u'llah, Prayers and Meditations by Baha'u'llah, p. 231
7.8 Baha'u'llah, Prayers and Meditations by Baha'u'llah, p. 235
7.9 Baha'u'llah, Tablets of Baha'u'llah, p. 252
7.10 Baha'u'llah, Tablets of Baha'u'llah, p. 254
7.11 'Abdu'l-Bahá, Selections from the Writings of 'Abdu'l-Bahá, p. 301
7.12 'Abdu'l-Bahá, The Promulgation of Universal Peace, p. 182
7.13 'Abdu'l-Bahá, The Promulgation of Universal Peace, p. 300
7.14 'Abdu'l-Bahá, The Promulgation of Universal Peace, p. 76
7.15 'Abdu'l-Bahá, The Promulgation of Universal Peace, p. 107
7.16 'Abdu'l-Bahá, The Promulgation of Universal Peace, p. 133
7.17 'Abdu'l-Bahá, 'Abdu'l-Bahá in London, p. 27
7.18 'Abdu'l-Bahá, 'Abdu'l-Bahá in London, p. 104
7.19 'Abdu'l-Bahá, 'Abdu'l-Bahá in London, p. 105
7.20 The Universal House of Justice, 24 July 1975 to an individual believer, , The Compilation of Compilations vol II, p. 370
7.21 The Universal House of Justice, 1988 May 31, Women and Universal House of Justice Membership
7.22 Bahá'í International Community, 1993 Apr 05, Equality of Men & Women A New Reality
7.23 Bahá'í International Community, 1989 Mar 30, Women Development
7.24 Bahá'í International Community, 1989 Mar 30, Women Development
7.25 Bahá'í International Community, 1990 Feb 27, Equality in Political Participation Decision-Making
7.26 Bahá'í International Community, 1992 Mar 11, Women Development
7.27 Bahá'í International Community, 1995 Aug 26, Educating Girls - An Investment in Future
7.28 Bahá'í International Community, 1995 Mar 03, *The Prosperity of Humankind*
7.29 Bahá'í International Community, 2008, For the Betterment of the World

Chapter 8
8.1 Bahá'u'lláh, Gleanings from the Writings of Bahá'u'lláh, p. 288
8.2 Bahá'u'lláh, The Hidden Words, Arabic #68
8.3 Bahá'u'lláh, Gleanings from the Writings of Bahá'u'lláh, p. 286
8.4 Bahá'u'lláh, Gleanings from the Writings of Bahá'u'lláh, p. 203
8.5 Bahá'u'lláh, Tablets of Bahá'u'lláh, p. 35
8.6 Baha'u'llah, Gleanings from the Writings of Baha'u'llah, p. 81
8.7 Baha'u'llah, Gleanings from the Writings of Baha'u'llah, p. 149
8.8 'Abdu'l-Bahá, Selections from the Writings of 'Abdu'l-Bahá, p. 69
8.9 'Abdu'l-Bahá, Selections from the Writings of 'Abdu'l-Bahá, p. 299
8.10 'Abdu'l-Bahá, Selections from the Writings of 'Abdu'l-Bahá, p. 246
8.11 'Abdu'l-Bahá, Selections from the Writings of 'Abdu'l-Bahá, p. 291
8.12 'Abdu'l-Bahá, The Promulgation of Universal Peace, p. 181
8.13 'Abdu'l-Bahá, The Promulgation of Universal Peace, p. 181
8.14 'Abdu'l-Bahá, The Promulgation of Universal Peace, p. 56
8.15 'Abdu'l-Bahá, The Promulgation of Universal Peace, p. 269
8.16 'Abdu'l-Bahá, The Promulgation of Universal Peace, p. 50
8.17 Shoghi Effendi, Citadel of Faith, p. 126
8.18 Shoghi Effendi, The Advent of Divine Justice, p. 33
8.19 Shoghi Effendi, The Advent of Divine Justice, p. 36
8.20 Shoghi Effendi, The Advent of Divine Justice, p. 39
8.21 Shoghi Effendi: Messages to the Bahá'í World, pp. 135-136
8.22 Written on behalf of Shoghi Effendi to two individual believers, March 19, 1944. Lights of Guidance, p. 525
8.23 From a letter written on behalf of Shoghi Effendi to an individual believer, February 9, 1942. Lights of Guidance, p. 533
8.24 The Universal House of Justice, 1985 Oct, The Promise of World Peace, p. 3
8.25 The Universal House of Justice, A Wider Horizon, Selected Letters 1983-1992, p. 37
8.26 Baha'i International Community, 1988 Aug 03, Combating Racism

Appendix: Sources and Bibliography ❓ 379

8.27   Baha'i International Community, 1988 Aug 03, Combating Racism
8.28   Baha'i International Community, 1993 Feb 18, Eliminating Religious Intolerance
8.29   Baha'i International Community, 1990 Jan 26, Combating Racism
8.30   Baha'i International Community, 1989 Feb 08, Eliminating Racism

Chapter 9
9.1   Bahá'u'lláh, The Kitáb-i-Aqdas, p. 71
9.2   Bahá'u'lláh, Tablets of Bahá'u'lláh, p. 220
9.3   Bahá'u'lláh, Gleanings from the Writings of Bahá'u'lláh, p. 215
9.4   Bahá'u'lláh, Gleanings from the Writings of Bahá'u'lláh, p. 255
9.5   Bahá'u'lláh, Gleanings from the Writings of Bahá'u'lláh, p. 288
9.6   Bahá'u'lláh, The Proclamation of Bahá'u'lláh, p. 94
9.7   Bahá'u'lláh, The Proclamation of Bahá'u'lláh, p. 95
9.8   Bahá'u'lláh, Gleanings from the Writings of Bahá'u'lláh, p. 171
9.9   'Abdu'l-Bahá, Selections from the Writings of 'Abdu'l-Bahá, p. 28
9.10   'Abdu'l-Bahá, Selections from the Writings of 'Abdu'l-Bahá, p. 20
9.11   'Abdu'l-Bahá, The Promulgation of Universal Peace, p. 95
9.12   'Abdu'l-Bahá, The Promulgation of Universal Peace, p. 145
9.13   'Abdu'l-Bahá, The Promulgation of Universal Peace, p. 420
9.14   'Abdu'l-Bahá, The Promulgation of Universal Peace, p. 180
9.15   'Abdu'l-Bahá, The Promulgation of Universal Peace, p. 97
9.16   'Abdu'l-Bahá, The Promulgation of Universal Peace, p. 128
9.17   'Abdu'l-Bahá, The Promulgation of Universal Peace, p. 298
9.18   'Abdu'l-Bahá, The Promulgation of Universal Peace, p. 396
9.19   'Abdu'l-Bahá, The Promulgation of Universal Peace, p. 86
9.20   Shoghi Effendi, The Advent of Divine Justice, p. 5
9.21   Shoghi Effendi, The Advent of Divine Justice, p. 88
9.22   From letter written on behalf of the Guardian to an individual believer, December 2, 1935;. Lights of Guidance, p. 561
9.23   From a letter written on behalf of Shoghi Effendi to an individual believer, February 17, 1956. Lights of Guidance, p. 421
9.24   The Universal House of Justice, 1985 Oct, The Promise of World Peace, p. 3
9.25   The Universal House of Justice, A Wider Horizon, Selected Letters 1983-1992, p. 35
9.26   Commissioned by The Universal House of Justice, One Common Faith
9.27   Baha'i International Community, 1993 Feb 18, Eliminating Religious Intolerance
9.28   Bahá'í International Community, 1995 Jan 10, Promoting Religious Tolerance
9.29   Baha'i International Community, 1993 Aug 03, Ending Religious Intolerance

Chapter 10
10.1   Bahá'u'lláh, Gleanings from the Writings of Bahá'u'lláh, p. 160
10.2   Bahá'u'lláh, Gleanings from the Writings of Bahá'u'lláh, p. 184
10.3   Bahá'u'lláh, Gleanings from the Writings of Bahá'u'lláh, p. 65
10.4   Bahá'u'lláh, Prayers and Meditations by Bahá'u'lláh, p. 330
10.5   Bahá'u'lláh, Tablets of Bahá'u'lláh, p. 69
10.6   Bahá'u'lláh, Gleanings from the Writings of Bahá'u'lláh, p. 265
10.7   Bahá'u'lláh, Gleanings from the Writings of Bahá'u'lláh, p. 162
10.8   Bahá'u'lláh, The Seven Valleys, p. 18
10.9   Bahá'u'lláh, Gleanings from the Writings of Bahá'u'lláh, p. 216
10.10   Bahá'u'lláh, Gleanings from the Writings of Bahá'u'lláh, p. 234
10.11   'Abdu'l-Bahá, Selections from the Writings of 'Abdu'l-Bahá, p. 146
10.12   'Abdu'l-Bahá, The Secret of Divine Civilization, p. 59
10.13   'Abdu'l-Bahá, Selections from the Writings of 'Abdu'l-Bahá, p. 283
10.14   'Abdu'l-Bahá, Selections from the Writings of 'Abdu'l-Bahá, p. 303
10.15   'Abdu'l-Bahá, Bahá'í Prayers, p. 71
10.16   'Abdu'l-Bahá, The Promulgation of Universal Peace, p. 226
10.17   'Abdu'l-Bahá, Paris Talks, p. 138
10.18   Shoghi Effendi, The Unfolding Destiny of the British Bahá'í Community, p. 451
10.19   The Universal House of Justice, A Wider Horizon, Selected Letters 1983-1992, p. 63

10.20	The Universal House of Justice, A Wider Horizon, Selected Letters 1983-1992, p. 93
10.21	The Universal House of Justice, A Wider Horizon, Selected Letters 1983-1992, p. 102
10.22	The Universal House of Justice, A Wider Horizon, Selected Letters 1983-1992, p. 144
10.23	Commissioned by The Universal House of Justice, Century of Light, p. 3
10.24	Commissioned by The Universal House of Justice, Century of Light, p. 90
10.25	Bahá'í International Community, The Bahá'í Statement on Nature
10.26	Bahá'í International Community, 1990 Aug 06, Environment Development
10.27	Bahá'í International Community, 1991 Aug 13, International Legislation for Environment Development
10.28	Baha'i International Community, 1995 Mar 03, *The Prosperity of Humankind*
10.29	Bahá'í International Community, For the Betterment of the World

Chapter 11

11.1	Bahá'u'lláh, Tablets of Bahá'u'lláh, p. 138
11.2	Bahá'u'lláh, Gleanings from the Writings of Bahá'u'lláh, p. 126
11.3	Baha'u'llah, Gleanings from the Writings of Bahá'u'lláh, p. 235
11.4	Bahá'u'lláh, The Hidden Words, Persian #53
11.5	Baha'u'llah, Gleanings from the Writings of Bahá'u'lláh, p. 138
11.6	Bahá'u'lláh, The Hidden Words, Persian #49
11.7	Bahá'u'lláh, The Hidden Words, Persian #54
11.8	Bahá'u'lláh, The Hidden Words, Arabic #57
11.9	Bahá'u'lláh, The Summons of the Lord of Hosts, p. 189
11.10	Bahá'u'lláh, Gleanings from the Writings of Bahá'u'lláh, p. 314
11.11	Bahá'u'lláh, The Proclamation of Bahá'u'lláh, p. 50
11.12	Bahá'u'lláh, Tablets of Bahá'u'lláh, p. 132
11.13	'Abdu'l-Bahá, Selections from the Writings of 'Abdu'l-Bahá, p. 300
11.14	'Abdu'l-Bahá, Some Answered Questions, p. 273
11.15	Abdu'l-Bahá, The Compilation of Compilations vol II, p. 341
11.16	'Abdu'l-Bahá, Some Answered Questions, p. 274
11.17	'Abdu'l-Bahá, The Promulgation of Universal Peace, p. 181
11.18	'Abdu'l-Bahá, The Promulgation of Universal Peace, p. 11
11.19	'Abdu'l-Bahá, The Promulgation of Universal Peace, p. 12
11.20	Shoghi Effendi, The World Order of Bahá'u'lláh, p. 33
11.21	From a letter written on behalf of Shoghi Effendi to an individual believer, October 28, 1927: Extracts from the Bahá'í Writings on the Subject of Agriculture and Related Subjects, a compilation of the Universal House of Justice.
11.22	From a letter written on behalf of Shoghi Effendi to an individual believer, June 10, 1930: Ibid. Lights of Guidance, p. 548
11.23	From a letter written on behalf of the Guardian to an individual believer, November 19, 1945: Bahá'í News, No. 210, August 1948, p. 3. Lights of Guidance, p. 550
11.24	From a letter written on behalf of Shoghi Effendi to an individual believer, December 26, 1935. Lights of Guidance, p. 550
11.25	The Universal House of Justice, 1985 Oct, The Promise of World Peace, p. 3
11.26	From a letter written on the behalf of the Universal House of Justice to the National Spiritual Assembly of Jamaica, April 5, 1982. Lights of Guidance, p. 253
11.27	Bahá'í International Community, 1995 Mar 03, *The Prosperity of Humankind*
11.28	Baha'i International Community, 1995 Mar 03, *The Prosperity of Humankind*
11.29	Baha'i International Community, 1993 Feb 12, Human Rights Extreme Poverty
11.30	Bahá'í International Community, 1994 Jan 21, Global Action Plan for Social Development
11.31	Bahá'í International Community, 1994 Jan 21, Global Action Plan for Social Development
11.32	Bahá'í International Community, For the Betterment of the World

Chapter 12

12.1	Bahá'u'lláh, Gleanings from the Writings of Bahá'u'lláh, p. 216
12.2	Bahá'u'lláh, Gleanings from the Writings of Bahá'u'lláh, p. 93
12.3	Bahá'u'lláh, Tablets of Bahá'u'lláh, p. 88
12.4	Bahá'u'lláh, Gleanings from the Writings of Bahá'u'lláh, p. 7
12.5	Bahá'u'lláh, Gleanings from the Writings of Bahá'u'lláh, p. 315

12.6	Bahá'u'lláh, Gleanings from the Writings of Bahá'u'lláh, p. 8
12.7	Bahá'u'lláh, Epistle to the Son of the Wolf, p. 45
12.8	Bahá'u'lláh, The Hidden Words, Arabic #30
12.9	Bahá'u'lláh, Gleanings from the Writings of Bahá'u'lláh, p. 7
12.10	Bahá'u'lláh, Gleanings from the Writings of Bahá'u'lláh, p. 92
12.11	Bahá'u'lláh, Gleanings from the Writings of Bahá'u'lláh, p. 93
12.12	Bahá'u'lláh, Gleanings from the Writings of Bahá'u'lláh, p. 32
12.13	Bahá'u'lláh, Gleanings from the Writings of Bahá'u'lláh, p. 34
12.14	Bahá'u'lláh, Gleanings from the Writings of Bahá'u'lláh, p. 45
12.15	Bahá'u'lláh, Gleanings from the Writings of Bahá'u'lláh, p. 93
12.16	Bahá'u'lláh, Gleanings from the Writings of Bahá'u'lláh, p. 16
12.17	Bahá'u'lláh, Prayers and Meditations by Bahá'u'lláh, p. 170
12.18	'Abdu'l-Bahá, Selections from the Writings of 'Abdu'l-Bahá, p. 92
12.19	'Abdu'l-Bahá, Selections from the Writings of 'Abdu'l-Bahá, p. 93
12.20	'Abdu'l-Bahá, Selections from the Writings of 'Abdu'l-Bahá, p. 93
12.21	'Abdu'l-Bahá, Selections from the Writings of 'Abdu'l-Bahá, p. 93
12.22	'Abdu'l-Bahá, The Promulgation of Universal Peace, p. 420
12.23	Shoghi Effendi, The Guardian's Epilogue to the Dawn-Breakers, p. 667
12.24	Shoghi Effendi, The Advent of Divine Justice, p. 41
12.25	From a letter written on behalf of Shoghi Effendi to an individual believer, June 30, 1923. Lights of Guidance, p. 603
12.26	From a letter written on behalf of Shoghi Effendi to an individual believer, October 13, 1947. Lights of Guidance, p. 115
12.27	From a letter written on behalf of Shoghi Effendi to an individual believer, December 5, 1942. Lights of Guidance, p. 404
12.28	Shoghi Effendi, Baha'i Administration, p. 130
12.29	Message from the Universal House of Justice to the Bahá'ís of the World, September, 1964: Wellsprings of Guidance, pp. 37-38
12.30	Message from the Universal House of Justice to the Bahá'ís of the World, Ridvan, 1966: Wellspring of Guidance, pp. 79-80
12.31	The Universal House of Justice, 1985 Oct, The Promise of World Peace, p. 5
12.32	From a letter written on behalf of the Universal House of Justice, August 13, 1980. Lights of Guidance, p. 90
12.33	Bahá'í International Community, 1993 Apr 05, Equality of Men & Women A New Reality
12.34	Bahá'í International Community, For the Betterment of the World

Chapter 13

13.1	Bahá'u'lláh, Gleanings from the Writings of Bahá'u'lláh, p. 215
13.2	Baha'u'llah, Gleanings from the Writings of Baha'u'llah, p. 196
13.3	Bahá'u'lláh, Gleanings from the Writings of Bahá'u'lláh, p. 270
13.4	Bahá'u'lláh, Gleanings from the Writings of Bahá'u'lláh, p. 183
13.5	Bahá'u'lláh, Tablets of Bahá'u'lláh, p. 168
13.6	Bahá'u'lláh, The Proclamation of Bahá'u'lláh, p. 50
13.7	Bahá'u'lláh, Tablets of Bahá'u'lláh, p. 92
13.8	Bahá'u'lláh, The Proclamation of Bahá'u'lláh, p. 51
13.9	Bahá'u'lláh, Tablets of Bahá'u'lláh, p. 27
13.10	Bahá'u'lláh, Gleanings from the Writings of Bahá'u'lláh, p. 218
13.11	Bahá'u'lláh, The Proclamation of Bahá'u'lláh, p. 63
13.12	Bahá'u'lláh, Gleanings from the Writings of Bahá'u'lláh, p. 56
13.13	Bahá'u'lláh, Gleanings from the Writings of Bahá'u'lláh, p. 182
13.14	Bahá'u'lláh, Gleanings from the Writings of Bahá'u'lláh, p. 143
13.15	Bahá'u'lláh, Tablets of Bahá'u'lláh, p. 138
13.16	'Abdu'l-Bahá, Selections from the Writings of 'Abdu'l-Bahá, p. 288
13.17	'Abdu'l-Bahá, Selections from the Writings of 'Abdu'l-Bahá, p. 318
13.18	'Abdu'l-Bahá, The Secret of Divine Civilization, p. 103
13.19	'Abdu'l-Bahá, Some Answered Questions, p. 119
13.20	'Abdu'l-Bahá, The Promulgation of Universal Peace, p. 451
13.21	Shoghi Effendi, Dawn of a New Day, p. 146

13.22	Shoghi Effendi, Dawn of a New Day, p. 114
13.23	From Shoghi Effendi's postscript to a letter written on his behalf to the National Spiritual Assembly of the United States and Canada, November 18, 1933. Lights of Guidance, p. 176
13.24	Shoghi Effendi, Principles of Bahai Administration, p. 10
13.25	Shoghi Effendi, From a letter to the Bahá'ís of America, February 23, 1924: Bahá'í Administration, p. 64. Lights of Guidance, p. 32
13.26	From a letter dated 23 February 1924 written by Shoghi Effendi to the Bahá'ís of America, , The Compilation of Compilations vol II, p. 52
13.27	From a letter dated 30 August 1930 written on behalf of Shoghi Effendi to the National Spiritual Assembly of the United States and Canada, The Compilation of Compilations vol II, p. 53
13.28	The Universal House of Justice, 1985 Oct, The Promise of World Peace, p. 4
13.29	From a letter of the Universal House of Justice to all National Spiritual Assemblies, March 27, 1978. Lights of Guidance, p. 326
13.30	From a letter of the Universal House of Justice to the National Spiritual Assembly of Canada, March 6, 1970:. Lights of Guidance, p. 177
13.31	Bahá'í International Community, For the Betterment of the World

Chapter 14

14.1	Bahá'u'lláh, The Kitáb-i-Aqdas, p. 29
14.2	Bahá'u'lláh, Compilation on the Local Spiritual Assembly, p. 6
14.3	'Abdu'l-Bahá, Selections from the Writings of 'Abdu'l-Bahá, p. 83
14.4	'Abdu'l-Bahá, Selections from the Writings of 'Abdu'l-Bahá, p. 87
14.5	'Abdu'l-Bahá, Selections from the Writings of 'Abdu'l-Bahá, p. 86
14.6	'Abdu'l-Bahá, Selections from the Writings of 'Abdu'l-Bahá, p. 86
14.7	'Abdu'l-Bahá: Selections from the Writings of 'Abdu'l-Bahá, p. 80
14.8	From a letter written on behalf of Shoghi Effendi to the National Spiritual Assembly of the United States and Canada, . Lights of Guidance, p. 5
14.9	Shoghi Effendi Principles of Bahai Administration, p. 48
14.10	Shoghi Effendi Principles of Bahai Administration, p. 41
14.11	From a letter dated 15 November 1935 written on behalf of Shoghi Effendi to two believers, The Compilation of Compilations vol II, p. 42
14.12	From a letter dated 14 May 1927 written by Shoghi Effendi to a Local Spiritual Assembly, published in "Bahá'í News" 18 June 1927, p. 9, The Compilation of Compilations vol II, p. 43
14.13	From a letter dated 19 October 1947 written on behalf of Shoghi Effendi to an individual believer, , The Compilation of Compilations vol II, p. 49
14.14	From a letter dated 28 October 1935 written on behalf of Shoghi Effendi to an individual believer, The Compilation of Compilations vol II, p. 50
14.15	From a letter dated 30 June 1949 written on behalf of Shoghi Effendi to the National Spiritual Assembly of Germany and Austria, The Compilation of Compilations vol II, p. 51
14.16	From a letter dated 23 February 1924 written by Shoghi Effendi to the Bahá'ís of America, published in "Bahá'í Administration: Selected Messages 1922-1932", pp. 63-63, The Compilation of Compilations vol II, p. 52
14.17	From a letter dated 17 October 1944 written on behalf of Shoghi Effendi to an individual believer, , The Compilation of Compilations vol II, p. 55
14.18	From a letter dated 19 October 1947 written on behalf of Shoghi Effendi to an individual believer, The Compilation of Compilations vol II, p. 58
14.19	From a letter dated 9 March 1934 written on behalf of Shoghi Effendi to an individual believer, The Compilation of Compilations vol II, p. 53
14.20	Prepared under the supervision of the Universal House of Justice, Notes to the Kitáb-i-Aqdas, p. 188
14.21	The Universal House of Justice, From a letter dated Naw-Ruz 1974 to the Bahá'ís of the World, The Compilation of Compilations vol II, p. 29
14.22	The Universal House of Justice, From a letter dated Naw-Ruz 1974 to all National Spiritual Assemblies, The Compilation of Compilations vol II, p. 30
14.23	The Universal House of Justice, From a letter dated 30 July 1972 to the National Spiritual Assembly of Bolivia, The Compilation of Compilations vol II, p. 31

Appendix: Sources and Bibliography 383

14.24 From a letter of the Universal House of Justice to all National Spiritual Assemblies, March 3, 1977. Lights of Guidance, p. 4
14.25 From a letter of the Universal House of Justice to the National Spiritual Assembly of India, February 8, 1972: see section, "Visiting Teachers -- What They Are Supposed to Do". Lights of Guidance, p. 3
14.26 The Universal House of Justice, 1994 May 19, response to US NSA
14.27 From a letter written on behalf of the Universal House of Justice to an individual believer, November 3, 1982. Lights of Guidance, p. 390
14.28 From a letter written on behalf of the Universal House of Justice to the National Spiritual Assembly of Brazil, April 13, 1983. Lights of Guidance, p. 4
14.29 Letter from the Universal House of Justice, dated September 18, 1968, to a National Spiritual Assembly
14.30 From a letter written on behalf of the Universal House of Justice to a National Spiritual Assembly, August 2, 1982 Lights of Guidance, p. 334
14.31 Universal House of Justice, in The Four Year Plan: Messages of the Universal House of Justice, dated Ridvan, 1996, Palabra Publications edition, p. 35, par. 3.26, NSA USA - Developing Distinctive Bahá'í Communities
14.32 From a letter of the Universal House of Justice to the National Spiritual Assembly of Italy, August 26, 1965. Lights of Guidance, p. 179
14.33 Bahá'í International Community, 1993 Apr 05, Equality of Men & Women A New Reality

Chapter 15
15.1 Bahá'u'lláh, Tablets of Bahá'u'lláh, p. 156
15.2 Bahá'u'lláh, Tablets of Bahá'u'lláh, p. 68
15.3 Bahá'u'lláh, Tablets of Bahá'u'lláh, p. 26
15.4 Bahá'u'lláh, The Hidden Words, Arabic #2
15.5 Bahá'u'lláh, Gleanings from the Writings of Bahá'u'lláh, p. 174
15.6 Bahá'u'lláh, Tablets of Bahá'u'lláh, p. 92
15.7 Bahá'u'lláh, Tablets of Bahá'u'lláh, p. 69
15.8 Bahá'u'lláh, Tablets of Bahá'u'lláh, p. 124
15.9 Bahá'u'lláh, Tablets of Bahá'u'lláh, p. 128
15.10 'Abdu'l-Bahá, Selections from the Writings of 'Abdu'l-Bahá, p. 215
15.11 'Abdu'l-Bahá, Selections from the Writings of 'Abdu'l-Bahá, p. 79
15.12 'Abdu'l-Bahá, Some Answered Questions, p. 172
15.13 'Abdu'l-Bahá, Selections from the Writings of 'Abdu'l-Bahá, p. 127
15.14 'Abdu'l-Bahá, Selections from the Writings of 'Abdu'l-Bahá, p. 132
15.15 'Abdu'l-Bahá, The Promulgation of Universal Peace, p. 455
15.16 'Abdu'l-Bahá, Paris Talks, p. 183
15.17 Shoghi Effendi, God Passes By, p. 332
15.18 Shoghi Effendi, The World Order of Bahá'u'lláh, p. 7
15.19 Shoghi Effendi, The World Order of Bahá'u'lláh, p. 8
15.20 Shoghi Effendi, The World Order of Bahá'u'lláh, p. 9
15.21 Shoghi Effendi, The World Order of Bahá'u'lláh, p. 153
15.22 Shoghi Effendi, The World Order of Bahá'u'lláh, p. 154
15.23 Shoghi Effendi, The World Order of Bahá'u'lláh, p. 156
15.24 The Universal House of Justice, The Constitution of The Universal House of Justice, p. 11
15.25 The Universal House of Justice, The Constitution of The Universal House of Justice, p. 13
15.26 The Universal House of Justice, The Constitution of The Universal House of Justice, p. 14
15.27 The Universal House of Justice, The Constitution of The Universal House of Justice, p. 14
15.28 The Universal House of Justice, The Constitution of The Universal House of Justice, p. 3
15.29 The Universal House of Justice, The Constitution of The Universal House of Justice, p. 4
15.30 The Universal House of Justice, The Constitution of The Universal House of Justice, p. 4
15.31 The Universal House of Justice, The Constitution of The Universal House of Justice, p. 7
15.32 The Universal House of Justice, The Constitution of The Universal House of Justice, p. 16
15.33 From a letter of the Universal House of Justice to as individual believer, May 27, 1966. Lights of Guidance, p. 317

Chapter 16
16.1   Bahá'u'lláh, Tablets of Bahá'u'lláh, p. 35
16.2   Baha'u'llah, Gleanings from the Writings of Baha'u'llah, p. 286
16.3   Bahá'u'lláh, Tablets of Bahá'u'lláh, p. 138
16.4   Bahá'u'lláh, The Kitáb-i-Aqdas, p. 82
16.5   Bahá'u'lláh, Tablets of Bahá'u'lláh, p. 138
16.6   Bahá'u'lláh, The Proclamation of Bahá'u'lláh, p. 73
16.7   Bahá'u'lláh, Tablets of Bahá'u'lláh, p. 207
16.8   Bahá'u'lláh, The Hidden Words, Persian #11
16.9   Bahá'u'lláh, The Hidden Words, Persian #36
16.10 Bahá'u'lláh, Tablets of Bahá'u'lláh, p. 96
16.11 Bahá'u'lláh, Gleanings from the Writings of Bahá'u'lláh, p. 79
16.12 Bahá'u'lláh, Gleanings from the Writings of Bahá'u'lláh, p. 213
16.13 Bahá'u'lláh, Gleanings from the Writings of Bahá'u'lláh, p. 58
16.14 Bahá'u'lláh, The Kitáb-i-Iqan, p. 187
16.15 'Abdu'l-Bahá, Selections from the Writings of 'Abdu'l-Bahá, p. 109
16.16 'Abdu'l-Bahá, Selections from the Writings of 'Abdu'l-Bahá, p. 269
16.17 'Abdu'l-Bahá, The Secret of Divine Civilization, p. 21
16.18 'Abdu'l-Bahá, Compilation on Scholarship, Prepared by the Research Department of the Universal House of Justice, p. 1
16.19 From the Writings of 'Abdu'l-Bahá The Importance of the Arts in Promoting the Faith, Compiled by the Research Department of the Universal House of Justice
16.20 'Abdu'l-Baha, The Importance of the Arts in Promoting the Faith, Compiled by the Research Department of the Universal House of Justice
16.21 'Abdu'l-Bahá, A Compilation on Bahá'í Education Compiled by the Research Department of the Universal House of Justice
16.22 'Abdu'l-Baha, Abdu'l-Baha in London, p. 93
16.23 'Abdu'l-Bahá, The Promulgation of Universal Peace, p. 226
16.24 'Abdu'l-Bahá, The Promulgation of Universal Peace, p. 227
16.25 'Abdu'l-Bahá, The Promulgation of Universal Peace, p. 30
16.26 'Abdu'l-Bahá, The Promulgation of Universal Peace, p. 454
16.27 'Abdu'l-Bahá, The Promulgation of Universal Peace, p. 49
16.28 'Abdu'l-Bahá, The Promulgation of Universal Peace, p. 231
16.29 'Table Talk' by 'Abdu'l-Bahá . Lights of Guidance, p. 412
16.30 From letter written on behalf of the Guardian to an individual believer, November 15, 1932 . Lights of Guidance, p. 412
16.31 From Letters Written on Behalf of Shoghi Effendi, 30 November 1932, to an individual The Importance of the Arts in Promoting the Faith, Compiled by the Research Department of the Universal House of Justice
16.32 From Letters Written on Behalf of Shoghi Effendi, 25 September 1942 to an individual believer Compilation on Scholarship, Prepared by the Research Department on the Universal House of Justice, p. 9
16.33 From a letter written on behalf of Shoghi Effendi to an individual believer, August 25, 1926. Lights of Guidance, p. 565
16.34 From a letter written on behalf of Shoghi Effendi to an individual believer, November 9, 1932. Lights of Guidance, p. 566
16.35 The Universal House of Justice, 28 December 2010, Letter To the Conference of the Continental Boards of Counsellors
16.36 The Universal House of Justice, 28 December 2010, Letter To the Conference of the Continental Boards of Counsellors
16.37 The Universal House of Justice, in Wellspring of Guidance, pp. 114-15
16.38 18 April 1989 on behalf of the Universal House of Justice to a National Spiritual Assembly Compilation on Scholarship, Prepared by the Research Department of the Universal House of Justice, p. 13
16.39 10 February 1995, on behalf of the Universal House of Justice to selected National Spiritual Assemblies Compilations, Scholarship

Appendix: Sources and Bibliography 385

16.40   From a Letter Written on Behalf of the Universal House of Justice, 19 October 1993 to an individual believer Compilation on Scholarship, Prepared by the Research Department of the Universal House of Justice, p. 4
16.41   The Bahá'í International Community, For the Betterment of the World

Chapter 17
17.1   Bahá'u'lláh, Tablets of Bahá'u'lláh, p. 68
17.2   Bahá'u'lláh, Tablets of Bahá'u'lláh, p. 89
17.3   Bahá'u'lláh, Tablets of Bahá'u'lláh, p. 128
17.4   Bahá'u'lláh, Tablets of Bahá'u'lláh, p. 168
17.5   Bahá'u'lláh, Tablets of Bahá'u'lláh, p. 220
17.6   'Abdu'l-Bahá, Selections from the writings of 'Abdu'l-Bahá: pp.77
17.7   'Abdu'l-Bahá, Selections from the Writings of 'Abdu'l-Bahá, p. 128
17.8   'Abdu'l-Bahá, Selections from the Writings of 'Abdu'l-Bahá, p. 136
17.9   'Abdu'l-Bahá, Selections from the Writings of 'Abdu'l-Bahá, p. 138
17.10   'Abdu'l-Bahá, Selections from the Writings of 'Abdu'l-Bahá, p. 128
17.11   'Abdu'l-Bahá, Selections from the Writings of 'Abdu'l-Bahá, p. 143
17.12   'Abdu'l-Bahá, Selections from the Writings of 'Abdu'l-Bahá, p. 127
17.13   'Abdu'l-Bahá, Selections from the Writings of 'Abdu'l-Bahá, p. 125
17.14   'Abdu'l-Bahá, Selections from the Writings of 'Abdu'l-Bahá, p. 140
17.15   'Abdu'l-Bahá, Bahá'í Prayers, p. 33
17.16   'Abdu'l-Bahá, The Promulgation of Universal Peace, p. 167
17.17   'Abdu'l-Bahá, Paris Talks, p. 138
17.18   From a letter written on behalf of Shoghi Effendi to an individual believer, July 9, 1939: Bahá'í Education, pp. 65-66. Lights of Guidance, p. 152
17.19   From a letter written on behalf of Shoghi Effendi, May 30, 1947. Lights of Guidance, p. 151
17.20   From a letter written on behalf of Shoghi Effendi to an individual believer, May 11, 1945. Lights of Guidance, p. 151
17.21   From a letter written on behalf of the Guardian to the National Spiritual Assembly of the United States, October 25, 1947. Lights of Guidance, p. 154
17.22   From a letter written on behalf of the Universal House of Justice to an individual believer, August 12, 1975. Lights of Guidance, p. 151
17.23   From a letter of the Universal House of Justice to the National Spiritual Assembly of El Salvador, December 14, 1970. Lights of Guidance, p. 75
17.24   From a letter written on behalf of the Universal House of Justice to the National Spiritual Assembly of the United Kingdom, July 19, 1982. Lights of Guidance, p. 152
17.25   From a letter written on behalf of the Universal House of Justice to the National Spiritual Assembly of Brazil, December 12, 1975. Lights of Guidance, p. 155
17.26   From a letter written on behalf of the Universal House of Justice to an individual believer, December 29, 1981. Lights of Guidance, p. 158
17.27   From a letter written on behalf of the Universal House of Justice to the National Spiritual Assembly of Canada, October 14, 1982. Lights of Guidance, p. 151

Chapter 18
18.1   Bahá'u'lláh, The Hidden Words, Persian #49
18.2   Bahá'u'lláh, Prayers and Meditations by Bahá'u'lláh, p. 33
18.3   Bahá'u'lláh, Gleanings from the Writings of Bahá'u'lláh, p. 275
18.4   Bahá'u'lláh, Gleanings from the Writings of Bahá'u'lláh, p. 275
18.5   Bahá'u'lláh, Gleanings from the Writings of Bahá'u'lláh, p. 279
18.6   Bahá'u'lláh, Gleanings from the Writings of Bahá'u'lláh, p. 278
18.7   Bahá'u'lláh, Tablets of Bahá'u'lláh, p. 71
18.8   Bahá'u'lláh, Tablets of Bahá'u'lláh, p. 156
18.9   Bahá'u'lláh, Tablets of Bahá'u'lláh, p. 156
18.10   Bahá'u'lláh, The Hidden Words, Persian #53
18.11   Bahá'u'lláh, The Hidden Words, Arabic #55
18.12   Bahá'u'lláh, The Hidden Words, Arabic #56
18.13   'Abdu'l-Bahá, Selections from the Writings of 'Abdu'l-Bahá, p. 72
18.14   'Abdu'l-Bahá, Selections from the Writings of 'Abdu'l-Bahá, p. 278

18.15   'Abdu'l-Bahá, Selections from the Writings of 'Abdu'l-Bahá, p. 115
18.16   'Abdu'l-Bahá, Selections from the Writings of 'Abdu'l-Bahá, p. 316
18.17   Letter written on behalf of Shoghi Effendi, in Bahá'í Funds: Contributions and Administration, p. 11, NSA USA - Developing Distinctive Baha'i Communities
18.18   Shoghi Effendi, from a letter dated 12 March 1923 to the Bahá'ís of the West, The Compilation of Compilations vol. I, p. 529
18.19   4 May 1932, From a letter written on behalf of Shoghi Effend to an individual believer, The Compilation of Compilations vol. I, p. 536
18.20   From a letter written on behalf of Shoghi Effendi to an individual believer, December 8, 1947:. Lights of Guidance, p. 121
18.21   Letter from the Universal House of Justice to the Bahá'ís of the World, Naw-Ruz 1974. Lights of Guidance, p. 250
18.22   From a letter of the Universal House of Justice to all National Spiritual Assemblies, August 7, 1985. Lights of Guidance, p. 251
18.23   From a letter of the Universal House of Justice to all National Spiritual Assemblies, August 7, 1985. Lights of Guidance, p. 251
18.24   From a letter written on behalf of the Universal House of Justice to an individual believer, June 6, 1985. Lights of Guidance, p. 262
18.25   Baha'i International Community, 1993 Feb 12, Human Rights Extreme Poverty
18.26   Bahá'u'lláh, The Kitáb-i-Aqdas, p. 54
18.27   Bahá'u'lláh, Compilation on the Huququ'lláh
18.28   Bahá'u'lláh, Compilation on the Huququ'lláh
18.29   Bahá'u'lláh, Compilation on the Huququ'lláh
18.30   Bahá'u'lláh, Compilation on the Huququ'lláh
18.31   Bahá'u'lláh, Compilation on the Huququ'lláh
18.32   Bahá'u'lláh, Compilation on the Huququ'lláh
18.33   Bahá'u'lláh, Compilation on the Huququ'lláh
18.34   Bahá'u'lláh, Compilation on the Huququ'lláh
18.35   Bahá'u'lláh, Compilation on the Huququ'lláh
18.36   Bahá'u'lláh, Compilation on the Huququ'lláh
18.37   Abbdu'l-Baha, Compilation on the Huququ'lláh
18.38   'Abdu'l-Bahá, Compilation on the Huququ'lláh
18.39   'Abdu'l-Bahá, Compilation on the Huququ'lláh
18.40   Shoghi Effendi, 23 June 1945 -- translated from the Persian, Compilation on the Huququ'lláh
18.41   Universal House of Justice, 18 August 1965 -- translated from the Persian, Compilation on the Huququ'lláh
18.42   Universal House of Justice, 25 October 1970 to the National Spiritual Assembly of Iran -- translated from the Persian, Compilation on the Huququ'lláh

Chapter 19
19.1   Bahá'u'lláh, Compilation on Youth, The Compilation of Compilations vol II, p. 414
19.2   Baha'u'llah, Gleanings from the Writings of Baha'u'llah, p. 93
19.3   Baha'u'llah, Prayers and Meditations by Baha'u'llah, p. 41
19.4   Baha'u'llah, The Hidden Words, Arabic #46
19.5   Abdu'l-Baha, Selections from the Writings of Abdu'l-Baha, p. 53
19.6   Abdu'l-Baha, Compilation on Youth, The Compilation of Compilations vol II, p. 415
19.7   Abdu'l-Baha, Selections from the Writings of Abdu'l-Baha, p. 203
19.8   Abdu'l-Baha, The Promulgation of Universal Peace, p. 438
19.9   'Abdu'l-Bahá, From a Tablet- translated from the Persian Compilation on Youth, The Compilation of Compilations vol II, p. 415
19.10   Shoghi Effendi, 9 June 1925 to the Spiritual Assembly of the East- translated from the Persian Compilation on Youth, The Compilation of Compilations vol II, p. 416
19.11   In the handwriting of Shoghi Effendi, appended to a letter dated 18 May 1926 written on his behalf to an individual believer Compilation on Youth, The Compilation of Compilations vol II, p. 416
19.12   [Postscript in the handwriting of Shoghi Effendi:] Compilation on Youth, The Compilation of Compilations vol II, p. 422
19.13   Shoghi Effendi, The Compilation of Compilations vol II, p. 422

Appendix: Sources and Bibliography ❷ 387

19.14   Shoghi Effendi, 12 March 1933 to an individual believer, The Compilation of Compilations vol II, p. 423
19.15   On Behalf of Shoghi Effendi, 8 December 1935 to an individual believer, , The Compilation of Compilations vol II, p. 425
19.16   On Behalf of Shoghi Effendi, 6 June 1941 to the Bahá'í Youth of Bombay, India, The Compilation of Compilations vol II, p. 429
19.17   On Behalf of Shoghi Effendi, 26 April 1923 to the National Spiritual Assembly of the Bahá'ís of India and Burma Compilation on Youth, The Compilation of Compilations vol II, p. 417
19.18   On Behalf of Shoghi Effendi, 28 December 1925 to the Bahá'í Youth of Baltimore, Maryland, U.S.A. Compilation on Youth, The Compilation of Compilations vol II, p. 417
19.19   From a letter written on behalf of the Shoghi Effendi to an individual believer, January 4, 1936. Lights of Guidance, p. 638
19.20   From a letter written on behalf of Shoghi Effendi to the Bahá'í children and youth of Peoria, May 8, 1942. Lights of Guidance, p. 638
19.21   On Behalf of Shoghi Effendi, 9 July 1931 to an individual believer Compilation on Youth, The Compilation of Compilations vol II, p. 419
19.22   From a letter dated 1 September 1933 written on behalf of Shoghi Effendi to an individual believer, The Individual and Teaching - Raising the Divine Call, p. 21
19.23   On Behalf of Shoghi Effendi, 7 December 1931 to an individual believer, published in "Bahá'í News" 64 July 1932, p 4Compilation on Youth, The Compilation of Compilations vol II, p. 420
19.24   Letter written on behalf of Shoghi Effendi October 2, 1951: Bahá'í Youth, p. 6. Lights of Guidance, p. 629
19.25   The Universal House of Justice, A Wider Horizon, Selected Letters 1983-1992, p. 38
19.26   From letter of the Universal House of Justice to Bahá'í Youth in every Land, June 10, 1966. Lights of Guidance, p. 214
19.27   From a letter of the Universal House of Justice to all National Spiritual Assemblies, March 25, 1975. Lights of Guidance, p. 632
19.28   The Universal House of Justice, 1966 Jun 10, Youth in Every Land

Chapter 20
20.1   Bahá'u'lláh, The Kitáb-i-Aqdas, p. 19
20.2   Gleanings from the Writings of Bahá'u'lláh, Sec. 153, p. 328
20.3   Bahá'u'lláh, Gleanings from the Writings of Bahá'u'lláh, p. 127
20.4   Bahá'u'lláh, cited in "The World Order of Bahá'u'lláh - Selected Letters", p. 132
20.5   'Abdu'l-Bahá, The Will and Testament of 'Abdu'l-Bahá", p. 11
20.6   'Abdu'l-Bahá, The Promulgation of Universal Peace, p. 322-23
20.7   'Abdu'l-Bahá, The Promulgation of Universal Peac p. 455-56
20.8   'Abdu'l-Bahá, , The Compilation of Compilations vol. I, p. 116
20.9   'Abdu'l-Bahá, Selections from the Writings of 'Abdu'l-Bahá, p. 207
20.10   'Abdu'l-Bahá, cited in "The World Order of Bahá'u'lláh - Selected Letters", p. 167
20.11   'Abdu'l-Bahá, , The Compilation of Compilations vol. I, p. 114
20.12   'Abdu'l-Bahá, The Promulgation of Universal Peace, p. 382
20.13   Shoghi Effendi, "God Passes By", pp. 237-38
20.14   Shoghi Effendi, from a letter of 8 February 1934, published in "The World Order of Bahá'u'lláh - Selected Letters" pp. 149-50
20.15   From a letter written on behalf of the Guardian to the National Spiritual Assembly of Canada, March 30, 1957. Lights of Guidance, p. 183
20.16   From a letter written on behalf of the Guardian to an individual believer, July 29, 1946. Lights of Guidance, p. 183
20.17   From a letter written on behalf of the Guardian to an individual believer, November 28, 1944: . Lights of Guidance, p. 184
20.18   From a letter written on behalf of the Guardian to the National Spiritual Assembly of India, May 8, 1948. Lights of Guidance, p. 184
20.19   From a letter written on behalf of Shoghi Effendi to an individual believer, May 16, 1925. Lights of Guidance, p. 185
20.20   From a letter written on behalf of the Guardian to an individual believer, February 7, 1947. Lights of Guidance, p. 187

20.21   From a letter written on behalf of the Guardian to the National Spiritual Assembly of the United States, April 11, 1949. Lights of Guidance, p. 188
20.22   From a letter written on behalf of the Guardian to an individual believer, April 15, 1949. Lights of Guidance, p. 182
20.23   23 March 1975, from a letter written by the Universal House of Justice to an individual believer, The Compilation of Compilations vol. I, p. 111
20.24   14 January 1979, from a letter written on behalf of the Universal House of Justice to an individual believer, The Compilation of Compilations vol. I, p. 119
20.25   From a letter of the Universal House of Justice to a National Spiritual Assembly, October 29, 1074. Lights of Guidance, p. 186
20.26   The Universal House of Justice, from a letter dated 9 March 1965, published in "Wellspring of Guidance: Messages 1963-1968" p. 44, The Compilation of Compilations vol. I, p. 122
20.27   9 November 1981, from a letter written on behalf of the Universal House of Justice to an individual believer, The Compilation of Compilations vol. I, p. 121
20.28   The Universal House of Justice, from a letter dated 27 May 1966, published in "Wellspring of Guidance: Messages 1963-1968", p. 90, The Compilation of Compilations vol. I, p. 123
20.29   The Universal House of Justice, from a letter dated October 1963, published in "Wellspring of Guidance: Messages 1963-1968, p. 13, The Compilation of Compilations vol. I, p. 123

Chapter 21
21.1   Bahá'u'lláh, Gleanings from the Writings of Bahá'u'lláh, p. 334
21.2   Bahá'u'lláh, Gleanings from the Writings of Bahá'u'lláh, p. 334
21.3   Bahá'u'lláh, Gleanings from the Writings of Bahá'u'lláh, p. 196
21.4   Bahá'u'lláh, quoted by Shoghi Effendi in Messages to the Bahá'í World 1950-1957, p. 101
21.5   Bahá'u'lláh, The Kitáb-i-Aqdas, p. 75
21.6   Bahá'u'lláh, Gleanings from the Writings of Bahá'u'lláh, p. 339
21.7   'Abdu'l-Bahá, Selections from the Writings of 'Abdu'l-Bahá, p. 243
21.8   'Abdu'l-Bahá: Selections from the Writings of 'Abdu'l-Bahá, pp. 280-281
21.9   'Abdu'l-Bahá, Tablets of the Divine Plan, p. 47
21.10   'Abdu'l-Bahá, Tablets of the Divine Plan, p. 21
21.11   'Abdu'l-Bahá, Selections from the Writings of Abdu'l-Baha, p. 214
21.12   'Abdu'l-Bahá, Selections from the Writings of Abdu'l-Baha, p. 250
21.13   'Abdu'l-Bahá, Tablets of the Divine Plan, p. 41
21.14   Shoghi Effendi, Citadel of Faith, pp. 25-26
21.15   Shoghi Effendi, The Advent of Divine Justice, pp. 57-58
21.16   From a letter written on behalf of Shoghi Effendi to the European Teaching Committee, May 24, 1954. Lights of Guidance, p. 573
21.17   From a letter dated June 30, 1952, written on behalf of Shoghi Effendi to a National Spiritual Assembly published in A Special Measure of Love, p. 7, Quickeners of Mankind, p. 56
21.18   From a letter dated June 29, 1941 written on behalf of Shoghi Effendi, published in Dawn of a New Day, p. 89
21.19   From a letter dated June 30, 1937, written on behalf of Shoghi Effendi to an individual believer, published in The Individual and Teaching, pp. 23-24
21.20   From a letter written on behalf of Shoghi Effendi to a National Spiritual Assembly, February 17, 1957: Lights of Guidance, p. 575
21.21   From a letter written on behalf of Shoghi Effendi to a National Spiritual Assembly, February 5, 1956. Lights of Guidance, p. 576
21.22   Shoghi Effendi, cited in a letter of the Universal House of Justice to the National Spiritual Assembly of the United States, July 2, 1965. Lights of Guidance, p. 571
21.23   From a letter of the Universal House of Justice to the National Spiritual Assembly of the United States, July 2, 1965. Lights of Guidance, p. 571
21.24   From a letter of the Universal House of Justice to the National Spiritual Assembly of the United States, July 2, 1965. Lights of Guidance, p. 572
21.25   From a letter of the Universal House of Justice to the National Spiritual Assembly of the United States, July 2, 1965. Lights of Guidance, p. 572

Appendix: Sources and Bibliography 389

Chapter 22
22.1 Bahá'u'lláh, Gleanings from the Writings of Bahá'u'lláh, p. 7
22.2 Baha'u'llah, The Hidden Words, Persian #76
22.3 Baha'u'llah, Gleanings from the Writings of Baha'u'llah, p. 96
22.4 Bahá'u'lláh, Tablets of Bahá'u'lláh, p. 173
22.5 Bahá'u'lláh, Tablets of Bahá'u'lláh, p. 237
22.6 Bahá'u'lláh, , Gleanings from the Writings of Baha'u'llah, p. 335
22.7 Bahá'u'lláh, The Individual and Teaching - Raising the Divine Call, p. 3
22.8 'Abdu'l-Bahá, Selections from the Writings of 'Abdu'l-Bahá, p. 205
22.9 'Abdu'l-Bahá, Selections from the Writings of 'Abdu'l-Bahá, p. 274
22.10 'Abdu'l-Bahá, Tablets of the Divine Plan, p. 13
22.11 'Abdu'l-Bahá, Tablets of the Divine Plan, pp. 52-53
22.12 'Abdu'l-Bahá, Tablets of the Divine Plan, p. 20
22.13 'Abdu'l-Bahá, Selections from the Writings of 'Abdu'l-Bahá, p. 121
22.14 'Abdu'l-Bahá, Selections from the Writings of 'Abdu'l-Bahá, p. 160
22.15 'Abdu'l-Bahá, The Individual and Teaching - Raising the Divine Call, p. 12
22.16 'Abdu'l-Bahá, The Individual and Teaching - Raising the Divine Call, p. 10
22.17 'Abdu'l-Bahá, Foundations of World Unity, p. 21
22.18 'Abdu'l-Bahá, Foundations of World Unity, p. 102
22.19 'Abdu'l-Bahá, The Promulgation of Universal Peace, p. 457
22.20 'Abdu'l-Bahá, Tablets of 'Abdu'l-Bahá v2, p. 374
22.21 Shoghi Effendi, The Advent of Divine Justice, p. 47
22.22 Shoghi Effendi, The Individual and Teaching - Raising the Divine Call, p. 15
22.23 Shoghi Effendi, The Advent of Divine Justice, pp. 42-44
22.24 Shoghi Effendi, Citadel of Faith, p. 148
22.25 From a letter dated 10 December 1942 written on behalf of Shoghi Effendi to an individual believer, The Individual and Teaching - Raising the Divine Call, p. 24
22.26 From a letter dated 21 September 1951 written on behalf of Shoghi Effendi to the Comite de Ensenanza Bahá'í para los Indigenas, The Individual and Teaching - Raising the Divine Call, p. 31
22.27 From a letter dated 28 December 1936 written on behalf of Shoghi Effendi to an individual believer, The Individual and Teaching - Raising the Divine Call, p. 22
22.28 From a letter dated 3 February 1937 written on behalf of Shoghi Effendi to an individual believer, The Individual and Teaching - Raising the Divine Call, p. 23
22.29 From a letter dated 14 January 1938 written on behalf of Shoghi Effendi to an individual believer, The Individual and Teaching - Raising the Divine Call, p. 24
22.30 From a letter dated 5 May 1943 written on behalf of Shoghi Effendi to an individual believer, The Individual and Teaching - Raising the Divine Call, p. 25
22.31 From a letter dated 14 October 1943 written on behalf of Shoghi Effendi to an individual believer, The Individual and Teaching - Raising the Divine Call, p. 25
22.32 From a letter dated 4 April 1947 written on behalf of Shoghi Effendi to the National Spiritual Assembly of Germany, The Individual and Teaching - Raising the Divine Call, p. 26
22.33 From a letter dated 5 July 1949 written on behalf of Shoghi Effendi to an individual believer, The Individual and Teaching - Raising the Divine Call, p. 28
22.34 From a letter dated 20 October 1956 written on behalf of Shoghi Effendi to an individual believer, The Individual and Teaching - Raising the Divine Call, p. 37
22.35 From a letter dated 22 August 1957 written on behalf of Shoghi Effendi to an individual believer, The Individual and Teaching - Raising the Divine Call, p. 39
22.36 Commissioned by The Universal House of Justice, One Common Faith

Chapter 23
23.1 Bahá'u'lláh, Gleanings from the Writings of Bahá'u'lláh, p. 286
23.2 Bahá'u'lláh, Gleanings from the Writings of Bahá'u'lláh, p. 118
23.3 Bahá'u'lláh, Gleanings from the Writings of Bahá'u'lláh, p. 214
23.4 Bahá'u'lláh, The Hidden Words, Persian #3
23.5 Bahá'u'lláh, Gleanings from the Writings of Bahá'u'lláh, p. 216
23.6 Bahá'u'lláh, Gleanings from the Writings of Bahá'u'lláh, p. 118

23.7   Baha'u'llah, The Hidden Words, Persian #56
23.8   Baha'u'llah, The Hidden Words, Persian #2
23.9   'Abdu'l-Bahá, Selections from the Writings of 'Abdu'l-Bahá, p. 181
23.10 'Abdu'l-Bahá, The Promulgation of Universal Peace, p. 66
23.11 'Abdu'l-Bahá, The Promulgation of Universal Peace, p. 158
23.12 'Abdu'l-Bahá, The Promulgation of Universal Peace, p. 168
23.13 'Abdu'l-Bahá, The Promulgation of Universal Peace, p. 344
23.14 'Abdu'l-Bahá, The Promulgation of Universal Peace, p. 457
23.15 'Abdu'l-Bahá, Paris Talks, p. 96
23.16 Shoghi Effendi, The Promised Day is Come, p. 114
23.17 Shoghi Effendi, Citadel of Faith, p. 124
23.18 Shoghi Effendi, The Advent of Divine Justice, p. 51
23.19 Shoghi Effendi, The Advent of Divine Justice, p. 30
23.20 Shoghi Effendi: Dawn of a New Day, p. 200
23.21 From a letter dated 6 September 1946 written on behalf of Shoghi Effendi to an individual believer, The Compilation of Compilations vol II, p. 16
23.22 Letter Written on behalf of Shoghi Effendi to an individual believer, 22 July 1933, The Compilation of Compilations vol. I, p. 84
23.23 From letter written on behalf of the Guardian to the National Spiritual Assembly of India, June 30, 1952: Dawn of a New Day, p. 153
23.24 From a letter written on behalf of Shoghi Effendi to an individual believer, December 23, 1942. Lights of Guidance, p. 412
23.25 From a letter written on behalf of the Universal House of Justice to a National Spiritual Assembly June 5, 1986. Lights of Guidance, p. 362
23.26 From a letter of the Universal House of Justice to an individual believer, March 14, 1973 . Lights of Guidance, p. 365
23.27 Letter from the Universal House of Justice to two individual believers, May 22, 1966. Lights of Guidance, p. 363

Chapter 24
24.1   Bahá'u'lláh, Gleanings from the Writings of Bahá'u'lláh, p. 249
24.2   Bahá'u'lláh, Gleanings from the Writings of Bahá'u'lláh, p. 280
24.3   Bahá'u'lláh, Gleanings from the Writings of Bahá'u'lláh, p. 303
24.4   Bahá'u'lláh, Prayers and Meditations by Bahá'u'lláh, p. 174
24.5   Bahá'u'lláh, Tablets of Bahá'u'lláh, p. 113
24.6   Bahá'u'lláh, Tablets of Bahá'u'lláh, p. 138
24.7   Bahá'u'lláh, Tablets of Bahá'u'lláh, p. 171
24.8   Bahá'u'lláh, Tablets of Bahá'u'lláh, p. 234
24.9   Bahá'u'lláh, Gleanings from the Writings of Bahá'u'lláh, p. 92
24.10 'Abdu'l-Bahá, Selections from the Writings of 'Abdu'l-Bahá, p. 3
24.11 'Abdu'l-Bahá, Selections from the Writings of 'Abdu'l-Bahá, p. 144
24.12 'Abdu'l-Bahá, Selections from the Writings of 'Abdu'l-Bahá, p. 26
24.13 'Abdu'l-Bahá, Selections from the Writings of 'Abdu'l-Bahá, p. 266
24.14 'Abdu'l-Bahá, Selections from the Writings of 'Abdu'l-Bahá, p. 271
24.15 'Abdu'l-Bahá, Selections from the Writings of 'Abdu'l-Bahá, p. 316
24.16 'Abdu'l-Bahá, The Promulgation of Universal Peace, p. 185
24.17 'Abdu'l-Bahá, Paris Talks, p. 60
24.18 From a letter written on behalf of the Guardian to the Bahá'í Youth of Lime, Peru, November 17, 1945. Lights of Guidance, p. 425
24.19 From a letter written on behalf of Shoghi Effendi to the National Spiritual Assembly of the United States and Canada, March 22, 1937 Compilations. Lights of Guidance, p. 623
24.20 From a letter of the Universal House of Justice to the Bahá'í youth of the world, January 1984. Lights of Guidance, p. 635

Chapter 25
25.1   Bahá'u'lláh, Tablets of Bahá'u'lláh, p. 37
25.2   Bahá'u'lláh, Tablets of Bahá'u'lláh, p. 38
25.3   Bahá'u'lláh, The Kitáb-i-Aqdas, p. 62

Appendix: Sources and Bibliography ❷ 391

25.4 Bahá'u'lláh, Gleanings from the Writings of Bahá'u'lláh, p. 270
25.5 Bahá'u'lláh, Gleanings from the Writings of Bahá'u'lláh, p. 296
25.6 Bahá'u'lláh, The Hidden Words, Persian #64
25.7 Bahá'u'lláh, Gleanings from the Writings of Bahá'u'lláh, p. 304
25.8 Bahá'u'lláh, The Kitáb-i-Aqdas, p. 139
25.9 Baha'u'llah, The Hidden Words, Persian #63
25.10 Baha'u'llah, Gleanings from the Writings of Baha'u'llah, p. 98
25.11 Bahá'u'lláh cited by Shoghi Effendi, The Advent of Divine Justice, p. 23
25.12 'Abdu'l-Bahá, Selections from the Writings of 'Abdu'l-Bahá, p. 318
25.13 'Abdu'l-Bahá, Selections from the Writings of 'Abdu'l-Bahá, p. 294
25.14 'Abdu'l-Bahá, The Secret of Divine Civilization, p. 55
25.15 'Abdu'l-Bahá, The Will and Testament, p. 14
25.16 'Abdu'l-Bahá, The Will and Testament, p. 15
25.17 'Abdu'l-Bahá cited by Shoghi Effendi, The Advent of Divine Justice, p. 25
25.18 Shoghi Effendi, Trustworthiness: A Cardinal Bahá'í Virtue, Compiled by the Research Department of the Universal House of Justice
25.19 Shoghi Effendi, Trustworthiness: A Cardinal Bahá'í Virtue, Compiled by the Research Department of the Universal House of Justice
25.20 In the hand writing of Shoghi Effendi, Trustworthiness: A Cardinal Bahá'í Virtue, Compiled by the Research Department of the Universal House of Justice
25.21 Shoghi Effendi, Trustworthiness: A Cardinal Bahá'í Virtue, Compiled by the Research Department of the Universal House of Justice
25.22 On behalf of Shoghi Effendi, Trustworthiness: A Cardinal Bahá'í Virtue, Compiled by the Research Department of the Universal House of Justice
25.23 On behalf of Shoghi Effendi, Trustworthiness: A Cardinal Bahá'í Virtue, Compiled by the Research Department of the Universal House of Justice
25.24 On behalf of Shoghi Effendi, Trustworthiness: A Cardinal Bahá'í Virtue, Compiled by the Research Department of the Universal House of Justice
25.25 The Universal House of Justice, Messages 1963 to 1986, p. 93
25.26 Baha'i International Community, 1995 Mar 03, *The Prosperity of Humankind*

Chapter 26
26.1 Baha'u'llah, Gleanings from the Writings of Baha'u'llah, p. 316
26.2 Baha'u'llah, Gleanings from the Writings of Baha'u'llah, p. 183
26.3 Baha'u'llah, Prayers and Meditations by Baha'u'llah, p. 86
26.4 Baha'u'llah, Tablets of Baha'u'llah, p. 190
26.5 Baha'u'llah, Gleanings from the Writings of Baha'u'llah, p. 206
26.6 Baha'u'llah, The Kitab-i-Iqan, p. 23
26.7 'Abdu'l-Bahá, Selections from the Writings of 'Abdu'l-Bahá, p. 26
26.8 'Abdu'l-Bahá, Selections from the Writings of 'Abdu'l-Bahá, p. 220
26.9 'Abdu'l-Bahá, Selections from the Writings of 'Abdu'l-Bahá, p. 318
26.10 'Abdu'l-Bahá, Selections from the Writings of 'Abdu'l-Bahá, p. 35
26.11 'Abdu'l-Bahá, Selections from the Writings of 'Abdu'l-Bahá, p. 35
26.12 'Abdu'l-Bahá, Selections from the Writings of 'Abdu'l-Bahá, p. 33
26.13 'Abdu'l-Bahá, The Promulgation of Universal Peace, p. 460
26.14 'Abdu'l-Bahá, The Promulgation of Universal Peace, p. 461
26.15 From a letter written on behalf of the Universal House of Justice to the National Spiritual Assembly of Italy, November 19, 1974. Lights of Guidance, p. 122

BIBLIOGRAPHY

Bahá'u'lláh. *The Seven Valleys.* Wilmette, Illinois, Bahá'í Publishing Trust: 1986 Edition
Bahá'u'lláh. *The Kitáb-i-Iqan.* Wilmette, Illinois, Bahá'í Publishing Trust: 1983 Edition
Bahá'u'lláh. *The Hidden Words.* Wilmette, Illinois, Bahá'í Publishing Trust: 2002 Edition
Bahá'u'lláh. *Tablets of Bahá'u'lláh.* Wilmette, Illinois: Bahá'í Publishing Trust,1983 Edition
Bahá'u'lláh. *Gleanings from the Writings of Bahá'u'lláh.* Wilmette, Illinois: Bahá'í Publishing Trust,1983 Edition
Bahá'u'lláh. *Prayers and Meditations by Bahá'u'lláh.* Wilmette, Illinois, Bahá'í Publishing Trust: 1987 Edition
Bahá'u'lláh. *The Proclamation of Bahá'u'lláh.* Wilmette, Illinois: Bahá'í Publishing Trust,1967 Edition
Bahá'u'lláh, *Epistle to the Son of the Wolf.* Wilmette, Illinois: Bahá'í Publishing Trust, 1988 Edition
Bahá'u'lláh. *The Kitáb-i-Aqdas.* Wilmette, Illinois: Bahá'í Publishing Trust, 1992 Edition
Bahá'u'lláh. *The Summons of the Lord of Hosts.* Haifa, Bahá'í World Centre, 2002 Edition

'Abdu'l-Bahá. *Selections from the Writings of 'Abdu'l-Bahá.* Haifa: Bahá'í World Centre, 1982 Edition
'Abdu'l-Bahá. *Tablets of the Divine Plan.* Wilmette, Illinois: Bahá'í Publishing Trust, 1993 Edition
'Abdu'l-Bahá. *The Promulgation of Universal Peace.* Wilmette, Illinois: Bahá'í Publishing Trust, 1982 Edition
'Abdu'l-Bahá. *Some Answered Questions.* Wilmette, Illinois: Bahá'í Publishing Trust, 1987 Edition
'Abdu'l-Bahá. *Paris Talks.* London: Bahá'í Publishing Trust, 1995
'Abdu'l-Bahá. *'Abdu'l-Bahá in London.* London: Bahá'í Publishing Trust, 1983
'Abdu'l-Bahá. *Secret of Divine Civilization.* London: Bahá'í Publishing Trust, 2007
'Abdu'l-Bahá. *Foundations of World Unity.* Wilmette, Illinois: Bahá'í Publishing Trust, 1968 Edition

Shoghi Effendi. *The Promised Day is Come.* Wilmette, Illinois: Bahá'í Publishing Trust, 1996 Edition
Shoghi Effendi. *The Advent of Divine Justice.* Wilmette, Illinois: Bahá'í Publishing Trust, 2003 Edition
Shoghi Effendi. *The World Order of Bahá'u'lláh.* Wilmette, Illinois: Bahá'í Publishing Trust, 1993 Edition
Shoghi Effendi. *Citadel of Faith.* Wilmette, Illinois: Bahá'í Publishing Trust, 2000 Edition
Shoghi Effendi. *God Passes By.* Wilmette, Illinois: Bahá'í Publishing Trust, 1974 Edition
Shoghi Effendi. *Dawn of a New Day.* New Delhi. Bahá'í Publishing Trust, 1974 Edition
Shoghi Effendi. *Directives from the Guardian,* New Delhi. Bahá'í Publishing Trust, 1955 Edition
Shoghi Effendi. *Summary Statement - 1947, Special UN Committee on Palestine.* Haifa, Bahá'í World Centre
Shoghi Effendi, *The Light of Divine Guidance,* Baha'i-Verlag Deutschland (Baha'i Publishing Trust Germany, 1985
Shoghi Effendi, *Baha'i Administration: Selected Messages 1922 - 1932,* Wilmette, Illinois: Bahá'í Publishing Trust, 2000 Edition
Shoghi Effendi, *The UnfoldingDdestiny of the British Baha'i Community,* London: Bahá'í Publishing Trust, 1981

The Universal House of Justice, *Wellspring of Guidance, Messages 1963 to 1986.* Wilmette, Illinois: Bahá'í Publishing Trust, 1970 Edition
The Universal House of Justice, *Century of Light,* Haifa: 2001
The Universal House of Justice, *One Common Faith,* Haifa: 2005
The Universal House of Justice, 1996 July 02, *Criticism of Institutions*
The Universal House of Justice, 2001 Apr 19, *Unity of Nations and the Lesser Peace*
The Universal House of Justice, 2001 May 24, *To Believers Gathered for Terrace Events*
The Universal House of Justice, *The Constitution of The Universal House of Justice*

Baha'i International Community, 1992 May 29, *Statement on Baha'u'llah*
Bahá'í International Community, 1993 Aug 03, *Ending Religious Intolerance*
Baha'i International Community, 1995 Oct, *Turning Point For All Nations*
Baha'i International Community, 1999 Mar 20, *Peace Among the Nations*
Bahá'í International Community, 1989 Jan 02, *Position Statement on Education*
Bahá'í International Community, 2008, *For the Betterment of the World*
Baha'i International Community, 1995 Mar 03, *The Prosperity of Humankind*

The Compilation of Compilations vol. I & vol II. Prepared by the Research Department of the Universal House of Justice. Maryborough, Victoria: Bahá'í Publications Australia, 1991
Lights of Guidance. Compiled by Helen Hornby. New Delhi. Bahá'í Publishing Trust, 1994 Edition
Consultation: Compiled by the Research Department of the Universal House of Justice
Bahá'í Prayers, Wilmette, Illinois: Bahá'í Publishing Trust, 1991 Edition
Principles of Bahá'í Administration, London: Bahá'í Publishing Trust, 1976 Edition
Trustworthiness: A Cardinal Bahá'í Virtue, Compiled by the Research Department of the Universal House of Justice

The copyright of this text in no way modifies the copyright status of the above publications.

WhyUnite?
because your journey matters to the world.

We hope you have enjoyed this WhyUnite? book. We are committed to providing quality introductory materials for the Bahá'í Faith across all mediums. To learn more about our products, find recommendations for further reading, and connect with more Bahá'ís, please visit: http://www.whyunite.com.

www.ingramcontent.com/pod-product-compliance
Lightning Source LLC
Chambersburg PA
CBHW020845090426
42736CB00008B/245